The Thirst for Wholeness

The Thirst for Wholeness

Attachment, Addiction,
and the Spiritual Path

CHRISTINA GROF

HarperSanFrancisco
A Division of HarperCollins Publishers

Grateful acknowledgment is made for permission to reprint excerpts from the following works:

Reprinted from: *The Kabir Book* by Robert Bly. Copyright © 1981, 1977 by Robert Bly. Reprinted by permission of Beacon Press. "New Heaven and Earth" and "Pax" from *The Complete Poems of D. H. Lawrence* by D. H. Lawrence. Copyright © 1964, 1971 by Angelo Ravagli and C. M. Weekley, Executors of the Estate of Frieda Lawrence Ravagli. Used by permission of Viking Penguin, a division of Penguin Books USA Inc. Excerpt from "Little Gidding" in *Four Quartets*, copyright 1943 by T.S. Eliot and renewed 1971 by Esme Valerie Eliot, reprinted by permission of Harcourt Brace & Company.

FIRST HARPERCOLLINS PAPERBACK EDITION PUBLISHED IN 1994
ISBN 0-06-250315-4 (pbk)

An Earlier Edition of This Book Was Cataloged As Follows:

Grof, Christina.
    The thirst for wholeness : attachment, addiction, and the spiritual path / Christina Grof. — 1st ed.
      p. cm.
    Includes bibliographical references.
    ISBN 0-06-250314-6 (alk. paper)
    1. Spiritual life. I. Title.
BL624.G763 1993
291.4—dc20
                               92-54616 CIP

94 95 96 97 98 ❖ RRD(H) 10 9 8 7 6 5 4 3 2 1

This edition is printed on acid-free paper that meets the American National Standards Institute Z39.48 Standard.

To my husband, Stan, with deep love and gratitude for your love, consistent support, gentle encouragement, and enduring patience. You opened your heart and your life to me from the beginning, and the gifts have been manifold.

To my daughter, Sarah, with my love and thankfulness for your insight, directness, beauty, and for the moment that you pointed the way. From day one, you have combined grace and strength, vitality and sensitivity, in a way that inspires.

To my son, Nathaniel, with my love and appreciation for your wisdom, perception, gentleness, and your creative compassion. Your unique blend of humor and seriousness, resoluteness and tenderness, have brought me great joy, and for that I am grateful.

Acknowledgments

This book brings together many threads of my life, and it could not have been written without the invaluable help and support of many others. Thank you to my sisters: Kathy for her love, openness, and willingness to hang in there with me, and to Peggy for years of humor, caring, and sweet companionship during many stages of this saga. Thank you to Lisa Livingston for holding my hand, always asking the perfect questions, and providing impeccable insights.

Thank you to my editor, Barbara Moulton, for shepherding this project from early on, championing it through its many phases, and for allowing me the room to find my own voice.

I am grateful to Cary Sparks, friend and angel assistant, whose consistent willingness, quiet presence, and dedicated work have made my life easier and brighter. Thank you to my friend Tav Sparks for being an insightful counsel and compatriot as I developed ideas for this book. And thank you to Kathy Altman and Lori Saltzman for their affection, laser-like perceptions, and expert direction.

I particularly feel grateful to Jack Kornfield, compassionate and gentle friend, colleague, and teacher, for helping me to learn about some of the themes in this book. A special thank you to Kit Wilson, for her loving guidance, wisdom, and thoughtful comments on the manuscript; to Frances Vaughan, for years of gentle friendship and unflagging confidence; to Eileen Sanchez, for personal inspiration, encouragement, and for feedback on the manuscript; to Angeles Arrien, for enthusiastic support and for trusting that I could do it long before I did; and to Mondy Bridges, for providing a safe and caring refuge.

I am also deeply grateful to many other friends who have offered their generous and kind support before and during this project: to Wyatt Webb, Roger Walsh, Brother David Steindl-Rast, Micky Reny, George Nash, Betty Monaghan, Jane Middleton-Moz, Father Thomas Matus, Roquelle Lerner, Pauline Kirby, Helen Gitkind, Patricia Dimitrios, John Buchanan, Susie Bower, Leroy Bishop, Kathy Colletti Bishop, Anne Armstrong, Rod Allison, and to Brigitte Ashauer for the term "militant altruism."

And finally, from the bottom of my heart, I would like to thank the community of people recovering from addictions of all kinds. It is my deep hope that in writing this book I will be able, in part, to give back even a tiny fraction of what they have given to me.

Contents

Introduction

Early in my recovery from alcoholism, I came across part of a letter from the famous Swiss psychiatrist Carl Gustav Jung to Bill Wilson, cofounder of Alcoholics Anonymous. Referring to one of his former patients, Jung wrote, "His craving for alcohol was the equivalent on a low level of the spiritual thirst of our being for wholeness, expressed in medieval language: the union with God."

As I read on, I realized that Jung was describing something that I know well. I have felt a nonspecific craving for most of my life. Many of us do. And I recognize it from my recovery. It is different from and more far-reaching than the physical craving for alcohol. A trip to the mall, a piece of cake, a cuddle: none of these momentary solutions quenches the deep thirst.

I have talked with numerous others, both nonaddicts and recovering addicts, and they describe the same underlying longing in their lives. It is a pervasive aspect of the human experience, and it has been misread, misunderstood, and acted upon in mistaken ways, some of them deadly. The only way we successfully satisfy this elemental craving for wholeness or for God is through an ongoing relationship with a vast inner spiritual source.

This book is for those who are aware of their own thirst for wholeness, struggle with it at times, and want to find ways to quench it. Much of my focus is on the problem of addiction; however, I believe that the addict's struggle is in many ways an exaggeration of a challenge we all face. The issues are similar, and so are the solutions. Whether you are a student, a parent, a professional, a person involved in active recovery from one or more addictions, or simply someone looking for a more fulfilling life, you may recognize yourself here.

When I was a child, the sacred beckoned to me. I found divine glimmers in nature, in church, and during private, interior interludes. In my midtwenties, I experienced a sudden and dramatic spontaneous mystical awakening that took me light-years away from everything I had always considered to be real and acceptable—it turned my life completely upside down. To better understand what was happening to me, I began to explore, to read, and to ask questions of people I thought might give me clues. I met a spiritual teacher from India whose teachings and practices helped to explain and support my experiences; I became his student and started meditating.

A short time later, I became acquainted with the relatively new field of transpersonal psychology, a branch of the field that offers a broad understanding of the human experience. Proponents of transpersonal psychology talked about the whole person, our physical, emotional, and intellectual capacities, and included our mystical nature as an essential element in our makeup. This theory was unlike any Western approach I had known about or experienced, and as someone who had always felt drawn to spirituality, I felt significant relief just knowing that there were people—serious people—who thought and lived this way. A whole new world began to open to me. I increasingly sought out transpersonal thinkers, spiritual teachers, and practitioners of various psychological approaches.

I listened and learned, and learned some more. I struggled with my own demanding inner process, which had turned into a true transformational crisis, or *spiritual emergency*, as I called it. I encountered very difficult and dramatic areas of my psyche. As I tried to comprehend and integrate what was happening to me, I felt particularly attracted to Eastern mystical traditions. And I found that transpersonal psychologists and theoreticians helped me to understand many of my insights and experiences by translating them into a language that a Westerner could comprehend.

Meanwhile, I traveled and worked at a hectic pace. With my husband, Stan, I began to organize and give lectures, seminars, and workshops around the world and to coordinate international conferences on transpersonal psychology. At the same time, I continued to struggle with the challenges of my own emotional and spiritual growth, as well as with the considerable pain I still felt with the separation from my children because of an earlier divorce. Somewhere along the way, I discovered temporary relief from it all; I began to use alcohol as an exceptionally effective tranquilizer.

I had never had a normal relationship to alcohol—being a controlled person, I had always used alcohol in a controlled way. Now, I discovered that a couple, or maybe a few, drinks would take the edge off, numb the intensity of my inner world, relax me, relieve the pain, and get me offstage temporarily. I did not realize until later that alcoholism has affected a number of my family members. My biochemistry, plus many other factors, created in me fertile ground for what was to come. The disease swept through me like wildfire, and within a relatively short time, I became a very sick alcoholic.

I found myself developing a deep conflict: as my alcoholism progressed, I remained involved in spiritual and transpersonal pursuits. I remember sitting at the feet of my guru and then going home to drink, feeling horrible and guilty and wretched. The misery of my drinking seemed as far from my concept of the divine as anything could be, and the alcoholic hell I was experiencing had nothing to do with the ecstatic mystical states and the expansive insights I had known.

Finally, in January of 1986, I checked into a twenty-eight-day treatment program for chemical dependency, where I hit bottom on the tenth day. My bottom was very low and extremely devastating. In this process, I felt that everything I had been or had been connected to had ended, that I had died.

Amazingly, waiting for me immediately on the other side of what felt like total desolation was a time of profound healing and guidance. For months, I felt connected with the world, with myself, and with a source of inner strength and inspiration that seemed boundless. I sensed that I had been given a second chance and that I was beginning to find the mystical connection I had been seeking for so long. I became aware of untapped creativity stirring within me and began to sense a renewed purpose to my existence. It was a wondrous, mystical period.

Standing on the edge of a new life, I at first felt sad as I reviewed what felt like endless days and months and years of wasted time and productivity during my active drinking career. But then my focus started to shift, and I began to see that the dark years of alcoholism had actually been an important stage in my spiritual journey. I had been given lessons and opportunities and gifts that could have come to me only through that experience.

Meanwhile, anywhere I went in the world, I found myself being welcomed into a global community of recovering people who offered me the love, understanding, and acceptance I had never known elsewhere. I became acquainted with the Twelve-Step programs and discovered that they contained, in ordinary Western language, many of the elements that had attracted me to various spiritual systems. Recovering alcoholics and addicts who actively worked these Twelve Steps were involved in an earthbound, practical daily program that was producing miracles in their lives. And they had a different commitment to their spirituality than I had seen before: their spiritual practice was about life and death, and most of them had confronted each deeply.

I also found myself thinking a lot about the Buddhist notion of attachment. According to Buddhist philosophy, the root of all human suffering is attachment or desire, and the way to liberation is through a daily practice that includes an element of surrender or letting go. I began to think that the terrifying inability to detach from the deadly cycle of addiction is perhaps simply an extreme and exaggerated form of the dilemma faced by every human being as we cling to the roles, relationships, activities, and material possessions in our lives. I realized that part of the effectiveness of the Twelve-Step programs is that they offer a way out of our attachments through a spiritual practice that includes, in the first three Steps, the essential experience of surrender.

I was impressed and genuinely excited about everything I was learning, feeling, and seeing. I wanted to know more. I was aware that in my personal experience, there was an important connection between spirituality and addiction, and I was meeting many others for whom this was also true. I initiated and co-coordinated a month-long seminar and two professional conferences with variations on the title "Yearning for Wholeness: Addiction, Attachment, and the Spiritual Quest" in order to further explore these topics and to give others the opportunity to do the same. I kept asking myself, How is all this related, and how can I articulate it to myself and others?

This book represents an attempt to do just that. It is divided into three parts: Part I defines the prevalent yearning for our own wholeness and relates it to addiction. I address such questions as, What is spirituality? What is a spiritual experience? How do we define and recognize our wholeness? What is the relationship between the individual self and a larger sacred identity?

Part II discusses the human state of existential alienation from the divine source and explores the role of abuse in deepening the sense of personal isolation. I look at our mechanisms for surviving in a nonsupportive or hostile world, our need to escape life's pain, and our tendency to seek solutions through potentially addictive activities and substances in the tempting world around us. We also travel through the dark night of addiction and examine the essential issue of surrender or letting go in the addictive process and the inner journey. Finally, I address the relationship between the universal problem of attachment and the cycle of active addiction.

Part III offers ways in which we can start to satisfy our inner longing. I look at the qualities of spiritual maturity and explore recovery as a path to the deeper Self. I survey some of the challenges and pitfalls of the path, as well as the complex issues of acceptance and forgiveness. The book concludes with a discussion of the rewards of the quest for wholeness and the importance of discovering the sacred dimensions in everyday life.

The journey through this book is a hero's or heroine's journey through some essential elements of the human dilemma, and my deepest hope is that it will be helpful to others along the way.

6

The Thirst for Wholeness

The Craving Behind Addiction

As FAR BACK into my childhood as I can remember, I was searching for something I could not name. Whatever I was looking for would help me to feel all right, at home, as though I belonged. If I could find it, I would no longer be lonely. I would know what it is like to be loved and accepted, and I would be able to love in return. I would be happy, fulfilled, and at peace with myself, my life, and the world. I would feel free, unfettered, expansive, and joyful.

I have tasted that possibility many times and in different ways: as I sat on a hill, infused with reverence and wonder, watching the splendor of a sunset spread across the sky; as I came upon tiny spring flowers pushing their way through the frozen earth; as my heart swelled with the power of the hymns and the voices and the beauty of the stained glass during a Christmas service in church; as, with joyous abandon, I galloped my horse bareback down the long, warm sandy beach and splashed into the ocean for a swim; and when as a new mother I looked into the perfect, miraculous face of my newborn child.

I saw glimmers of that prospect during those moments, however fleeting, in which each filament in my experience suddenly seemed to come together; it all appeared to work; everything made some sort of nonverbal sense. It might happen as I worked in my garden, when I prayed or meditated, while I was walking with a friend in nature or sitting at the feet of a wise elder.

I also remember sampling what seemed to be the promise of freedom, connectedness, and love as I received praise from a revered teacher, a colleague, or appreciative guests after hours or days of frantically working to prove myself. I thought I felt it as I nestled into the arms of lovers, swallowed a Valium, devoured yet another brownie, or drove my car too fast.

And I *knew* I found it in the delicious oblivion of alcohol. My boundaries melted, the pain disappeared, and I was, I thought, free. I felt comfortable within my own skin and felt connected with a carefree vitality that told me I could do anything. I was at ease with people in a way that was impossible in my daily life. I felt included, accepted, and cherished—until alcohol turned against me.

The Addict as Spiritual Seeker

Since I began my recovery from alcoholism, I have listened to many recovering people discuss their search for some undetermined experience of unity and freedom and remember the territories to which their quest has taken them. They have described the clear, uplifting, and loving moments in their lives as well as the destructive or self-destructive periods in which they convinced themselves they were on the right track. In other peoples' stories and observations, I have recognized numerous familiar elements and themes that appear repeatedly in my own history.

Many alcoholics and addicts portray themselves as dreamers or as creative in some way, sensitive to the intensity as well as the beauty of life. We are idealists; legions of us talk about wanting to assist others or about helping to solve the world's problems. Some have been graced with spiritual experiences, often starting in childhood. We may find it difficult to deal with the complex and demanding world around us, as well as with the intricate emotional, psychological, and spiritual mosaic within. We have responded by developing elaborate and ingenious mechanisms that allow us to survive or to escape the challenges of our existence. Most of us feel different from other people, isolated and lonely, as though we are on the outside looking in at the rest of the world. We often experience ourselves as inadequate, shameful, and less important, intelligent, or effective than other people.

And we frequently feel a pervasive restlessness, a desire for something more. This yearning takes us into destructive or self-destructive relationships, activities, or substance use that may seem temporarily to provide the missing piece. Rationalizing or denying the implications of our conduct, we go back for more and more. At first, our sexual encounters, eating binges, use of alcohol or other drugs, gambling, or other potentially addictive behaviors seem to satisfy us. I have heard many people say, "When I took my first drink or my first drug, I felt that all my problems were solved. I was home."

A woman who grew up in an alcoholic home recounts that as a child, she vowed never to touch alcohol, having experienced first-hand its devastating potential. Finally, as a young bride, she gave in "because my husband drank, and I didn't want him to be lonely." With her first glass of wine, she said, "A whole new world opened up to me. I realized what I had been missing all my life. At that moment, I felt complete."

Eventually, we find ourselves caught in a ruinous addictive cycle that threatens our physical, emotional, mental, and spiritual well-being. We can no longer control our relationship with whatever substance, activity, or relationship we have chosen as the answer to our problems. We think about it incessantly, plan for it, and habitually participate in it. We become increasingly helpless when faced with the object of our obsession, until something forces us to change.

When we *hit bottom*, when we are confronted with the realization that we can no longer continue our addictive activities, many of us begin for the first time to find what we have been searching for. By surrendering, by releasing our old, ineffective ways of being, we slowly discover acceptance, love, inner harmony, serenity, and a sense of fulfillment. These qualities do not develop all at once. It takes time, courage, patience, willingness, and a great deal of attention. But once we gain a sense of the possibilities, we readily commit ourselves to a new life.

The Universal Thirst for Wholeness

There are many symptoms and problems related to addiction that are specific to this condition, but the deeper, core attributes and impulses seem to be part of the overall human experience. At one time or another, most of us feel some degree of emptiness, loneliness, inadequacy, idealism, or spiritual longing. We recognize the discontent, the desire to escape pain, and the tendency to seek answers in activities, substances, or relationships.

Here, I focus on the sense of restlessness and the spiritual longing familiar to many of us. People talk about a nonspecific hunger for something that seems to be missing in their lives. They describe a gnawing emptiness within that is never filled. This insistent stirring from within is so intense that it can, at times, be painful. It seems to originate at one's very core, and for some of us, it feels even stronger than our sexual drive or our hunger for food.

I was aware of it as a child, and I tried somehow to fill it by becoming active in the local church, spending time around horses, or participating in sports. I struggled with it as an awkward teenager; it was more potent than my desire to be liked and accepted by the other kids or to be noticed by the boy in my literature class. I remember its pain as I sat in my darkened college room listening to music. I felt it as a young adult when I looked at a particularly magnificent painting, read an eloquent poem, or watched an exquisite dance. And it manifested during a multitude of other restive moments.

The pit of my stomach felt empty, my heart hurt, and my entire being aspired toward something I could not identify. As I grew, the ache in my soul increasingly permeated all aspects of my life. I felt monumentally homesick for something undefined, for an unnamed entity, place, or experience. Nothing I did seemed to alleviate the yearning within me.

There are, I am sure, some fortunate people who feel this longing but do not act upon it in painful ways. However, many people identify the spiritual yearning as a persistent voice in their lives, one they often confuse with their everyday aspirations. At first, they identify it as the desire to excel on the playing field, to develop their intellect, to get into the right college, or to meet the man or woman of their dreams. Perhaps they feel an overwhelming craving for a certain model of automobile, for a new outfit, or for sexual contact.

This fundamental appetite might manifest in the use of food, alcohol, nicotine, or other drugs. Some people feel a general dissatisfaction in their marriage and find themselves longing for something more: a new house, a significant change in their partner's behavior, a completely different relationship. The grass looks greener on the other side of the fence. They feel discontented, as though something is lacking. Perhaps more money would bring happiness, or a better social position, or a new job.

Tom is a prime example of someone who wrestled with this prevalent feeling of restlessness. He is a successful businessman who married his steady girlfriend from college and with her had two daughters and a son whom he loves deeply. For a number of years, he excelled in an essentially creative and rewarding job. He worked hard to achieve the lifestyle he had envisioned for himself and his family. He owned his home and had money in the bank. In spite of all Tom's accomplishments, he felt unsettled and unfulfilled.

He said, "I couldn't put my finger on it. Rationally, I knew that I had everything I needed to be happy. I loved my wife and kids, was satisfied with my job, and felt reasonably good about my accomplishments. But something was missing. I found myself thinking about moving to another state or trying another line of work. I began to drink too much. After a while, I realized that none of those things would help my feelings of emptiness, and in fact, they had the potential to cause more problems than they would solve. I felt stuck."

The irony is, no external activities or substances satisfy the initial craving or the feelings of emptiness. Many people attain the object of their desire, and the incessant ache remains. One person may win the player-of-the-year award for football, another earn an advanced degree from a prestigious college. Someone else might capture the heart of a perfect mate, make enough money, and live in the style he or she has always wished for. Yet, even in the midst of the bounty that is meant to bring satisfaction and fulfillment, the yearning persists, perhaps even magnified by the achievements, which only remind us of the emptiness within.

In a frantic effort to fill the void, some people consume enormous quantities of alcohol, smoke increasing numbers of cigarettes, ingest or inject drugs in a wide variety of combinations; however, many recovering addicts and alcoholics report that once the physical craving for the drug is eliminated, a deeper craving still remains.

In February 1991, Antonia Novello, Surgeon General of the United States, issued a report titled "Alcohol Practices, Policies, and Potentials of American Colleges and Universities." According to her, the average college student consumes over 34 gallons of alcohol a year, or 430 million gallons total. This is enough to fill 3,500 Olympic-size swimming pools, roughly one for each college or university in the country. Most of the alcohol consumed is beer—just short of 4 billion cans per year. College students spend $5.5 billion a year on alcohol, which is more than they spend on textbooks and far exceeds the operating costs of college and university libraries. The paper goes on to discuss the growing trend toward drinking with the intent to get drunk and the increased alcohol-related violence and crime on campus. It states, "More of our current college students in America will die of cirrhosis of the liver than will ever get doctorates in Business, Management, and Communications combined."

This report illustrates how the positive inner impetus toward wholeness can go in the wrong direction. Rather than indicating degeneration among the college-age population, these statistics reveal a group of human beings who are searching intensely for a connection with something beyond the ordinary, limited scope of their existence. Those who attend college represent only a fraction of their age group; other young people share the same addictive problems. As a culture, we do not have many sanctioned frameworks in which to deeply experience and satisfy the yearning for wholeness. As a result, people of all ages distort and misdirect this immensely strong impulse into addictions of all kinds, not only addictions involving the use of chemicals, but also eating disorders, sexual addictions, and addictions to power, money, relationships, gambling, and countless other addictive activities.

What is this free-floating yearning? I believe that Jung was right. This intense and at times painful craving is deep thirst for our own wholeness, our spiritual identity, our divine source, or God. Perhaps inspired artists such as Rembrandt or Mozart were able, in a momentary rapture of creative expression, to capture a piece of that source in their art, and I, as an observer, recognize this. Even for the great artists that moment is fleeting, however, and I, sensing that, am left with a gnawing, dissatisfied ache in my soul because I cannot get to that experience and stay there.

This place of wholeness we seek is our spiritual core, an essential component of our nature. Development of a relationship with this inner source is a common, and necessary, aspect of human existence. Throughout history, the connection between the divine and the individual or the community has been encouraged and celebrated in a multitude of ways, through various forms of spiritual practice, rituals, and creative expression. Entire cultures have recognized the importance and value of the spiritual component of our lives and actively supported the emergence and refinement of this deep and influential divine aspect of our makeup. The desire to reach our full capacity is natural. The "thirst of our soul for wholeness . . . the union with God," as Jung called it, is a fundamental impetus within us that has great power in our lives. The drive to know our true selves elicits a kind of divine discontent within.

In his book *The Natural Mind*, the physician Andrew Weil speaks about the human need to alter consciousness. He says, "It is my belief that the desire to alter consciousness periodically is an innate, normal drive analogous to hunger or the sexual drive." He goes on to describe the activities of children who experiment with nonordinary states by whirling around until they fall down in a stupor, hyperventilating and having a playmate squeeze them around the chest until they faint, or holding their breath until they feel dizzy or pass out. I believe that this deep need to change consciousness reflects our natural desire to transcend the daily ego-centered identity and experience a larger sense of self.

How Do We React to Our Spiritual Craving?

Some individuals are able to recognize and pursue the thirst for wholeness with relative ease. They quietly and patiently involve themselves in activities that gradually bring them in touch with their deeper Selves. As they progress, the lessons they are learning begin to manifest through the manner in which they live their lives. Many feel drawn to a regular spiritual practice, such as prayer, meditation, performance of sacred rituals, or community worship. Others may discover artistic expression as a means to develop their relationship with the divine source. Still others find their spiritual identity through participating in the simple activities of their everyday routine, engaging in work they enjoy, caring for themselves and their loved ones, or creating a nourishing environment around them.

There are also those who exist unaware of their spiritual potential, either through lack of direct experience or because they actively attempt to disown that part of themselves. When we seek to deny or repress the drive toward our true potential, it is often because allowing our divine nature to express itself involves the change that comes with growth and expansion. We feel that if we change, we might lose control of our familiar, secure belief systems. Even if we are not particularly happy, at least we have been able to depend upon our perceived reality as safe.

If we suddenly feel propelled to redefine ourselves and our existence, we might also have to confront new and difficult aspects of ourselves. For many of us, altering our self-definition and our experience of the realms around and within us is frightening—uncharted territories *are* scary—so we construct for ourselves a limited and often rigid worldview and defend it at any cost. But the very nature of our lives challenges us to let go of who we thought we were and allow ourselves to be carried into the unknown.

Our craving for the divine is spoken of in the devotional poetry of mystics from many traditions. The intensity of the imagery and the urgency of the tone reflect the passionate nature of the spiritual longing. Mirabai, an Indian saint, writes to the Lord of the Universe, "My body is in pain, my breath burning. Come and extinguish the fire of separation. I spend the night roving about in tears." The Christian theologian Augustine writes in the *Confessions*, "Thou Movest us to delight in praising Thee; for Thou hast formed us for Thyself, and our hearts are restless till they find rest in Thee."

Kabir, a fifteenth-century Indian master and poet, says, "I am restless indoors and outdoors. The bride [seeker] wants her lover [God] as much as a thirsty man wants water." Psalm 42 declares, "As the deer pants for the water brooks, so pants my soul for You, O God. My soul thirsts for God, for the living God" (v. 2). The late twentieth-century Roman Catholic monk and poet Thomas Merton writes about "the living water of the spirit that we thirst for, like a hunted deer thirsting after a river in the wilderness."

Of course, it is not my intention to imply that any of the extraordinarily spiritual people who wrote these lines were addicts. They understood and accepted their longing as spiritual. I believe, however, that this fervent thirst for wholeness, as well as the discomfort with it, is the underlying impulse behind addictions. This deep yearning goes beyond the very real physiological craving of those of us who become hooked into the cycle of chemical addiction, and it is different from our desire to escape pain through addictive behavior. Our innate longing to rediscover our spiritual nature is an often unconscious driving force that many of us feel throughout our lives.

Until we acknowledge its presence, until we give way to its vital potency, we will experience a disquieting undercurrent of dissatisfaction with our existence. Poets repeatedly use the metaphors of thirst and hunger as they describe the power of this yearning for God. Thirst, hunger, and our impulse to know our true selves are essential drives within us. Just as we need to pay attention when our bodies tell us we need water or food to sustain our health, so we must respond to the inner thirst that, when quenched, will bring us spiritual well-being and a connection with our unlimited potential.

I am aware this statement might be difficult for some people to accept. I have said that the craving for our own experience of wholeness or union with God is the underlying impulse *behind* addictions. I might even say that it embraces all the other elements of the addictive process. I will qualify this concept and put it into a proper context.

I emphasize that when I discuss the spiritual dimensions of addiction, I am in no way invalidating the other aspects of this complex condition. I feel strongly that addiction affects all levels of a human being, and in order to understand and treat people suffering from this potentially fatal malady, we must address each aspect of our makeup: the physical, emotional, cognitive, social, *and* spiritual. Over the years, there has been a great deal of important work in the addictions field that has helped to completely revolutionize and transform the understanding and treatment of chemical dependency and other addictions. During this time, much of the emphasis has been on the physical, psychological, and social aspects of the addictive process. Professionals from a variety of disciplines have written numerous insightful books and papers about each of these areas. Therapies and other forms of treatment that focus on these levels have been developed and implemented with much success, significantly contributing to the healing of many thousands of people.

The mosaic of addiction has many facets that exist simultaneously. Recovering addicts regularly discover that their addictions may have resulted, in part, from their genetic disposition, the habit-forming chemical reaction of their bodies with their drug or drugs of choice, or their family history. They acknowledge their need to escape reality, to numb the pain in their lives, or purge unpleasant feelings. In addition, many recognize that the stress of living in a culture that encourages a compulsive, selfish, acquisitive lifestyle is also a factor in their addictive behavior. Those who have the insight that they are also dealing with a deep spiritual craving say that this divine discontent exists under and around all the other elements. Even as they acknowledge and deal with the other aspects of their addiction, if they do not directly address the spiritual craving, they are not adequately confronting their dilemma.

There are also those who believe that the entire problem is a spiritual one. This depends to a great extent on the way we define ourselves; if we accept that deep within we each have a divine core, then in essence we are individual representatives of the divine. From that very broad perspective, any challenge we face, any level on which we are affected or afflicted, is sacred.

The success of Alcoholics Anonymous (AA) and the many Twelve-Step fellowships that have modeled themselves after its program attests to the power and importance of the spiritual dimension in the understanding and treatment of addiction. Although there are other spiritually oriented recovery programs that claim a similar success in addictions treatment, I will focus on the Twelve-Step model as currently the best known and one that has been extremely effective in helping addicts to recover for over fifty years.

Twelve-Step programs talk about the addict's experience of *soul sickness* when he or she is caught in the throes of the addictive process. Addicts face *spiritual bankruptcy* as they reach the bottom, as they approach the time when they have finally had enough of the destructive and self-destructive addictive behavior. These fellowships offer an inspired spiritual program that allows its members not only to stop their addictive activities but also to heal the soul sickness and move past the devastating internal bankruptcy.

As individuals practice the Steps, with support from the community of other recovering people, they begin to move toward a spiritual way of being. The emptiness slowly fills; the yearning gradually subsides. Over time, they develop a life infused with happiness, peace, and compassion.

In his famous letter to Bill Wilson, Jung wrote, "Alcohol in Latin is *spiritus,* and you use the same word for the highest religious experience as well as for the most depraving poison. A helpful formula therefore is: *spiritus contra spiritum.*" The Spirit of the divine heals the ravages of the alcohol or the "spirits." This prescription specifically encourages the development of spirituality as an antidote to alcoholism, but it can also apply to other forms of addiction, including addiction to drugs, food, sex, relationships, power, or gambling. If we begin to quench our thirst with the experience of God instead of with our addiction, we will eventually know the satisfaction for which we have been longing.

2

The Self and Wholeness

I‌N DISCUSSING THE craving for wholeness, I have used terms such as *God, divine,* or *spirituality.* For some individuals, these words have positive connotations and represent something very desirable. Such people have no trouble with the concept of a sacred presence in their lives. They may have even had experiences that demonstrate its existence and its influence, and they may be actively seeking to develop a relationship with that force.

These terms provoke deep emotional discomfort for many people, however, for a multitude of reasons. I recently attended a symposium at which politicians, educators, psychologists, social workers, and anthropologists discussed the problems facing American youth. Almost all the participants agreed that in order to more fully comprehend the issues and ameliorate the problems, we needed to address the spiritual requirements of adolescents as well as psychological, physical, and social considerations. But most of the speakers found the subject difficult to approach. One presenter talked about the "s-word," or spirituality, as a frequently forbidden topic. It is an often-hidden, unspoken, but central quality of life that is often surrounded by more taboos than more obviously controversial areas such as sexuality and money.

Many of us have been in denial about our spirituality. Just as we have repressed or repudiated the terrible things we do to ourselves and others, we have refused to recognize our own mystical capacities. In the past few decades, with the resurgence of interest in spiritual systems, their teachings, and their practices, we have started to come out of denial and recognize this essential aspect of our human experience. Why do so many of us have such problems with it?

The issues are complex and multifaceted. Just as there are numerous forms of religious belief, there are also many different religious attitudes and preferences. Some people have found the experience of a specific theological model profound, moving, and influential in a significant, positive manner. Others were brought up in homes or communities where an accepted ideology and religious structure was forced on them, even though it may not have resonated with them personally. Still others may have initially responded to a certain religious institution and its teachings but later questioned or rejected its precepts and dogma.

My family did not identify itself with a specific faith when, as a nine-year-old, I found my way to the Episcopal church in my neighborhood. Much of what I learned there was very important to me at the time, but eventually I moved away from the church to find my fulfillment elsewhere. A major reason for my defection was the exclusivity I was being taught. I remember a priest telling my confirmation class that only those who were baptized into the Christian church would go to heaven. At the time, one of the most important people in my life was a kind and generous Japanese-American woman who was a Buddhist. She was like a grandmother to me, one of the most loving, giving people I had ever met. Her ample lap, her nurturing arms, and her compassionate manner provided me with comfort on many occasions.

When I questioned the minister about Kayoko, he confirmed that because she was not a Christian, she would not enjoy the same salvation I would. This simply felt wrong to me. It was unfair that someone who was consistently practicing the love Jesus talked about would be damned because she identified with another belief system. After several years and a number of similar incidents, I decided that if my church's God discriminated that way, I would have nothing more to do with that form of God or that particular doctrine.

Some children run into difficulty with religion when the tenets of their religious faith do not match the actions of the people who presumably exercise them. Father is the perfect image of a God-fearing, churchgoing man on Sundays. He serves as an upstanding Christian deacon and during the worship service reads passages from the Bible about love and honor. But behind closed doors at home, he frequently gets drunk and beats his wife and children. In this situation, the father literally does not practice what he preaches. His religious pretense juxtaposed with his abusive behavior confounds a child's image of God.

A child victim of incest who repeatedly hears stories about a benevolent God cannot imagine how a loving, holy presence could allow such violence and violation. By contrast, people who are taught that God is judgmental and vindictive and will send us to hell for what seem to be minor infractions might become so frightened that they eventually disengage themselves from anything to do with religion or spiritual practice.

Many individuals become confused and angry as a result of their exposure to rigid concepts and attitudes about God, as well as actions carried out in God's name or behind a religious facade. They naturally develop negative reactions to and defenses against anything religious but, in doing so, insulate themselves against the possibility of a meaningful, life-enhancing experience of their spiritual potential.

Names and Attributes of the Divine

The object of our thirst has many names: the Self, the creative energy, the force of love, the divine Mother, our Buddha nature, the Tao, or Cosmic Consciousness. Worshipers have referred to it as the Great Spirit, the Christ, the Beloved Within, our source of inspiration, our Higher Power, or God, to name only a few. Although it is an indescribable power that is beyond labels, we must use words in order to communicate about it.

When I write about the divine essence, or God, I am discussing something available to all of us. Spirituality in this context does not refer to some vague or exotic or New Age phenomenon. Nor is it the dogma, the politics, and the hierarchies present in some religious arenas. Spirituality is a simple but powerful element of existence that is available to anyone. It involves a direct, personal experience of realities beyond our ordinary, limited perception of who we are. These hallowed realms give meaning to our lives by adding a sacred dimension; they expand our sense of identity and of where we fit in the scheme of things.

The sacred force is at once transcendent and immanent. We can find it both outside us and deep within us. A friend told me of a neighbor's three-year-old son, Russell, who was obviously aware of this divine dichotomy. One afternoon, Russell surprised his mother by saying, "I've been thinking about God. God must be very, very, very big."

His amazed mother softly responded, "Why do you think that?"

"Well, if God made everything in creation, God has to be very, very big," the child mused. "And do you know what else?"

"What?" she asked.

"God must be very, very, very tiny."

"Why do you say that?"

"Well," said Russell, "God has to be very tiny because God has to fit inside me, right in the middle. And I am a very small boy."

These innocent observations reflect the conclusions of many religious and spiritual traditions. They describe one aspect of God as supreme, celestial, omnipresent, and transcending all finite forms. God is also manifest in creation, infusing the sacred spirit within and around us. God is at once both impossible to comprehend and knowable through our own increased awareness.

At the center of every religion is its mystical core. The founders of these systems were historical figures who had powerful firsthand encounters with the divine. For centuries, the mystical branches of these traditions have continued to believe in a spiritual reality we can interact with through direct contact. In the course of this book, I will refer to that personal contact with our own sacred potential. We will venture beyond the multitude of holy names and theological systems into a very personal experience of God. In this process, we will not negate the rich and varied religious and philosophical ideologies, but in an effort to simplify our discussion, we will seek to bypass the differences and focus on the mystical domains, which appear to share a common ground.

Mystics of the great spiritual systems call the Higher Power eternal and everlasting. They use such words as *infinite, boundless, universal,* and *imperishable.* Ancient Indian texts describe the all-pervading Self that exists beyond and behind the human drama of life and death. Unlike our bodies, which eventually wear out like old coats, the divine essence remains unchanging, the same forever.

The Spirit is ineffable, impossible to describe. When people experience it, they can approximate only a fraction of that encounter in words. Capturing God in language is like trying to distill a star-filled sky into a few words. We can point to it only with the use of metaphor. Artists have tried to paint it; musicians have attempted to render it in their music; architects have endeavored to evoke it in their sacred monuments. And still, the vastness and all-encompassing power of the divine is impossible to capture. Alan Watts writes that "the highest image of God is the unseen behind the eyes—the blank space, the unknown, the intangible and the invisible. That is God!"

This spiritual force represents complete oneness. It offers us wholeness and a sense of connection with ourselves, with others, and with the world around us. Sacred unity exists beyond the differences and oppositions in the universe. It transcends limitations and weaves together many diverse threads into the fabric of all existence.

In its vastness, the deeper Self is benevolent, loving, and wise. Those who experience it describe feelings of grace that suddenly enter their lives, a kind of divine intervention and help. They might feel overwhelmed with a sense of the unending generosity and goodness that emanates from the spiritual source. This does not mean that life will always be happy or easy; by definition, our lives are full of fluctuations and challenges, ups and downs. We can feel blessed by spiritual assistance during everyday activities, however. A general sense of peace, harmony, and equanimity periodically graces us, even in the midst of difficulty.

In addition, many traditions characterize this supreme principle as infinitely creative. This force is the Creator of the universe, in all its diversity and complexity, and the creation is continual, expressing itself through the play of existence and all the players; it orchestrates the unfolding of the cosmic drama and exists simultaneously beyond and within creation. The rhythm of this divine conductor is the rhythm of our lives.

Some musicians and artists acknowledge the Higher Power as their source of inspiration. Sports figures credit it with their extraordinary performances. Healers designate it as the source behind their healing gifts. Those who spend time in nature—at the beach, walking in the woods, or hiking in the mountains—might refer to it as the force behind Mother Nature or the mystery of life. Some define it as the love, compassion, and nurturing that comes from another person or a group of people who care. Still others say that it represents our potential, the unlimited possibilities and gifts that may lie hidden from us much of the time.

An important point here is that even though the sacred force is boundless, eternal, and universal, it is accessible. We can tap into it, no matter who we are or where we come from, because this deeper Self exists within each of us. Because we have the capacity to contact our deeper Self, we do not have to rely on intermediaries to guarantee our spiritual development. Our firsthand relationship with the divine has nothing to do with dogma or politics or personal grandeur. It is not about looking exclusively outside ourselves toward some vague, detached entity that is judgmental and critical. Spirituality has to do with our own private and intimate connection with the limitless and constant essence that dwells within. This is what we yearn for.

The Deeper Self and the Small Self

For thousands of years, mystics, philosophers, and poets have described human beings as having two essential components: we exist simultaneously as limited individuals who identify strongly with our bodies, our lives, and the material world and as spiritual entities who are unlimited, universal, and eternal. We live with a paradox: we are at once human and divine, limited and eternal, the part and the whole. We are both the small self and the deeper Self. I have already described the deeper Self. Let us now look at the aspect of ourselves that we know well, the small self.

The small self is our ego-centered personal identity. We are contained, limited organisms with well-defined physical parameters and distinctive characteristics. We exist enclosed within our bodies, and we display a constellation of traits that are specific to each individual in the same way that every snowflake is unique. Each of us has an ego: a sense of myself as *me*, who *I* am in relation to other people and my surroundings. Our individual egos are valuable, indeed essential, as we operate in the material world. They help us to determine what we need to achieve in order to get through our lives: how to plan, how to survive, and how to relate socially and physically to our external reality.

The small self is bound by time and space. We have a limited life span that reaches from conception to death. When the body dies, our existence ends. We are contained within certain spatial limits and can experience only events and objects that are present in our immediate environment, within the range of our senses. The world we can see, taste, touch, hear, and smell is the real world. Anything beyond that is unavailable to us.

We can directly experience these two aspects of our nature, the small self and the deeper Self. Most of the time, we are aware of the small self. We live within a world that demands that, in order to function, we treat it and ourselves as material and tangible. We require a sense of individuality, with our own particular boundaries and personal characteristics, in order to successfully accomplish our daily tasks, conduct our relationships, and operate within our environment. The small self is the part of us that drives the car during rush hour, pays bills, goes to the supermarket, cooks and eats dinner, conducts business meetings, negotiates financial contracts, or visits the gym to lift weights.

However, there are times in our lives when we perceive ourselves as something more than our daily, finite identity. Our deeper Self breaks through, and we transcend our limitations. Suddenly we become aware that we are something much more than our ordinary perception tells us. This is a spiritual or mystical state, a direct awareness of our deeper Self.

Spiritual experiences can occur in many ways. They are extremely significant, pointing toward our deepest source of power and recognition of our unity with the rest of creation. It is easy to assume that because they are not part of our regular routine, mystical states are somehow out of reach for most of us. We might think they are grand and glorious visitations available only to those whom we define as religious personages, mystics, or saints. In fact, most of us have spiritual experiences, whether or not we recognize them as such. Because our ideas about sacred events are limited, we may not identify them for what they are; we may think of such events as special and rare times when God speaks to us, when we are enveloped by divine illumination and swim in the glory of the Cosmic Consciousness.

Such states are certainly possible, and there are many descriptions validating them, but spiritual experiences also take place during everyday life. Sometimes they take the form of sudden inspiration. You might be diligently trying to figure out a solution to a problem. Eventually, after working on the question from every possible angle, you admit that a solution is hopeless. You give up and turn to other things. Immediately, when you stop trying so hard, the answer pops into your head. You are caught off guard, disengaged from your ego involvement, and you might even have a sense that the answer did not come from you.

Dancers and athletes talk about times when they excel beyond their normal performance, when something seems to take over and they feel propelled by a profound sense of energy, power, and creativity. A dancer told me, "I was no longer the one doing the dance. The dance was doing me. Something else was in charge." The golfer shoots a hole in one; the basketball player makes an impossible shot; the runner finishes a race in record time. At times like these, athletes and artists say, they were somehow able to step aside as individuals, and the deeper Self surged past their usual limitations.

There are also times when we feel blessed. For a while, everything in our lives seems to work. We feel we are on track. All is right with the world. These are the times when we seem to unconsciously tune in to the rhythm of the day: parking places are easier to come by; our work is inspired; the right people show up at the right time. Perhaps, even for a brief moment, we open to the clear flow of creation.

Most of us are familiar with those periods when, for a little while, we seem to be led by meaningful coincidences, or *synchronicities,* as Jung called them. You have lost track of a former schoolmate, for example, and for some reason, you cannot get him out of your mind on a particular day. That night, you reluctantly accompany a friend to a party, and suddenly, across the room, you spot your old friend. He, too, has been wondering about you, because he is developing a new creative project and feels you are the natural one to join him as a partner. You just happen to be at a juncture in your life when you are trying to find a new direction for yourself; your friend's venture is perfect for you. That night at bedtime, as you close your eyes, you feel grateful and blessed.

There are also times when we feel protected as well as guided. In the early morning hours, a mother abruptly awakens out of a deep sleep and feels drawn to her child's room. She opens the door just in time to witness the first tiny flames of an electrical fire. An adolescent survives a serious automobile crash in which the car is demolished but he completely escapes injury. As he replays the accident in his mind, he cannot understand how he survived. His only explanation is, "A guardian angel must have been watching over me."

Many alcoholics and addicts speak of the times when, in the grip of their addiction, they could have seriously harmed themselves or someone else. There is the drug-addicted parent who drives safely for miles in a blackout with a carload of children or the closet drinker who, alone at home, combines alcohol and tranquilizers until she passes out fractions of an inch from the sharp corner of a table. A sex addict might consistently place himself in jeopardy with unsavory strangers or a bulimic abuse herself by repeatedly bingeing, vomiting, and ingesting large doses of laxatives. When they come into recovery, such individuals often begin to realize that, left to their own devices, they easily could have seriously injured themselves. They might have even died. But they did not, and they credit their Higher Power or deeper Self with their delivery from self-destruction and their introduction to recovery, often expressing profound gratitude for having been given a second chance.

We have been examining spiritual experiences that can occur during our everyday lives, when we feel inspired, guided, or protected by a force beyond our limited individual capacities. There are also mystical states that are sudden, overwhelming events that transport us to realms far beyond our common reality. This kind of direct, personal divine communion can dramatically transform and expand our worldview, completely changing our concept of who we are. They represent the "Cecil B. deMille" form of spiritual experience: Moses enraptured, humbled, and transformed before the glory of the burning bush. I have heard some people refer to them as "white light" experiences. These sacred occurrences are not exclusively available on a mountaintop, in a hermit's cave, or in the sanctuaries of the grandest temples. They can happen in the course of a normal human life, in relatively ordinary circumstances, to ordinary people.

We can have a mystical experience during the birth of a child, a loving sexual encounter, or a private moment of contemplation, during meditation or during a time of stress in our lives. When we witness or participate in beautiful artistic expression, music, or movement, we might suddenly find ourselves catapulted into a transcendent state of awareness. With the growing interest and research into near-death experiences, increasing numbers of people have been willing to disclose their own powerful, life-changing mystical episodes during operations, accidents, or health crises. Some individuals have profoundly tapped the deeper Self while in nature: during a walk on the beach, in the desert, on a beautiful day in the backyard.

A few months before she died at the age of ninety-three, my grandmother, knowing of my interest in such things, told me of two mystical experiences she had had as a young woman, when she was in her twenties. One sparkling sunny morning, we sat close together on her garden bench as she related her story in a hushed voice. She had been visiting a favorite meadow near her home, and as she walked along, drinking in the beauty of the day and her surroundings, she felt an insistent inner urging to lie down and look up into the clear, boundless sky.

As she sank into the grass, she whispered, "I was lifted out of myself, and I became one with everything that is. It was a beautiful feeling." Her individual limitations and distinctions had faded, and she had felt intimately connected with all of existence. This happened to her again in the very same meadow. Although she had never mentioned them to anyone, the memory of those events never left her. Seven decades later, as she prepared for her death, the understanding that her identity extended beyond her physical limitations allowed her to greet her eventual passing with grace.

Bill Wilson, the cofounder of Alcoholics Anonymous, had a dramatic spiritual experience at the bottom of his drinking career. He was an ordinary man, a New York stockbroker, whose life and alcohol intake were out of control. As he sat in his hospital bed, once again under treatment for severe alcoholism, he desperately prayed to an unknown God to help him. Suddenly, he felt surrounded by white light and infused with mystical ecstasy, strength, and peace. "I became acutely conscious of a Presence which seemed like a veritable sea of living spirit," he wrote. "I lay on the shores of a new world. 'This,' I thought, 'must be the great reality. The God of the preachers.'" This event, described in the book *Pass It On*, was so profound and significant that it brought Wilson the strength to stop drinking and completely altered the course of his life. During this brief episode, the healing power of the divine flooded past the small, helpless self.

There is also a form of spiritual experience that the recovering community acknowledges as the "educational variety," in the words of the psychologist William James. This is the inner awareness that develops gradually over time, perhaps without our consciously realizing it. People close to us may comment on behavior changes and positive qualities they observe in us, and if we look back over the preceding few months or years, we recognize we have grown significantly. These changes may be partially due to our own efforts, our own personal work. However, as we review and compare our old and new selves, we realize that a source beyond our limited possibilities guided our transformation.

The Treasure Hunt

We have been discussing the presence of the spiritual force in our lives and its potential for expanding our understanding and definition of ourselves. Now, a logical question might be, If we exist simultaneously as small, ego-centered selves and as the deeper Self, why don't we have easier access to our source of inspiration, healing, and guidance? If our sacred identity already exists within us at this present moment, why can't we recognize it immediately and consistently? Why instead do we feel a relentless drive, a searching for something we cannot easily identify? And why are many people completely unaware of their possibilities, their potential for wholeness? Seekers have wrestled with such issues for centuries.

There is a story from Swami Muktananda's book *Kundalini: The Secret of Life* I have thought of many times as I have asked myself questions like these: Before the creation of the world, only God existed. After some time, God became bored with being all alone and wanted someone to play with. So God created the world from Himself and Herself and formed lesser gods to help operate the universe. But the beings in God's creation knew they were divine, and they knew how to merge back into the source from which they came. Within a short time, they lost interest in the world, and all thronged back to God in heaven. God's game was ruined. God once again became bored.

God called a council of the other gods and asked them for their help. One suggested, "Why not throw everyone out of heaven, close the gates, and hide the key? And erect the veils of forgetfulness, so that these beings do not remember easily where they came from?"

God thought this was an excellent idea. "But where should we hide the key to heaven?" God asked.

"In the deepest depths of the Pacific Ocean," suggested one god.

"How about the top of the Himalayas?" said another.

"No, no. Put it on the moon. It is so far, no one will ever reach it."

God sat in meditation to see the future. God appeared to be discouraged, saying, "None of our ideas will work. Humans will explore the far reaches of the universe. Not only will they dive to the bottom of the ocean and climb the highest mountain, but they will visit the moon, explore the planets, and attempt to discover the workings of the cosmos."

The gods became silent. Suddenly, God said, "I have the answer! I know the one place humans will never look for the key to heaven. That place is within themselves, right in the core of their being. They'll travel millions of miles into space, but they will never take two steps within themselves to find the key to heaven."

The gods all applauded God's brilliant plan. And God has delighted in watching our search for the way home ever since.

Could it be that this all-involving human drama is really a long and complex treasure hunt for the key that will unlock the gate to our true nature? Perhaps every step we take is part of a wondrous divine game that keeps the human condition vital and dynamic and involved. Could it be that we are each wandering or trudging or skipping or dancing along a path that is the path of remembering who we really are? The restlessness we feel in our lives is the inbuilt initiative that propels us toward our spiritual possibilities. Our thirst for wholeness is the dynamic drive that will eventually unite our individual selves with our deeper Self, in the way that a drop splashed ashore by a wave ultimately reunites with the vast ocean.

6

Walking in the Desert

3

Alienation, Abuse, and the Human Experience

LET US FOLLOW the idea that we are each individual units, segregated from the ocean of our true nature, and that a major impulse in our makeup is to reunite with our source. As we continue, keep in mind that what I will discuss is only a story, a metaphor, in the way that the last chapter's tale of creation is a story. I am not saying this is how things are, but that perhaps this is a useful way of thinking about our experience. This portrayal of our heroine's or hero's journey describes the path that leads us through tests and challenges but promises healing and transformation for those who choose them.

In this chapter, we will look at alienation from our spiritual identity as an essential element of our humanity. As we do this, we will begin to follow the journey each of us travels from conception through our prenatal life, birth, and into our existence in the world. We will explore the qualities inherent in our state of isolation and examine the ways in which they manifest in our lives. How do we feel when we are cut off from our deeper Selves? What do we do to ourselves and to each other that increases and intensifies this general sense of disconnection from our divine identity? And what is the role of abuse in the story of our odyssey?

In this context, our separateness is not a negative or discouraging fact of existence from which we have no recourse. This is not a description of our lives as the *angst*-producing no-exit sentence of futility and absurdity that the existentialists talked about. From the perspective I am presenting, we exist in a state of cosmic amnesia. By disengaging from our potential, we have forgotten who we really are. And we are each involved in an intricate universal game in which our mortal identity is just as divine as the transcendent mystical realms. Our limitations, our finite perceptions, our inability to remember our true identity: these are all part of an exquisite drama in which we each play a distinctive role.

From this point of view, our state of separation is a divine condition, even though its depths feel far from sublime. It is part of the unique spiritual experience that we can only discover in our humanness. Just as the darkness of night is essential for the illumination of dawn, so the predicament of our cosmic loneliness is necessary in order to create the instinctive incentive that will eventually drive us toward our sacred source.

The Lessons from Holotropic Breathwork™

As we begin to explore our divine alienation, I will briefly describe the work I have done, because some of what I will discuss is based on my observations from and experiences with it. My involvement in this approach, coupled with my own spiritual journey and personal therapeutic pursuits, have led me to speculate that perhaps many of the great spiritual systems are right when they say our estrangement from the deeper Self begins before we are born.

In 1976, my husband, Stan, and I began to develop and offer what we now call Holotropic Breathwork™, a tool for self-exploration and self-healing that combines animated breathing, evocative music, and focused release work. Holotropic Breathwork™ provides a safe and supportive setting in which participants may discover the rich spectrum of experiences that exists within each human psyche. During our workshops and training seminars, we employ a very broad, inclusive model of the human psyche that emerged from reports of individuals involved in deep experiential work. This theoretical framework has many similarities to the observations of C. G. Jung, Roberto Assagioli, and Joseph Campbell and the inner cartographies of various spiritual traditions.

Holotropic Breathwork™ is usually done in a group. We encourage participants to turn inward and, with our support, to go wherever their inner meanderings take them, without editing. With comprehensive preparation and within a supportive, caring context, people regularly access deep levels within themselves. In this way, Holotropic Breathwork™ employs principles similar to Jung's active imagination, Fritz Perls's Gestalt practice, and other approaches that allow unrestricted expression of the unconscious realms, including the spiritual and archetypal.

Often, people come to Holotropic Breathwork™ to address specific emotional and psychosomatic issues, as well as problems of living such as marital difficulties, addictive tendencies, and stress. However, most of the individuals who practice this form of deep self-exploration eventually move beyond their original dilemma into a quest for a larger self-definition, a spiritual search. They each recognize that they have an innate wisdom and healing capacity that is effective, trustworthy, and at times, persistent. They discover that the healer is within.

The kind of material that regularly becomes available in Holotropic Breathwork™ sessions covers a very wide spectrum, and its broad scope tends to give participants a sense that their inner world is vast, complex, and full of possibilities. People regularly confront memories, experiences, emotions, and physical sensations from their earlier histories, from the circumstances before, during, and after their biological birth (Stan Grof calls them *peri-natal* experiences). They encounter the cycle of death and rebirth, as well as the extensive realms referred to as *transpersonal*. Our transpersonal qualities exist beyond the personal, that is, beyond the materialistic and limited self, in the realm of the deeper Self. Transpersonal experiences that emerge in the Holotropic Breathwork™ include realistic archetypal or mythological sequences, psychic phenomena, episodes that seem to come from past lives, mystical and devotional states, and others.

Repeatedly, participants in Holotropic Breathwork™ have reported that, after confronting some of the problematic areas of their unconscious, they realize how much of their lives have been dominated or motivated by them. These individuals are usually ordinary, functional people, many of them professionals. Like many others, they work on marital stress, psychosomatic illness, emotional tension, addictive behavior, or depression. Very regularly, during the breathwork sessions, they discover that the roots of these difficulties lie in unexpressed emotions, unrecognized experiences from the past, unacknowledged archetypal influences, or spiritual yearnings. In a safe and supportive environment they can confront these aspects of themselves, and a caring community of like-minded individuals with a broad understanding of the human being allows them to explore themselves without conceptual limitations.

The experiences I am about to describe happened in Holotropic Breathwork™ sessions. I focus on this approach because it is the one I am most familiar with. The same kinds of states can occur spontaneously or in many other contexts for self-exploration. I have seen a large number of people relive their prenatal life and/or their birth, including distinctive details they had no way of knowing and were later able to confirm. No one directed them to relive these early memories. Participants simply opened themselves to the possibilities within, and, with the breath and the music, these states emerged. Some people were even skeptical going into the session. They did not believe they could access their prenatal life or their birth, yet they had a convincing experience of being in their mother's womb, of fetal distress, of the induction of labor, of being born in the breech position or with the umbilical cord around the neck.

During the reliving and afterward, they felt amazed at the intricate details of the experience. Many people have subsequently checked their birth records or contacted their parents to verify their revelations and found out they were right. Frequently, their mothers had forgotten the information they had discovered, deemed it insignificant, or denied or repressed particular aspects of it as difficult and painful parts of an otherwise joyful occasion.

Every once in a while, people who are reliving the birth struggle or embryonic life, or even connecting with what they call a cellular memory of conception, will also describe another experience that produces enormous emotion: they talk of the deep and pervasive grief that comes with taking a human form. They say they feel cut off from their true nature, that somehow conception has wrenched them away from an expansive sense of freedom and unity and ensnared them in an individual, material body. Coming through the birth canal, they feel even further defined and confined, as though birth is the gateway from the transpersonal to the personal.

Abuse and Further Alienation

According to these reports and in keeping with the musings of the mystics, we begin to disengage from the sea of spirit at conception. We are estranged from our celestial roots as our essence becomes contained in matter. Our state of separation is now part of our new condition, an innate component of our nature as human beings. If, in our isolated individual form, we are abused at any time during our ensuing existence, our sense of isolation deepens and becomes cemented into place.

What is abuse? It is the invasion of our physical, sexual, emotional, intellectual, or spiritual integrity. It is the violation of our own sacred identity as individuals, an active intrusion through the boundaries that define us as unique. Healthy boundaries constitute the frontier between us and the rest of the world. They are the borders that define our identity, the characteristics that rightfully belong to us. My boundaries state who I am as separate from other people and the influences of my surroundings. Boundaries are essential as I perceive and interact with the environment.

As we continue, we will look at the role of abuse in various developmental stages. If we are systematically shamed or violated or betrayed, not only do we feel an increased sense of separation from our deeper Self, but we also become isolated from ourselves, our parents, other people, and the world at large. We feel alienated from the elements in our lives that should be sources of nurturance and support. In some cases, this alienation may have begun even before we were born.

Prenatal Patterns and Their Effect on Development

As recently as a couple of decades ago, most Western medical practitioners regarded a fetus as an unconscious, unfeeling, inferior mass of matter that did not respond to external stimuli until some time after birth. With the assistance of modern research, we now know what mothers have known for centuries: we know that an unborn child reacts very sensitively to influences within the maternal organism as well as to the outside environment.

Most of the studies on prenatal life have concentrated on the fetus's physiological reactions to the external world. We now know that loud noises affect infants in the womb. With sensitive machines, health practitioners can monitor periods of fetal distress in utero. And we are finally beginning to pay attention to the importance of diet during pregnancy and to the effect of alcohol, nicotine, and other drugs on our unborn children. We have witnessed the heart-wrenching tragedy of tiny babies who begin their lives agonizingly addicted to crack cocaine, heroin, or other drugs that have been passed to them through the mother's bloodstream.

Although medical researchers have made strides in understanding the physiological influences in the womb and during childbirth, they have largely ignored the psychological components. The work of the obstetrician David Cheek is an exception. Dr.

Cheek delivers babies and keeps detailed records of the circumstances of the delivery and any complications that arise. Dr. Cheek is also a trained hypnotherapist. Years later, when the children have grown into young adults, he hypnotizes them and directs them back to their perinatal experiences. He has found many accurate correlations between the actual delivery and the reliving of that event, and he has written and spoken about his findings.

As I have watched people reliving various aspects of their prenatal life, I have become convinced that this part of our history is important. I have heard many descriptions of the interior atmosphere of existence before birth. A number of people have depicted life in the womb as "an experience of oceanic bliss," a time of comfort and freedom and expansiveness. When they attempt to verify the details of their experience, they usually discover their mothers were relatively happy and healthy during the pregnancy. Often she enjoyed the exclusively feminine experience of carrying a baby, was emotionally supported by the child's father, and eagerly anticipated the arrival of the new family member.

But this is not always the case. Often the mother's health, her behavior, or the pressures and problems of her daily existence or of her marriage have negatively affected the child in utero. Many people, until they relived the experience, did not know about these factors in their mother's life. Perhaps the mother was a heavy drinker or smoker, or she felt trapped by her impending motherhood, or she and her partner, if there was one, did not want the child. Her body may have threatened a miscarriage. Maybe her husband was abusive, causing her to suffer emotional, physical, or sexual violence during her pregnancy. She might have been abusive to herself or to others. All these conditions are reflected in the child with whom she is so intimately connected for nine months. One woman reflects on her breathwork sessions:

> *Every once in a while, my experience would take me to a place where I found myself floating in a toxic, hostile atmosphere. I could see purple and red images that had a synthetic, chemical cast. I felt dizzy and nauseous, as though I was being poisoned. This happened*

several times, and it seemed to be related to the period around birth. I finally realized that this must have been my mother's womb, and that she was very likely having problems in her life while she was carrying me.

When I asked my mother about the pregnancy, I told her that I had had several dreams about it. After some time, she reluctantly told me about the prevailing circumstances. I was her first child. Deep down, neither my mother nor my father wanted a baby, even though, as a young married couple, it was the culturally accepted thing to do. They were young, and there was tremendous tension in their marriage, for a number of reasons. My mother reacted with severe anxiety attacks, for which she was later treated. And she used alcohol and tranquilizers to cope with her life. Hearing her story, there is no doubt in my mind that her constant stress, as well as her use of drugs, had affected my well-being before birth.

If we take this kind of experience seriously, it challenges us to accept that our parent's conduct and their physical, emotional, and spiritual well-being during our prenatal life are important pieces in the mosaic of factors that shape our personality and our behavior.

Of course, there are less than ideal conditions that can threaten or complicate a pregnancy that are part of the natural course of events. Unexpected physical complications or emotional responses to various life situations can affect the child. Even though they may feel disruptive to one who relives them later, there is a different quality to their impact. These difficulties are part of the life process. In spite of the challenges they present, in such cases the birth experience is still undergirded with the generally positive, loving attitude of the parents.

Our Passage Through Birth

We continue to be influenced by external conditions through birth and into our infancy, childhood, and later life. Professionals in various fields are now beginning to explore and accept the idea that the way in which we are born also has an important effect on our development. It is obviously not the only factor in who we become, but it is an essential one.

Individuals who relive their birth discover that certain patterns in their behavior make sense only in terms of the details of their delivery. Previously, they had felt mystified by these aspects of themselves, and trying to understand them in relation to their childhood was like trying to fit a round peg into a square hole. It simply did not fit. Once they start to open up to the possibility that the birth experience is at the root of some of their personal dynamics, their questions begin to be answered. The peg suddenly slips into place.

For most of us, the birthing struggle is intense and difficult, and at times, violent. Our world suddenly changes drastically. We are trapped within narrow confines, rhythmically pressured by unforgiving contractions, and often cut off from the generous supply of oxygen through the umbilical cord. Sometimes this goes on for hours or even days. However, many people who as adults work on memories of relatively uncomplicated births experience the passage through the birth canal as the first major challenge of their existence, a challenge from which they can ultimately emerge victorious. Birth is part of life, a natural rite of passage we all encounter. Moving through this ordeal and emerging into a new world is a major accomplishment. We learn that even though we confront difficulties as part of being human, we have the strength to overcome them.

Unnecessary human intervention that complicates the initial challenge of birth is abusive. There are many compassionate, gentle health professionals who do not engage in such practices and do everything they can to ease the transition for both mother and child. But some do not, perhaps largely because of the outdated bias that the infant does not register sensation. Labor may be induced for the convenience of the parents or the physician. Forceps are sometimes used automatically and unnecessarily to extract the infant. Heavy anesthetics may be administered indiscriminately.

Immediately after birth a child may be held by the heels or slapped in order to start the breathing rhythm. Males are routinely circumcised without anesthetics, regardless of the pain it produces. Babies are separated from their mothers and forced into feeding schedules that have nothing to do with their natural functioning or their individual needs.

Some of us were born when many such measures were routine. Thankfully, there have been important changes in Western birthing practices that have allowed for a return to a more humane treatment of mothers and children. However, though the last few years have offered prospective parents increasing options for non-invasive childbirth and early infant care, there is still a long way to go before this becomes the norm.

Over the years, I have seen many people relive vivid birth sequences, complete with minuscule details and visceral reactions. I have also had convincing experiences of my own birth. I have seen a slow-motion film of a newborn as the umbilical cord is cut before it stops pulsating. The pain momentarily distorts his tiny features, and he wails to express his anguish. Many medical professionals believe that a child does not feel pain when the cord is cut, because the umbilicus does not have nerves. The camera told me something else.

I have also witnessed the smile and the expression of deep satisfaction on the face of another infant as the doctor, and later, her father, gently cradled her in warm water as she unfolded and relaxed into her new existence. As a result of encounters such as these, I have reluctantly had to accept that the way in which we come into this world really *does* affect us—just as our later history affects us. We develop patterns of behavior not only as a result of our childhood conditioning but also from our prenatal and perinatal experiences.

A significant number of recovering chemical addicts and alcoholics have told me they have discovered a link between the use of general anesthesia at birth and the development of their later addictions. They say that, though this is not the only factor in their use of chemicals, it seems to be a major one. If the drugs that are introduced into the mother also reach the child, they discourage a victorious release after an infant's passage through the birth canal. Feelings of dizziness, nausea, and disorientation confound the infant's entry into the world. When adults with this history relive birth, they frequently report that during that event they received an emotional and psychological imprint that freedom from pain means the involvement of chemical substances. In addition, they are given the message that drugs are a necessary component when confronting challenges, a new chapter in life, or the promise of personal liberation.

Childhood and Beyond

Once we have met the challenge of our birth, we are introduced into our life in the world. It may even be that in our early life, we still maintain some contact with our origins (with the possible exception of those who have faced extreme difficulties prenatally and at birth). This is a fairly common experience for people who relive a relatively uncomplicated birth. They describe their initiation into the world as the entry into an existence that has similarities to the state of spiritual freedom or the sense of expansion and comfort in the amniotic ocean of the womb. If loving, nurturing parents welcome them, if they receive warmth, security, and nourishing physical contact, the connection to their vast potential remains strong and vital.

As I watch some infants in the first few months of life, I wonder as I observe their openness and trust, their long, intense gazes at the world around them, what it is they are perceiving and what they know that I do not. Are they open to realities not easily available to adults? I think about the number of parents who have made the observation, "My baby looks like a little Buddha," referring to the fresh, open, all-knowing quality of their infant's presence.

Or consider young children who spend long hours playing games with so-called imaginary friends or daydreaming about fantastic adventures. Although some children engage in such activities to escape severe problems, most children enter the world of fantasy and fairy tales as a normal part of childhood. Do they have a foot in the other realms that so many of us forget as we grow older?

This is not a new idea. Wordsworth wrote of it in his classic poem "Ode: Intimations of Immortality from Recollections of Early Childhood." He writes beautifully of the infant who comes into the world and perhaps maintains some faint connection with the original source before becoming completely confined by his or her humanity.

> Our birth is but a sleep and a forgetting:
> The Soul that rises with us, our life's Star,
> Hath had elsewhere its setting,
> And cometh from afar:
> Not in entire forgetfulness,
> And not in utter nakedness,
> But trailing clouds of glory do we come
> From God who is our home:
> Heaven lies about us in our infancy!
> Shades of the prison house begin to close.

Professionals from various fields have done a great deal of valuable work on the dynamics of our family life, abuse, and social influences as they affect our development. Virginia Satir, Alice Miller, Jane Middleton-Moz, Charles Whitfield, Sharon Wegscheider-Cruse, John Bradshaw, and many others have written sensitively and skillfully about the family of origin. They have described both functional and dysfunctional behavior, its results, and the paths toward individual and family healing. It is very clear that the kinds of human responses and other stimuli to which we are exposed, day after day for years of our lives, have a profound effect on our self-image, on our values, and on how we conduct ourselves.

Some children have the great fortune to be born to loving, aware parents who can encourage and celebrate their children's unique gifts while recognizing and nurturing their spiritual nature. In such families, both mother and father care deeply for their child. They respect the child's personal integrity and support the emergence of his or her unique personality and creative expression. They take time to guide, comfort, teach, and be taught by their children. They are emotionally available to each other and to their family. And they have the humility to admit to and learn from their mistakes. They openly discuss problems as they arise and honor the full range of emotions that exist as part of the human experience. The atmosphere at home is infused with love, acceptance, tenderness, flexibility, and honesty; there is a consistent sense of positive mutual regard.

Many individuals who grow out of this kind of background generally experience the world as welcoming, nourishing, and exciting. They are able to easily connect with the beauty and joy within and around them. They often feel blessed to be alive, and regard life, with all of its imperfections, as there to be lived as fully as possible. Most days are welcome and imbued with richness. Difficult situations are challenges rather than problems. The glass is half full, not half empty.

Those who are nurtured and cherished as children usually make their way in the world more easily than those who are not. They feel at home. They are more likely to be self-confident and competent in their endeavors. Through loving and accepting parents, they preserve and cultivate their contact with their divine origins and, as a result, are likely to develop an expansive sense of themselves and the world.

However, as we know, many people are not born into such a nurturing environment. Many of us are born into the desert, jolted into painful survival as human beings. From our very beginnings, we are surrounded by physical, emotional, intellectual, sexual, or spiritual abuse, by violent emotions, and by a world that not only does not support us, but tells us we are bad, over and over again.

When I started to acknowledge and to work on my own childhood history, I began with a very narrow definition of violation.

With my limited knowledge and with my substantial denial system cemented firmly into place, I thought that childhood sexual abuse meant genital contact imposed by an adult on a child. Incest was the same explicit act committed toward children by older family members. I was suspicious of and astounded and outraged by reports that told me one in every three women and one in every five or six men had been sexually abused as children. How could that be? What does this say about us as human beings? In the case of incest, how can people commit such horrible acts toward their own precious children? What kind of God would allow such an abomination?

As I continued my own recovery from incest, I began to see the broader picture. I began to let myself absorb, feel, and respond to the awful truth that there are many faces to the phenomenon of sexual abuse. I realized that the so-called *covert* sexual acts toward children can be just as damaging as the direct, *overt* ones. I started to understand that I needed to expand my definition of sexual abuse. Sexual abuse is one individual imposing himself or herself sexually on another person without that person's consent, whether it be physically, emotionally, or verbally. Sexual abuse includes a wide spectrum of behavior, from covert acts such as exposure to inappropriate nudity or the spilling over into the family atmosphere of the parents' sexuality, to overt acts such as mutual masturbation and rape.

According to this expanded definition, a child who is given no privacy in the bathroom or is repeatedly tickled until he or she cries is being sexually abused. A girl who is subjected to family members' comments about her breasts or a young boy who endures jokes about the size of his penis are being sexually abused. A spouse who is exposed to pornography or forced into sexual activity by his or her partner without consent is being sexually abused. And a child who is used for the sexual pleasure of any adult is being sexually abused.

Just as my definition of sexual abuse is very inclusive, so, I believe, must be our general definition of abuse. Earlier in this chapter, we defined abuse as an active and damaging intrusion beyond the physical, sexual, emotional, intellectual, or spiritual boundaries that define individuals. Physical abuse means violation of physical integrity, whether it is hitting or touching without asking. Emotional abuse invades the emotional parameters. People suffer emotional abuse when their unique emotional truth is discounted or rejected, when they are subjected to ridicule, to rageful outpourings, or to judgmental and derogatory comments. Emotional abuse also occurs when a person is repeatedly treated with silent withdrawal and lack of attention.

During intellectual abuse the thinking process is disregarded, disrupted, or discouraged. For example, when people's ideas or thoughts are subjected to destructive criticism, when they are harshly judged or punished for errors in reasoning, when they are authoritatively and rigidly told how and what to think without room for creativity or error, they are being intellectually abused.

Religious abuse occurs when religious precepts, teachings, or rituals are imposed without permission. Children who are forced to accept their parents' unwavering and stringent belief systems, while their own spiritual truth is undermined or discarded, are being subjected to religious abuse. So are communities that are forced to follow specific theological programs under threat of punishment.

Spiritual abuse is different from religious abuse. Spiritual abuse includes all the other forms of abuse and more. Anyone who is being violated in any way is also being spiritually abused. If we accept the possibility that our deepest roots are sacred, that we do come into our lives "trailing clouds of glory," as Wordsworth put it, then when we abuse each other, we are violating a sacred share of the divine. Mystics tell us that God dwells within each of us. Every one of us is a precious piece of the deeper Self incarnate, a drop temporarily separated from the ocean. Those who selfishly and violently impose themselves on their children are trespassing into the sanctity of their specialness. If we recognize that we are each a miraculous, unique thread in the fabric of creation, then we are all parts of the same cosmic cloth. When we violate others, we are also committing an act against the very core of our own being, against the eternal and creative source of our existence.

When we abuse someone, we are wounding another human being. We are imposing pain. By hurting or exploiting someone, we engender fear and anger, hopelessness and victimhood, confusion, guilt, and shame. And often those we abuse are the people whom we ostensibly love the most. When we inflict suffering on others, we are assisting in the creation of profoundly blemished individuals. These individuals become adults who carry within them unrecognized wounded children. They are hollow men and women, cut off from their sense of worth and their source of inspiration. As their sense of cosmic loneliness deepens, it becomes secured into place. This, in its deepest sense, is spiritual abuse.

There is nothing like abuse such as incest to scar a child so deeply that even if he or she works very hard to get rid of the resulting shame, fear, confusion, mistrust, and anger, it takes a long time. Incest cuts to the deepest layers of our beings. It instills in us a sense of cellular humiliation and outrage. The counselor and lecturer John Bradshaw talks about the difference between guilt and shame: when we feel guilty, we feel that we made a mistake; when we feel ashamed, we feel that we *are* a mistake.

A survivor of childhood incest or abuse walks through life feeling like one big mistake, like the elephant man or woman amid others who seem untouched—a far cry from our origin as beings who know they are divine. Those with a history of abuse often find themselves isolated and withdrawn. Their original divine estrangement has been overlaid by a human-wrought expulsion from a reality in which they may have had a chance to remain in touch, however tenuously, with their sacred origins. They have been cast loose.

The most frequent theme I have heard from those recovering from addictions is, " I always felt different." "I have always been on the outside looking in." "I have never felt at home, as though I belong." "I feel less than other people." I heard one person say, "For years, I thought I was adopted because I never felt that I fit in my family." Another mentioned that as a child his feelings of displacement were so strong that for a while he imagined he was an extraterrestrial, literally from another planet, a stranger in a strange land.

So many addicts come from addictive, abusive homes. Where there is excessive use of alcohol or drugs, there are also other forms of abusive behavior. Where there is manipulation and control by codependent family members, there is abuse. Where there is the pain and fear that accompanies any kind of self-centered, uncontrolled, compulsive activity, whether it is an obsession with sex, money, power, gambling, or food, there is abuse.

Abuse of Cultural and Religious Groups

We can apply everything we have said about the abuse of individuals to the way we treat other cultural groups. Horrifying and disgraceful examples of this violation of others, based on their gender, age, racial, religious, sexual, or social differences, are strewn throughout history. Those who are entrenched in the illusion that they are better than others regularly impose physical, emotional, intellectual, sexual, religious, and spiritual abuse on those whom they consider to be inferior.

A blatant and prevalent example is the abuse of indigenous peoples around the world. For centuries, entire societies or segments within them have been uprooted from their culture, traditions, and religion by neighboring communities or foreigners in search of power, control, or material wealth. Conquering forces, missionaries, or traders intent upon domination impose unfamiliar, unnatural social and religious attitudes and ideologies on the subjects of their exploitation. The vanquished are wrenched from their spiritual roots and their sources of inner inspiration and sustenance, as well as from their rich cultural reference points. They are alienated from sacred lands and meaningful relationships with the natural elements, one another, and the sacred. The histories of Africans, Australian aborigines, Tibetans, Polynesians, and natives of North, Central, and South America, among many others, are deeply marred by this kind of abuse.

In her book *Children of Trauma*, Jane Middleton-Moz sensitively and movingly portrays the difficulties encountered by different minorities. She writes of the "ethnic shame," self-hatred, and "learned helplessness" that result from discrimination against those who are identified as inferior. In addition, the accepted agenda of the dominant culture is unfamiliar, placing those who are part of an identified minority at a greater disadvantage by further removing them from their own values. Referring to Native Americans, she states, "There are many expectations of the majority culture that Indian children will face as they move into the broader world. It will be unlikely that they will be able to attain them without denying their own culture. Competition, success, and independence are not Native values. In a traditional Native home, children will be taught lessons of modeling, cooperation, interdependence, and the value of silence."

When anyone is violated, his or her identity as a representative of the divine is threatened and compromised. No one has the authority to impose an agenda on others, whether individuals or groups. Why do we do this? Although this is a complex issue, one of the central reasons is that by finding fault in other people and subjugating them, we do not have to address our own shortcomings. In his book *Faces of the Enemy*, Sam Keen writes, "We do, in fact, love or hate our enemies to the same degree that we love or hate ourselves. In the image of the enemy, we will find the mirror in which we may see our own face most clearly." We project our own unclaimed anger, fear, shame, and judgments onto those we ignore, despise, or exploit.

What Can We Learn About Love and Respect?

As I write about this very inclusive definition of abuse, I can hear the anticipated reactions: "Come on. You're splitting hairs. Rape and sodomy are much worse than ribbing my daughter about her date last night." "You mean to tell me that if I slap my son on the back during the ball game, I am physically abusing him?" "If all this is true, we are going to end up walking on eggshells. We're going to have to watch how we treat one another."

Exactly. It is already happening. Some manifestations of abuse appear to be more serious and damaging than others. For a while, I felt tempted to rate the spectrum of intensity, from mild intrusion to active abuse to torture. However, I believe that each time we violate another person, no matter what the severity, it is a serious matter. We are living in a time when we frequently disregard the life around and within us. We have forgotten how to honor ourselves, other people, other species, and our environment. As a result, our world is facing an unparalleled crisis.

With the increase of interest in various therapeutic and spiritual approaches, and especially with the courageous work being done by people recovering from abuse and from addictions, our attention has turned to the reality of the abuse that we visit upon one another and upon ourselves. We have begun to exhume the dark secrets we have furtively fueled and adapted through generations. Recent attention to issues such as sexual harassment, incest, date rape, and racial, gender, and social inequality have made many people uncomfortable. The blatant reality of such problems has pried us out of our automatic, often unconscious ways of conducting ourselves. We are being called to return to a basic reverence for ourselves, for others, and for our world.

I find great hope in the increasing numbers of people who are courageous enough to discover and examine the influences in their development, willing to explore the sources of their difficulties, as well as the painful individual, family, and social secrets that have kept them locked into blind repetition of harmful patterns. As more of us become aware of these factors in our experience, we begin to heal. We change the way we conduct our lives, the way we treat ourselves, other people, and the world around us.

A much saner and happier option than continuing in the destructive patterns so many of us have known firsthand is to approach our internal and external worlds with care and respect: to treat one another with a loving, devoted attitude; to love our sisters and brothers the way we love ourselves, as Jesus commanded; to honor the Self within one another, as Siddha Yoga suggests; to recognize our Buddha nature and the Buddha nature in every sentient being; to perceive the Christ within each person, as Mother Teresa of Calcutta quietly implores.

My dear friend Angeles Arrien is a cross-cultural anthropologist who works with myths, rituals, and symbols, tells wondrous stories, and helps her students to discover their natural ethics. Angeles is a Basque who was raised biculturally with family both in the Pyrenees mountains and in the American Basque community in Idaho. When she talks about her heritage and upbringing, she tells an ancient Basque myth about the origin of the Basques and their possible beginnings. She describes a lovely mermaid who would only swim in the lighted waters of the sun:

> *Gradually, the sun fell in love with this beautiful creature and stuck out his tongue, which was a beautiful rainbow, and pulled her up to him. They unified, and there were seven tear drops of joy. Then, he spat her back out; and she grew and grew to become the moon. At twilight you see neither the sun nor the moon, but you see their children, which are the stars, to whom the Basques were born.*

To this day, in less modern regions of the Basque countryside, when a baby is born, he or she is acknowledged as a "walking star" on a giant star, the earth. Children are highly revered among the Basques. Infants are regarded as "living treasures," an image that follows them throughout life. Every child is given a name that encapsulates his or her attributes and ancestral qualities. For example, the Basque name "Mendiola" means "of the mountain," a powerful symbol for certain personal attributes. Each time a member of the family or community speaks the name, the person is honored for both individual uniqueness and ancestral heritage. During childhood, adolescence, adulthood, and into death, members of the community are repeatedly honored, through various major and minor rituals, for the original contributions they are making spiritually to both family and community.

Can you imagine the difference in our lives as individuals and communities if we regarded one another as "living treasures" or "walking stars," as embodiments of the heavens? What if, each time we called for our children or spouses or friends, we payed homage to them by repeating their names, their own personalized emblems that remind us of their spiritual roots? This attitude may be far from the everyday reality of our lives today, but it is an inspirational example of what is possible.

4

How Do We Survive?

I HAVE BEGUN THE story by following the passage from an expansive state of freedom, through conception, prenatal life, and birth, until we emerge as functioning individuals. This journey has taken us from the gates of heaven, as the creation tale in the last chapter describes them, through our increased definition in human form. We have explored some of the elements and influences that contribute to molding our personalities and behavior and have depicted both the safe and nourishing atmosphere and the abusive, threatening environments to which we may be exposed.

As we continue, we will review an area that has received much attention from the fields of psychology and addiction recovery: our mechanisms for survival, the ways we learn to adapt in an unstable world. In the last chapter, I defined some of the characteristics of individuals whose history is relatively uncomplicated, people who have consistently received the nurturing, support, and understanding that they need. Here, I focus on the others, on the multitudes who have not been fostered in this way; I have a reason for this.

Some time ago, I heard a lecture on the diverse roots of addictive problems that was presented to a general audience by a counselor from an addictions treatment center. At the beginning of his talk, the lecturer asked his listeners this question, "How many of you come from dysfunctional families?" He went on to explain that a dysfunctional family is one that creates a behavioral structure in which its members avoid, rationalize, or cover up problems and carefully guard or deny secrets. Individuals within this system also have the tendency to indulge in exaggerated and destructive emotions, conceal their true feelings, or evade their own issues by judging, criticizing, blaming, or attempting to control others. In addition, they regularly violate one another's personal boundaries or remain aloof and unavailable behind well-fortified emotional and psychological defenses.

In answer to our speaker's question, almost everyone in the room raised a hand. He went on to tell us that according to some studies 96 percent of us come from dysfunctional families. From somewhere behind me, a male voice murmured, "It's gotta be more like 99.9 percent."

When I heard those numbers, I was still struggling to accept the statistics that reflect the high rate of sexual abuse, so my mind automatically rejected the large figures I was hearing. How could 96 percent of families be dysfunctional? But as I have continued my personal work, and as my general definition of abuse has expanded, I have reflected on this interchange many times. I have become convinced that because our behavior toward one another is often invasive, whether motivated consciously or unconsciously, many of us have been violated or have violated others. Unfortunately, this often happens at home. In rereading the definition of a dysfunctional family system, we can see that almost all families fit that category to a greater or lesser degree.

Because a large number of us have been raised in dysfunctional family systems, when we create our own households, we often automatically repeat the patterns we learned growing up. Our parents have probably done the same thing. It is a multigenerational pattern. Because we have lived so long within a certain emotional climate, we have accepted as normal some values and behaviors that are in fact destructive and self-destructive. According to this definition, we are all dysfunctional sometimes.

Again, we display our dysfunction over a very wide spectrum of intensity and behavior. Some actions are mildly intrusive, others are overtly violent, and still others involve equally devastating covert forms of invasiveness, deprivation, or abandonment. One family might create a controlled, inexpressive, unyielding structure that, from all appearances, is unruffled and cheerful. It presents a different profile from an extremely violent family in which verbal, physical, and sexual abuse is regularly visited upon a spouse and children. Yet both are dysfunctional.

In another family, one or both of the parents may be absent because of their worldly obligations, general inattention, or lapses into oblivion through alcohol or drug use. It is different from a family in which the adults silently radiate subterranean anger, furtively criticizing each other and the children while upholding rigid and impossible expectations for everyone. In yet another family system, parents may feel overwhelmed by their responsibilities and become unable to set any boundaries or guidelines. This is dynamically different from a family in which the mother and/or father establish themselves as the undisputed, unwavering authorities who occupy elevated, superior positions and expect their spouse and/or children to obey their demands without question.

We may recognize various elements of these descriptions in our own backgrounds, whether manifested in extreme or in subtle ways. Whatever the differences, each of these families has as part of its complexion an occasional or consistent disregard for the uniqueness and integrity of the people within it. This attitude is significantly different from that of an open family system in which individuals talk honestly about their concerns, honor one another's experience, emotions, and thoughts, and live in an atmosphere of mutual respect and love.

Our disrespect for one another is not specific only to family systems. We carry the lessons from our upbringing into a modern social structure that often engenders the same lack of reverence for individuals, communities, and nature as the dysfunctional family does for its members. We hear the stories all the time. How many children receive report cards that focus on what they *will* become, according to the teacher's perceptions and judgments, without acknowledging or accepting their current uniqueness? My student appraisal form from the seventh grade lists the behavior that, in the teacher's opinion, was either acceptable or objectionable. It then spells out what needs to happen in order for Christina to "develop into a top-flight personality." What about the already existing personality? What about the special gifts and contributions that are already present but may or may not fit the expectations of the teacher or the school? Doesn't the child have some special qualities that may be obscured by his or her difficulties?

There are numerous examples of situations in which the integrity of others is ignored, devalued, or violated; it happens all the time. We all know about children who have no hope of discovering and developing their talents in crowded classrooms with overworked, exasperated teachers. Many college and university systems reduce candidates to test scores and accept or reject them on that basis. Numerous employers expect a regimented conformity that successfully discourages or denies the creativity of their employees.

Every day, individuals are subject to discrimination on the basis of their race, gender, age, religious beliefs, or sexual preferences. In addition, we are entrenched in a cultural attitude that regards human beings as superior to other life forms and that gives us the right to unlimited exploitation of the natural bounty of our earth. We live in a global power system that has fostered development of weapons capable of destroying life as we know it many times over.

I realize I have been painting a rather bleak portrait. Although it is clear to me that this is only part of the story, these issues desperately deserve our attention and remedial efforts. On the other side of this picture are the many caring, compassionate individuals who respect and honor other people, other species, and the world. It seems that this kind of awareness is becoming more widespread as we are increasingly willing to recognize, address, and act on the problems within and around us. One of the ways we do so is through courageous efforts to extract ourselves from the fogbank of denial about actions that cause pain and fear to us and to others. Our discomfort when we discuss such issues usually points directly to the issues that need attention, to what must be changed.

Living with Abuse

Let us now return our attention to the individual as he or she progresses through life. Accepting the reality that most of us have tasted abuse in some form, we will explore how we learn to live with it. How do we survive in a world that does not recognize or respect our sacred individuality? We will begin by describing the atmosphere in an abusive household. Although this portrayal might seem more extreme than most people's experience, the common attitudes it represents may be familiar.

How does it feel to live in an abusive home? Remember yourself as a child who is completely dependent upon the protection of your parents, large presences who are presumed sources of nourishment, comfort, guidance, and love. You are impressionable, vulnerable, and trusting. You are like a little sponge, eagerly absorbing whatever your complex environment offers you. You love to explore, experiment, and discover.

But your caretakers are unwilling or unable to provide the warmth and the nurturing that you need. They have become too entangled in their own problems, too preoccupied with their own pursuits. Their quest for drugs, alcohol, power, or money may absorb them. Together or separately, they might act out their rage or their exaggerated sexual needs, focusing on you and on other family members. Perhaps they subject you to violence, to periods of silence or withdrawal, to secrecy, or to overattentive control. They might impose unyielding expectations on you or give you very little attention and guidance. They might regularly belittle, ridicule, or talk you out of your feelings and opinions. Instead of receiving the generous love, attention, and support to which you are entitled, you are diminished, ignored, violated, or unnecessarily restricted.

If there is no consistency in your life or if you are regularly dominated by others, you can easily feel out of control, as though you have no reliable reference points. You may learn that you cannot depend upon others. As a result, your ability to trust gradually diminishes, and you feel lonely in the midst of the disharmony in your life. Over time, you develop specific fears or a general sense of anxiety. You may feel confused about who you are and where you fit, where you end and the world begins.

In addition, you may increasingly experience a deep sense of shame. If someone repeatedly discounts you, you begin to believe the messages they are giving you. If you have been physically or sexually abused, you might find it is easier to accept that you are at fault than to painfully affirm the truth: that people who are supposed to be dependable are capable of such violent acts. Your confidence gradually erodes, and in response, you regularly denigrate yourself, regarding yourself as the problem.

Many articulate, thoughtful professionals in the fields of psychology and addictions treatment have written and spoken eloquently, in great detail, about the abusive elements in our family and social histories and the reactions we have to them. When I suggest that the human unconscious contains many layers beyond biographical memories, I am aware that I am stepping into controversial territory. It is true that many people have experiences of other levels, however, either spontaneously or within the context of self-exploration; I have seen it happen many times. And these experiences can bring about important insights, change, and growth.

People who engage in self-exploration and therapy often discover that these other levels of experience often act as underpinnings or umbrellas for their biographical issues, adding potency and depth to them. They might encounter familiar themes and emotions in association with memories of birth or their prenatal life: profound layers of guilt, loneliness, anger, or confusion. They may find, on the transpersonal level, archetypal and mythological elements, even sequences that seem to come from other cultural and historical contexts, underlying their own history of abuse and adding power to it. Someone who is working through the aftermath of physical violation by a stepfather, for example, might reach another level within that contains a realistic identification with the suffering of humanity.

An expanded model of the human psyche offers the possibility of deeper understanding and assistance for those who need it. Many transpersonal psychologists have done solid, reputable, and well-documented work that offers valuable insights into our makeup. In the context of this book, we will focus on our biographical history against the background of our vast psychological, emotional, and spiritual potential. We will not attempt to specifically explore the many layers of our minds; that would constitute another volume, one that a number of well-qualified authors have already written from different perspectives. For our purposes, we will focus on our histories, behaviors, and reactions, knowing that the mosaic of the psyche is complex and multileveled.

How Do We Survive?

How do we survive? How do we take care of ourselves? What do we do to make our lives acceptable and safe? How does a child who lives day after day in an uncertain or abusive atmosphere find what it takes to endure her or his existence? How does someone who carries the imprint of a complicated prenatal life or birth, or who feels deeply influenced by a powerful mythological theme, get along in a world that may be reinforcing those patterns?

We sustain ourselves by becoming extraordinarily creative. Because we cannot depend upon others, we learn to rely upon ourselves. I have felt deeply moved, even awed, by the impressive power and ingenuity of the human spirit. It helps us to endure the most unthinkable situations and the more constant minor transgressions. Our ability to preserve ourselves in the face of our trials is truly impressive. Because creativity springs from spirituality or, as some people believe, is the same as spirituality, we employ the deeper Self as we learn to manage and cope with our lives.

Traditional psychiatry defines *defense mechanism* as an often unconscious psychological process that enables the ego to reach compromise solutions to problems. We all create defense mechanisms, whether we encounter relatively mild difficulties or severe ones. By that definition, our defenses are solely a function of the ego. More recently, however, many psychological approaches have expanded their understanding to include physical and spiritual mechanisms, as well as psychological.

Let us look at some of the more familiar defense mechanisms. We employ each part of us to construct them: the spirit, the mind, the emotions, and the body. We automatically mobilize all our reserves in order to provide safety and comfort for ourselves. Because many of these survival strategies are ultimately inspired by the deeper Self, they are all, by their deepest definition, spiritually motivated. For the sake of clarity, however, I will divide them into three general categories that of necessity will overlap. The first are strategies that specifically employ our spiritual resources; the second, the psychological (emotional and mental); and the last category, the physical.

As we will see, there are two sides to these inventive designs for self-preservation. At first, they bring us valuable and necessary gifts, but as we continue to grow, they often turn against us as we carry them through our lives and into our relationships. We begin by quickly and deftly generating survival strategies to defend us against the external sources of our difficulties by removing, numbing, or circumventing our pain. As we test these new schemes, we discover that many of them work well, so we repeat them. Eventually, they become so familiar that we may mistake our new conduct for the reality of who we are. In addition, our behavior might impede relationships with others, lead us to develop addictive qualities, or eventually harm us in other ways.

Spiritual Survival Strategies

Children in threatening situations often depend upon capabilities not always recognized and accepted within our limited human self-definition. One very common reaction of abused children is to develop *intuition*. Many of them develop a well-tuned radar, an intuitive or psychic scanner that helps them anticipate, outguess, and outmaneuver those who represent a threat. Intuition comes from our deeper Self, from the spiritual resources that exist beyond our ordinary capacities. Robert, a man in his late thirties, grew up in an alcoholic home. He describes his radar as an ACOA (Adult Child of Alcoholics):

> Both my mother and my father were drunks. My father became quiet and mean when he drank, making scathing comments to everyone within earshot. My mother would get violent, often hitting us kids or slamming objects around in the house. They fought a lot. It was like living in a constant battle zone, never knowing when the next incident would happen. I was always on alert, and I learned pretty fast to read the signals that my parents gave. I became able to anticipate what they were about to do and figure out something either to placate them or to get my sisters and myself out of their way. I knew by the look in my father's eye or by certain minute gestures from my mother when there would be trouble. Even today, as an adult, my intuition is very strong. The problem is that I am often so attuned to other people and their needs that I neglect my own. For so long, I have been so sensitive to the world around me that I have lost touch with myself.

In the face of danger, Robert developed his intuitive skills and used them to survive. Later, when he was an adult, that exceptional capability remained. This is an example of a highly developed ability that can ultimately become a gift or a hindrance. Even now, Robert's intuition provides valuable insight about the reality around him. He has become very adept at sensing the dynamics of a situation and uses his frequent "hunches" to his advantage on the job. But, as he says, if he focuses solely on the external world, he ultimately distances himself from his own needs. When this happens, he feels off balance, constantly vigilant and guarded against the possibility of the next intrusion. He becomes so absorbed by other people's behavior and requirements that he finds it difficult to focus on himself.

Another common survival strategy for an individual is to *split off* when confronted with a highly traumatic situation. We escape the pain around us by retreating into the safe haven of fantasy, illusion, or the transpersonal realms. By temporarily retreating from daily life, wounded children defend, preserve, and nurture themselves. They protect themselves by separating their awareness from the rest of their being, so that they do not have to register or confront the reality of their circumstances. A young girl who is sexually abused quickly and instinctively learns to detach emotionally and psychically. She retreats into another world so that she does not have to experience the violation of her body and her soul. In this way, she not only protects herself from the impact of that event, but she also maintains an identity that is accessible to no one but her. In the face of a violent threat to her entire being, she is able to salvage a piece of her selfhood that is inviolate.

This inner refuge provides the child with safety and comfort. It reflects her unconscious attempt to nourish and care for herself. She may simply become numb, blank out her experience, or protect herself so strenuously that she has no conscious recollection of the event. Or she might propel herself into an expanded experience of her deeper Self, into a place that is beyond the despicable activity to which she is being subjected. In this realm, she can feel a kind of divine support, a mystical guardianship that provides an unconditional sense of solace and communion that is unavailable in her external world. This may even be her first mystical experience.

Detaching from present reality was one of my favorite survival strategies, and I now believe it gave me an early introduction into the spiritual realms. It began during the ordeal of sexual abuse and then became something that worked in many situations beyond it. I went to a sanctuary in which I felt invisible arms wrapping around me, welcoming, embracing, and protecting me. Sometimes Jesus appeared, holding out his hands to help and comfort me. My haven was a dreamy, light-filled place of freedom and expansion. When I was there, I was all right. No one could hurt me. I was safe.

Some researchers have studied political prisoners who, after their capture by the enemy, were subjected to torture. They found that there is a mechanism by which, when the pain reaches a certain point, the victim's consciousness detaches from his or her plight. He or she suddenly flips into a state of mind that exists beyond the pain. The prisoner transcends the agony, often experiencing an ecstatic state in the midst of chaos.

In a number of cultures there are rituals, such as the Native American Sun Dance, that include elements of physical or emotional suffering. Occurring within a ceremonial framework, such rites often mark important transitions in the participants' lives. At a certain point during the proceedings, the initiate's anguish turns into spiritual rapture as he or she moves beyond the everyday restrictions of consciousness.

During such ceremonies, participants choose to use suffering as a gateway to transformation. Although children who are abused or traumatized in other ways have no choice in the matter, I believe that a similar mechanism exists. I do not mean to say that because of the possibility of a mystical glimpse there is anything positive or desirable about a traumatic event. Nor, as some people have suggested, am I saying that incest is an experience of initiation for a child, a notion that is insensitive and offensive. By juxtaposing the examples of the prisoners and the rituals with a child's ordeal, I mean to reveal a sense of wonder and appreciation for the wise force within us; it is able to automatically provide nurturing amid devastating, painful conditions.

Victims of incest are not the only ones who learn to split off in order to protect themselves. This happens to children who go through any trauma, whether it be verbal, physical, or emotional abuse, an accident, war, or famine. Whether a child is subjected to extreme trauma or a milder form of abuse, the mechanism of dissociation works the same way. As we become increasingly proficient at it, we learn to use it regularly. We discover that we can check out of present reality whenever there is pain. We absent ourselves when our social or sexual interactions are difficult, when conversations contain uncomfortable information, when we are visiting a place where we do not want to be.

Consider the child whose report card from school reads, "Cynthia is a good student, but she would do even better if she didn't spend so much time looking out the window." My question is, When did that child learn to dissociate, and why? What is it about this situation that motivates her to detach herself? Is she sitting in class without the proper stimulation? Is she so filled with shame that she cannot adequately perform for the teacher, unable to bear the pain of her humiliation? Or is she steeling herself against the reality of the home life to which she must return that afternoon?

Not long ago, my husband and I asked a lawyer to help us draw up our wills. Sitting across the massive desk from us, the attorney recited a litany of the possible ways in which we each could die. In the midst of his recitation, I abruptly realized that I had completely missed a significant portion of his advice. I had automatically escaped into some corner of reality rather than face the stark fact of our eventual death. My once useful and creative coping mechanism interfered when I needed to pay attention.

There seems to be a relationship between *splitting off* and the phenomenon of *spiritual emergency,* the sudden, often dramatic breakthrough of mystical or transformative experiences. For years I have been interested in spiritual emergency: I have spoken about it, written about it, and lived it. It seems that the more extreme forms of spiritual emergency often happen to those who have a serious history of abuse.

Such individuals exist with the weakened or shattered self-definition of someone who has been repeatedly violated. Their small self exists as a loosely constructed structure, and through dissociation, they have already become familiar with the spiritual arena. Consequently, they are perfect candidates for the powerful transformative power of the deeper Self. They become open channels for experiences from the deeper realms, but they do not have the boundaries to contain them. Frequently, they have difficulty functioning in daily life, and unfortunately, they cannot always find a sympathetic and supportive environment where caring professionals encourage them to go through and grow from their experiences. All too often, they are misunderstood and given unwarranted psychiatric labels and treatment.

Kenneth Ring, Ph.D., a prominent researcher of near-death experiences (NDE), has come to a similar conclusion. Ring and others have found that people who report NDEs often describe an encounter with nonordinary realities, including mystical states. In a study called *The Omega Project*, he and fellow investigator Christopher J. Rosing used a questionnaire called the Home Environment Inventory (HEI) in order to measure the relationship between childhood abuse and trauma and susceptibility to NDEs. They discovered there was a high correlation between the two and postulated that "a history of child abuse and trauma plays a central etiological role in promoting sensitivity to NDEs." They also acknowledged the role of dissociation in familiarizing an individual with alternative realms.

People who dissociate often become so detached and isolated that they cannot enjoy the riches their lives offer them. They miss the beauty of the world and the joy of participating in it. And they forfeit the potential of a loving connection with others and with themselves. On the positive side, they may discover and become comfortable in the mystical realms or develop easy access to spiritual experiences, something that some of us can only wish for.

Before we move away from the survival strategies that directly involve our spiritual resources, I want to mention another common behavior: *the desire to save the world.* This is less a survival mechanism than a reaction, but it is something I hear about regularly. Many people who are recovering from addictions talk about their lifelong desire to save the world, to become involved in some activity that would bring about justice, love, and harmony. They often chuckle apologetically and say that they realize this is a manifestation of their grandiosity, an inflated character defect.

I see it differently. Many individuals who later suffer with addictions come from abusive environments. They also have good hearts, carrying within them a reservoir of kindness and compassion. As they lived through the disruptive inconsistency of their childhoods, they repressed the unspoken voice that said, "Somebody *do* something! Someone has got to stop this! Please, stop this!" They felt an urgent need for some larger force, an older and bigger person, to bring peace, control, and love to the chaos around and within them. As they grow, they may even act out that role in their family or their community; they may become the identified peacekeeper, the one who steps in and attempts to placate others or defuse tense situations.

It is only a small step to a larger stage. From the familiar stance of the family pacifist, fueled by the intense desire for love and serenity, such people can easily throw themselves into causes or crusades that promise the peace and unity they crave. If they have felt repeatedly frustrated in their localized efforts, their passion to "make it okay" in their external reality increases. The more they lack tranquility and order within themselves, the more vehement their efforts become to achieve it elsewhere. It is easy to extend this well-motivated fervor to a very profound and benevolent vision of planetary peace and well-being that is not much different from the formulations of the mystics and pacifists throughout history.

Again, this reaction has both positive and negative sides. To be able to conceive of ways in which we can realize more compassion and harmony in the world is a much-needed altruistic gift. Our efforts to effect such changes may bring about many good results. If nothing else, our activities put us in touch with our capacity to love and to feel compassion, qualities that spiritual traditions encourage us to develop.

However, our efforts to achieve harmony may be completely outward-directed. We might focus so intensely on global difficulties and needs that we neglect our own. Arms outstretched and hearts wide open, we reach so fiercely toward the anguish of the world that we lose our balance. In addition, the positive emotions that motivate us may become infused with our anger, shame, and fear. When this happens, a potentially humanitarian activity becomes a vehicle for our unacknowledged personal agenda, often turning against itself and bringing about the very thing we are protesting. Those who furiously demonstrate against one cause or another eventually engender an angry response. Those who feel compelled to offer help out of their own fear may ultimately serve only to instill fear in others.

Psychological Survival Strategies

A wounded child often feels out of control. He or she feels defeated, swept from one unexpected situation to the next. A little boy might not know from day to day whether someone will be there when he arrives home from school, if anyone has had the time or the inclination to cook an evening meal, or if mother or father has been drinking. A young girl may be uncertain whether she will receive too little or too much attention, whether there will be a fight at the dinner table, or whether Daddy will sneak into her room that night to touch her in the wrong places. Sometimes the fear, the anger, or the shame feel overwhelming. "If I let it out, I will explode. If I even admit to it, I will feel crazy."

And so what do children like this do? We create psychological defense mechanisms based on our mental and emotional reactions to our plight. In order to shield ourselves against the threats around us, we develop behavioral defenses. We construct safeguards that are largely responses to our fear, shame, and anger. We shield ourselves against our sense of guilt, our sadness or hurt.

Repression is a common method of self-defense. Have you ever met someone who tells you she cannot really remember much of her childhood? She might even say, "It must have been happy or at least pretty uneventful, otherwise I'd remember it." Not necessarily. Often those who have forgotten large segments of their history have used psychological defense mechanisms to successfully store traumatic memories safely out of reach somewhere in their inner repository. At the time a trauma occurred, the child was not strong enough to withstand its full impact and truly absorb its devastating consequences; instead, the child learned to tuck it safely away out of sight and memory. At the same time we repress an event, we might also split off, that is, propel our awareness out of the situation altogether.

Some children who repeatedly experience abuse or other forms of trauma learn to escape the outer chaos through ordered and logical thinking, particularly if they are intelligent to begin with. By retreating into the protected confines of their minds, they not only create a sense of control over uncontrollable situations but also effectively remove themselves from their physical and emotional reality. These children discover that the power of the mind is so great that it can successfully distract and distance them from bodily pain and the intensity of their fear, anger, sadness, and confusion. Frequently, they lock their emotions and physical needs safely out of reach in favor of an overactive intellect.

A T-shirt around the recovering community reads, "Denial is not a river in Egypt." *Denial* is a very common, much-discussed psychological defense mechanism. If we deny to ourselves or others the reality of our experience, we do not have to feel the full extent of it. If we believe that it did not happen, that it was not the way others perceived it, we can protect ourselves. If we deny there is an elephant in the living room, there is a good chance we can remain blind to the implications of its existence.

Related to denial are the psychological defense mechanisms of minimizing, idealizing, and rationalizing. We *minimize* when we tell ourselves that it was not really *that* bad: "Maybe it was all in my mind." "Perhaps it did not really have much of an affect after all." "Oh, this happens in every family." We minimize when we tell ourselves that what has happened to us is nothing compared to the dilemmas others face; after all, there are people whose lives are a lot worse. We can always find someone whose story appears to be more dramatic and devastating than ours. We protect our emotional reality when we minimize, keep ourselves from recognizing and absorbing the painful truth.

Rationalization is another defense mechanism. When we rationalize, we make excuses. If our parents leave us alone without much contact with them, we explain to ourselves that mother or father have very important jobs. They have to work hard; we are all right by ourselves. If we are subjected to verbal or physical abuse, we justify the behavior by thoughts such as, "She yelled at me because she had a bad day at the office," or "He didn't mean to hit me. He was just feeling sick today." In the midst of a situation that seems irrational, we seek logical reasons for behavior.

When we *idealize* our circumstances, our minds become storytellers. A child in a dysfunctional family might tell himself and others that his family is wonderful and happy, perhaps even better than others. He may idealize his parents, seeing them as the perfect mother and father who always do the right thing. Everyone gets along famously, and they have a great time together. He hangs on to the pleasant memories and blows them out of proportion, generalizing them to represent his entire reality. This is a remarkably creative endeavor that helps him to survive. However, it also leads to a pattern of false optimism, avoidance, or unrealistic idealism that will sooner or later become a burden in his relationships or daily functioning.

Another common and seemingly effective mechanism that brings an air of order into our lives is the attempt to *manipulate* or *control* a situation and the people within it. As wounded children who are dominated or victimized by others, we rally our forces to somehow climb out of our subjugated role and exert some semblance of strength. This effort can take many forms. Some of us react by hanging on tightly to our reality, by desperately trying to control as much of it as we can. I have seen children whose straight, taut bodies and well-behaved rigidity belie the pain and internal chaos they carry. It is as though they are saying to themselves, "Hang on. Put on a happy face. Don't move. Don't even breathe too hard. If you do, it will all fall apart."

Some children become overbearing and demanding in order to gain a sense of power over their lives. They might use whatever force they can muster to coerce others into behaving according to their demands. Friendships become vehicles for a demonstration of strength. These individuals intimidate younger siblings or weaker schoolmates and get away with it because of their size.

If we do not find ourselves in a recognized position of power, we can still exert some control through less overt means. We might learn to be cute, flirtatious, playful, or even seductive to get what we want. We turn on our charm. We become extra agreeable, virtuous, or attentive to someone else's needs in order to get the other person to respond. Soon they want something from us that only we can give them: our attention, our assistance, or our favor.

When we have assumed a measure of command over the situation, we feel safer. We are in charge. This is the little boy who develops intricate ways of enticing the older people in his life to give him what he wants by exaggerating or dramatizing his charm. These are the children who become identified as the family mascots, the ones who are masterful at adopting positive responses as a method of controlling others. By acting cute or clowning, they also divert attention away from the pain or stress within the system.

We may mobilize our resources to mold ourselves into the perfect person, a "good girl" or "good boy," the apple of Mommy's or Daddy's eye. We do everything to please others. We anticipate and act on their expectations of us and make an enormous effort to build a facade of excellence and capability. We study hard in school, present ourselves as model students, and work to appear flawless in our behavior. It is a very lonely stance. Somewhere within, we are aware of the disparity between our well-polished image and the reality of our inner turmoil. We have set ourselves apart from other less exemplary individuals, and we have probably created for ourselves a set of extremely difficult expectations impossible to reach.

Another form of controlling behavior is a constant attempt to take care of others. We anticipate their every whim, making sure we are there to assist them whenever necessary. We need to be needed, and we make ourselves indispensable so that we can feel dominant. We may also believe we can change the people we help according to our expectations. As painful and unrewarding as this role may be, it often becomes as necessary for the caretaker as for the person being cared for. Our charges need our supervision. Without us, where would they be? For some time, we do what we can to make sure they remain dependent on us, because without them, we would not have a function. Our world would fall apart. We would lose our sense of power.

Children are often forced into this role out of circumstance. They live with a parent who has a serious illness or disability or who is an alcoholic or addict. They become responsible for ministering to the patient or alcoholic, for cleaning up after him or her, for assisting the parent to bed. As these children leap in to help, they feel strong and important by contrast to the disheveled addict or the infirm parent. As adults, many of them gravitate toward work in the helping professions, such as nursing, social work, or psychology, in order to play out their need to help.

As we know, many children of alcoholics, addicts, or other dependent parents eventually reach a point at which they can no longer endure the painful and deceptive situation in which they find themselves. However, if the addict stops his or her addictive behavior and moves into recovery, the attendant is suddenly out of a job. He or she is no longer necessary, no longer has a semblance of control over an uncontrollable condition. In the midst of the joy and celebration over a loved one's healing process, the caretaker feels fear and anxiety. The known reality, as terrible as it was, has suddenly shifted.

We might also attempt to control others by becoming *martyrs* or *victims*. True historical martyrs are those who selflessly give up their lives, their stature, or their possessions for the sake of a conviction or belief. They do this out of a sense of ethical commitment and goodness. The sort of martyrs that I am talking about here sacrifice too, sometimes greatly, but they are motivated by fear, shame, and anger. They become deeply identified with their suffering, and they use their wretchedness in order to get people's attention and love.

The martyr is the person who says, "Don't worry about me. I'm not that important. Just as long as the rest of you are happy." This is the mother who gives her family members the largest portions of food at dinner, ostentatiously reserving only a small amount for herself, or the father who perpetually reminds his children of the tremendous sacrifices he has made so they can go to college. People like these give to others, but usually with a tangle of strings attached.

A martyr's behavior often serves as a sad caricature of his or her low self-esteem. Because martyrs feel so undeserving and so unable to respect themselves, they forcibly promote the gratitude of others. Sometime early on, they learned that if they behave like martyrs, they receive a great deal of attention from others. Harboring weighty expectations, they exert a great deal of power and influence as they coerce people around them to respond with reassurance and commitment: "Oh, but you *are* important to me." "Thank you *so much* for your generosity. I hope to do the same for you someday." Martyrs evoke expressions of the love, concern, and appreciation they crave but that never fill the emptiness within. This void is left over from a past that robbed them of their sense of self or could not give them what they needed.

A martyr may also be a victim. Victims identify themselves as those to whom great injustices have been done. The world conspires against them. They feel completely at the mercy of the designs of people around them. This is the way they abdicate responsibility for their problems. The difficulties are always someone else's fault, and the victim simply endures and suffers. It is easy for a victim to slide into an inferior stance within a relationship. It makes sense that another person is dominant. As with other survival mechanisms, victimhood is often an exaggeration of the reality of this individual's history; he or she has probably been victimized to such an extent that this role has become familiar.

Related to some people's tendency to control themselves and others is a need to rigidly control their immediate surroundings. We develop unwavering ideas about how we want our world to work. We discover that if we do things in a certain manner, we feel safe and ordered. We evolve a routine, and as long as we stick to it, we maintain some feeling of security. However, if our sense of continuity changes, we often feel fearful and anxious. If, for example, we are used to beginning our mornings in a certain fashion and a modification in our school schedule interrupts our daily ritual, we may become anxious or frightened. Or if we do our job our way and someone comes along and does it differently, we might feel strangely insecure and out of control.

We might like to maintain our possessions in a certain order or disorder, placed around the room the way *we* want them. This way, we feel that the place is really ours, a familiar haven. We do not welcome the interference of anyone, even a well-motivated offer to help us clean up. Individuals whose jobs require frequent travel regularly enter new situations, unfamiliar hotel rooms or homes. Some describe a feeling of anxiety each time they relocate. They discover that once they unpack a little, hang clothes in the closet, place books and a travel clock on the bedside table and the toothbrush in a bathroom cup, they feel more at home. By making the place theirs, they feel safer.

Of course, this need for security and structure can be taken to an extreme, leading to obsessive behavior. But even in its less severe, garden-variety forms, our drive toward safety and invulnerability can lead to rigidity and the need to become authoritative. An inflexible attitude can get us in trouble with ourselves and the people we are trying to form relationships with.

There is another means of dealing with our fear, shame, and anger, as well as with our feelings of being out of control: we may learn to *act out*. We react to the anger and judgment and hurt that comes our way by becoming angry, resentful, judgmental, and hurtful ourselves. We "get" other people before they get us. We blame them before they blame us. The best defense is a good offense. We erect a wall of aggressive emotion that shields us from potential harm. This is the roughneck on the playground who says, "Don't anyone mess with me!" This is the wounded kid who acts tough and dresses in rugged clothing. In a less obvious form, such people may be obstinate and headstrong, bossy, or excessively demanding.

If we become judgmental and self-righteous, we effectively distance and defend ourselves while building the illusion of self-worth and importance. In our judgmentalism, we separate ourselves from the person or the situation we are judging and assume a superior role. If we can convince ourselves our judgment is correct, we might cover our shame or insecurity with a self-righteous facade.

This kind of behavior can begin early in childhood. It seems to manifest itself on a grand scale in junior high and high school, when we are making the transition from child to adult. This is a time when we manufacture cruel jokes about people who do not fit our standards: computer nerds, people who come from the wrong neighborhood or do not keep up with the latest fashions. Standing around the school yard, many of us have made or heard comments such as, "Did you see Emily? Her dress looks like a shower curtain." Or, "How can Ralph hang around with those guys? They look as though they crawled out from under a rock somewhere." Or, "Who would ever join the marching band? The band is for geeks."

Judgments keep people away. They sustain us in our illusion of superiority and perfection. By judging others, we hide our fear; we give expression to our anger and sense of injustice; we mask our shame, our feelings of inadequacy. I believe that judgments also conceal our possible attraction to the person or situation we are judging. Perhaps we feel too drawn to an individual or a situation and are afraid to admit it, even to ourselves. If we condemn whatever appeals to us, we create a distance. A gaggle of girls gossiping about someone's short skirt may in fact reflect their jealousy, their desire to look as great as their enemy does. The derogatory comments about the marching band might disguise a secret wish to play the trumpet, even though the in-group does not consider it to be socially acceptable.

While some individuals maintain their defenses and a sense of control through anger and judgment, others accomplish the same thing by crying, and still others, through compulsive joking. While one guarantees attention and sympathy from others through frequent tears, another seeks to gain recognition through the ability to make people laugh. The melancholy child maintains a distance by encouraging others to treat him or her gingerly and with pity; the class clown hides behind the illusion of merriment.

Another survival strategy is *withdrawal* from dangerous or painful circumstances by removing ourselves physically or emotionally. We might run away, isolate ourselves from other people, or become silent. We refuse to admit to the emotions we feel. We repress them, store them well away in deep and hidden recesses of our being. In this way, we protect ourselves. We avoid the reality of the pain around and within us and hide our responses. We deny our abusers the satisfaction of a reaction. And we give ourselves a sense of mastery: whether or not we participate in the world around us or the relationships at hand depends upon *us*. We have the power to decide if and how we will favor others with our physical or emotional presence. Anyone who has ever received "the silent treatment" or been locked out of someone's room and someone's thoughts knows the kind of power the absent person has at that moment.

Though we can appreciate the ingenuity that originally created these survival mechanisms, they have a shadow side that eventually catches up with us. Whether we angrily blast away at anyone within range, maintain an excessively judgmental attitude, or retreat into silence and isolation whenever there is discomfort, we separate ourselves from others. We set it up for ourselves so that we cannot possibly find the loving contact we so desperately crave; we have created too many barriers between ourselves and those close to us.

If we can manage our fear, shame, and anger by acting out, we can do the same by *acting in*, by turning them against ourselves. Unloading on ourselves is often much easier than projecting onto other people. It does not seem as risky. If we let someone know how we really feel, he or she might hurt us. If we have an investment in that person's liking and accepting us, we are more comfortable internalizing undesirable emotions, even though they are self-destructive. If we are dependent on our image as a good girl, a churchgoer, or an effective employee, expressing so-called "negative" sentiments is not suitable.

Rather than expressing anger, we become furious with ourselves or turn our rage into depression. Fear of concrete situations becomes a constant generalized anxiety, and the shame that originated with another person's actions stagnates within us. We prefer to judge, criticize, and hate ourselves rather than turn these feelings toward someone else. If we have been abused, we learn to abuse our own bodies, minds, emotions, and spirits rather than striking back. Instead of holding a friend or family member accountable for his or her actions, we blame ourselves. We feel saner condemning our own perceptions than believing that those we depend upon to protect and love us are wrong.

Although such an approach may provide a certain measure of safety and protection at first, its drawbacks are manifold. We are harder on ourselves than on others, and we damage our own integrity in the process. By constantly internalizing undeserved emotions and opinions, we diminish our sense of worth and self-esteem. This can lead to further isolation or self-destructiveness through stress, addiction, illness, or suicide.

Physical Survival Strategies

The body usually plays an essential role in successfully helping us to endure difficult or threatening conditions. Beside producing the muscle power, the reflexes, and the adrenaline necessary to fight or flee from potentially harmful circumstances, our bodies are also adept at taking care of us within the situation itself. Rather than facing the full power of a painful event or further endangering ourselves by reacting spontaneously, we commonly learn to *somatize* the experiences and the emotions associated with them. Any massage therapist recognizes that this protective function can eventually take a tremendous toll on the body.

Soma is the Greek word for body. Many traumatic events, such as operations, injuries, birth, sexual and physical abuse, have strong *somatic*, or bodily, components. Some aspects of these events can become encoded in our muscles, our tissues, or perhaps even in our cells. We can also somatize experiences that are not specifically physical. We might somatize our reaction to verbal humiliation by locking our anger, fear, shame, or guilt into our bodies rather than expressing them. Unaware that we are carrying these memories or emotions, we become conscious of them when they manifest in forms such as muscle tension, headaches, digestive problems, skin rashes, numbness, or heightened blood pressure. When we dissociate from an abusive encounter, chances are the event leaves its impact on the body, even though we have separated our awareness from it.

The connection between the body and a person's history and emotional condition came as a surprise to many professionals who began to use experiential methods of self-exploration as part of their therapeutic work with clients. Earlier, mental health professionals had acknowledged that traumatic memories could become buried in the unconscious mind. They knew that, spontaneously or through therapy, clients could release hidden experiences and events as part of the healing process. However, few considered it possible that the physical trauma, as well as the psychological trauma, could be stored in the body. As practitioners added approaches such as Reichian work, bioenergetics, and Gestalt practice to the therapeutic toolbox, they began to realize that the physical as well as the emotional needs of their clients needed to be addressed.

This discovery is consistently evident in the work I have done with Holotropic Breathwork™. Innumerable times I have watched individuals release years of tensions as they focus inward, gaining insight about the various experiences they have somatized. I have felt impressed and moved by the freedom they gain when they allow themselves to relive traumatic memories from the past. In that context, they express the emotions and physical reactions that were impossible to express during the original situation.

For example, a young boy whose drunken father repeatedly beats him may feel like fighting back, but he cannot. His father is bigger and more powerful than he is. If he hits back, he is likely to attract even more violence. Instead of striking out at his abuser, the child withholds his impulses, clenching his teeth, swallowing his anger, setting his jaw, and forming his fists into tight little balls. Repeatedly, he has the urge to strike out in retaliation, and over and over, he represses his reflexes.

Where do these reactions go? In part, he internalizes the emotions and the experiences by mentally repressing them. But he also locks them securely into his body. As a result, he may develop physical symptoms such as digestive problems or tension in his arms and his jaw. He might grind his teeth or have trouble expressing himself with his hands. He may not be able to rid himself of these symptoms until, in a supportive and therapeutic setting, he can fully express all the unexpressed emotional *and* physical tension.

This child used his body to survive by somatizing part of his response to distressing circumstances, enabling him to make it through the event without completely losing his integrity. As with other survival strategies, his approach is necessary and extremely beneficial at the time. But as years pass, his originally creative and resourceful response begins to obstruct and perhaps even become harmful to his well-being.

In the context of Holotropic Breathwork™, I have also seen a number of people who have linked various medical problems to important psychological issues. They have struggled for years with a variety of stress-related physical ailments, such as frequent colds and flu, infections, or chronic fatigue. Through therapy or other forms of self-exploration, they realize there is a psychosomatic component to their difficulties. They also discover that somewhere in their lives, they learned to divert emotional pain into their bodies and somatization became an important escape mechanism for them.

One woman said, "I realized I had one foot out the door. Life had become extremely difficult for me. I really didn't want to be here because it hurt too much. What easier way to completely remove myself from the pain and responsibility of living than to become ill? I began to wonder if I would die if I kept getting sick. In a sense, death would be the final escape from my pain. I feel that my unattended illnesses were taking me in that direction." Once again, an originally useful and ingenious method of survival had become problematic.

Cultural and Social Survival Strategies

Entire segments of the population may creatively employ many of the same defense mechanisms used by individuals. In order to preserve themselves and maintain some degree of sanity, they construct behavioral defenses against the threat from outside and as responses to their fear, shame, anger, pain, and grief. They might repress, deny, or minimize the situation they are in or turn their oppression into self-righteousness and judgmentalism. They can act out their emotions against each other or other groups or turn them against themselves. Jane Middleton-Moz writes and speaks movingly about the "cultural self-loathing" that can be found in demoralized and humiliated populations.

These social groups might also conceal or safely vent their feelings through humor, in the way that individuals do. For example, during the communist occupation of the former Czechoslovakia, political circumstances smothered creative personal and social expression. The oppression also discouraged any open reaction to the fury, hurt, anxiety, and dishonor felt by millions of people. Instead, in the privacy of their homes, many Czechoslovak citizens would tell caustic jokes about the regime, couching their emotions in bitter humor. Under communist rule, this pained jesting was one of the few outlets they had for many years.

Some native peoples have incorporated or fused their beliefs or spiritual traditions with that of the oppressors, creating *syncretistic* systems. Syncretistic religions are combinations of beliefs or practices, and there are many examples of these hybrid religions. African slaves who were abducted from their homes and taken to Brazil took their sacred beliefs with them. In a life dominated by Roman Catholicism, they kept some of their own faith and customs alive by incorporating them into those of their captors. Over time, and with the inclusion of some elements from Brazilian Indian traditions, a unique form of religion emerged, with several different variations: Condomblé, Umbanda, and Macumba. These new systems reflect the creativity of survival, but they also represent a sad compromise.

A painting of the much-loved Virgin of Guadalupe hangs in the Mexico City cathedral. This portrait represents the Virgin Mary standing in a prayerful pose on a crescent moon, the golden rays of the sun radiating from behind her. Cathedral guides proudly state that she is eclipsing the sun and stamping out the moon, which the church regards as symbols of "paganism." They go on to tell visitors how Spanish conquerors built the cathedral on the site of a primary and powerful ancient temple to the sun and enumerate the thousands of Indians that were killed in the process. In spite of the obvious violation of a rich and vital culture of their ancestors, many Indian pilgrims still relate to the Virgin, although in a somewhat different way than the Christian faithful. They simply translate the symbols of the sun and the moon, as well as a beautiful representation of the feminine goddess, into meaningful representatives from their own spiritual and cultural traditions.

These are testimonials to the strength and creativity of the human spirit. Whenever we are subjected to some form of violation, either as individuals or as groups, we miraculously summon our resources and care for ourselves.

Survival and Divine Alienation

It is a reality that most of us have been exposed to some form of dysfunction. We have all endured some degree of violation or disregard for our integrity as unique and gifted individuals, whether from our families or from the world at large. And we have developed specific creative responses. As useful and important as these survival strategies have been, they can eventually stand in the way of our living as healthy individuals or groups. What does this have to do with our thirst for wholeness?

Let us return to the theme of our story, that we are individual representatives of the divine essence who are cut off from our source. By the nature of our humanness, we already exist separately from our true Selves. That sense of isolation increases further if we suffer abuse. And we become even further alienated from our intrinsic source of wholeness through the defenses, escapes, and denials that we create in order to protect and care for ourselves.

When we discover a survival mechanism that works, we repeat it. Before too long, we begin to rely upon it as a method of coping with the stress and pain in our lives. We incorporate it into our way of being, believing we are gaining control of ourselves, other people, or the life process. Eventually, the survival strategies that were originally so very ingenious, useful, and necessary become burdens. Gradually, we begin to identify ourselves with our behavior, with our defenses, reactions, and denials.

As time passes, we patch together a convincing social mask, enshroud ourselves in veils of illusion, and build protective walls of behavior. Little by little, layer by layer, we construct a counterfeit self that successfully shields us from the world so we can survive but also increasingly isolates us from the deeper Self or God. As we move farther and farther away from the gates of heaven, the original thirst to reunite with our wholeness becomes intensified. The more isolated we become, the more we consciously or unconsciously crave our divine roots.

5

The Dark Night of Addiction

So HERE WE are, most of us, in the
desert. Fueled by our remarkable ingenuity and resourcefulness,
we do what we can to create stability in our unpredictable world
and to keep ourselves from hurting too much. In spite of the challenges in our lives, we may enjoy periods of genuine contentment
and well-being. Sometimes our hearts fill with joy as we greet a
clear spring day or share good news with a friend. We experience
surges of excitement as our child's team wins the game or we gain
exciting opportunities at work. We may feel a quiet delight whenever we help someone in need. We might become impassioned
about accomplishing a task or exhilarated as we fall in love with
someone who seems to be perfect.

We also enjoy moments when we tap our source of guidance
and inspiration, times when we seem to be deeply connected to
the workings of creation. We may feel uplifted as we gaze into the
starry sky or transported as we temporarily break out of our ordinary inhibitions during an all-consuming dance or song or during
our favorite sport. We might have moments when everything
seems to work or when we excel beyond our usual limits. Perhaps

we feel piloted through a project by an unusual surge of creativity that seems to exceed our everyday capacity.

But we have noticed that the good times do not last and that sooner or later we return to a general sense of discomfort or a familiar feeling of pain. Try as we may to maintain the pleasant feelings, they always change. That fact alone, the fact that our reality is constantly in flux and undependable, increases any insecurity and fear.

Depending upon the extent of the abuse we have endured, our perception of reality can be shrouded by a veil of unhappiness. Many of us look at the world through a selective unfavorable filter, often without being aware of it. Much of the time, we are unknowingly affected by an unconscious reservoir of disowned emotions and experiences. No matter how blessed we might be with unique talents or with possibilities for harmony in our lives, we cannot adequately feel or see them. Nor can we trust them as worthwhile and dependable.

We live much of our lives under the influence of our repressed, denied, or uncontrolled feelings. We may feel swept by waves of loneliness or by an intense sense of our own inadequacy. We become ashamed of who we are. Somewhere deep within we recognize that we are hiding, living a lie behind the false identity we have created. Guided by our own shame, we keep ourselves more or less isolated and protected. We shield ourselves from the pain of relating to people. We hide so that others do not discover the glaring truth of our inadequacies.

Some of us may be governed by undeclared anger, allowing it to seep into our relationships. Some may frequently vent our obvious rage toward anyone in our path. At times, we might briefly slip into a state of confusion during which our thoughts, emotions, and reactions seem tangled and indecipherable. We may routinely experience an unremitting sense of grief, sadness, or pain. We cry easily, carry a deep sorrow about the suffering in the world, or feel depressed.

For many people, the most prominent motivating force in life is fear. Many of us feel it daily. It may manifest in small increments in our everyday lives: we feel afraid of failing at our job or being abandoned in a relationship. Or overwhelming anxiety may immobilize us as we realize our mortality or fear the potential harm that might come to us through violence; we may feel a free-floating terror that emanates from an unknown source. Just as shame engenders our mistrust of ourselves, fear feeds our mistrust of other people, the life process, even God.

Yet, in spite of our afflictions, we are prodded by an intense stirring from deep within. We feel the thirst for our own wholeness without knowing what it is. According to the story I am telling here, during the journey into life, we have progressed step-by-step into our own individuality. We have traveled from a spiritual state of undifferentiated unity, through ever more alienating circumstances that generate the need for coping devices, until we have lost touch with the consistent experience of our divine identity. Still, we feel an insistent and unspoken drive to reunite with our deeper Self. In fact, the more distant we are from that promise of wholeness, the more pronounced our yearning becomes. This motivating power or cosmic momentum urges us toward our spiritual home, toward our own inner oasis of well-being, expansiveness, ease, freedom, and love.

Not only do we long to be included as human beings in our immediate world, to be touched and cared for by the people around us, but we also harbor an insistent restlessness in our souls. Many of us already feel a deep craving for the love and acceptance we did not know as children. As the unacknowledged, unfulfilled child within us reaches out, a deeper eddy of yearning amplifies the wistful hunger from our past. From the depths of our being, we feel a monumental nostalgia or homesickness for something we cannot begin to name. Feeling deficient and incomplete, we crave something that will make us complete. We feel restless, empty, unsatisfied. What do we do with this impulse?

What Do We Do with Our Spiritual Thirst?

If we attend a traditional church or synagogue, we might feel a deep response to the ritual or the music or the beauty of the stained glass. The spiritual depths within us stir, and we feel a genuine sense of connection with something greater. But we become confused. Chances are, there will be a priest preaching salvation by some vague external entity, or a rabbi talking about some God who is removed and unavailable and grand compared with us miserable human beings. In some portrayals, the Creator is omnipresent and judgmental, watching our every move and punishing us if we misbehave.

Even if God is represented as a loving God, he is almost exclusively male, and he exists apart from us. Whatever love and grace come into our lives emanate from this external source. He is the image that Michelangelo painted on the ceiling of the Sistine Chapel: a kind but intense old man with a flowing white beard floating skyward in the company of celestial multitudes, separate from humankind. As a child, I used to confuse God with Santa Claus. They looked similar, and the words from the Christmas song applied to both: I'd better watch out because he'd know if I'd been naughty or nice.

Our existence is sometimes described by religious texts as a vale of tears, a plane of darkness. They often emphasize the negative: human beings are sinners, lost souls in need of redemption. We are delinquents who were expelled in shame from the Garden of Eden, berated by God with these words: "Cursed is the ground for your sake. . . . For dust you are and to dust you shall return" (Genesis 3:17–19). Masses of humanity live in sin and toil helplessly toward a nameless goal, waiting for the moment they will be saved by some absent force. At times, we are like Job on the dung heap, bewailing our condition to a heedless God. The ordained representative of the church or synagogue is there to mediate our contact with that external entity, to describe him, and to shepherd us toward his redemptive power. We cannot relate to God alone.

This kind of spiritual assumption is a perfect context for a shame-based person, for someone who already feels inferior or sinful. People who have been repeatedly shamed through verbal abuse, have suffered the humiliation of physical violence or the degradation of incest, already feel impure and corrupt. Because they feel so deeply polluted, the last place they would look for guidance, love, or nurturing is within themselves. They then find themselves in a religious setting that tells them they are worthless and need to look toward some unseen entity for divine guidance. This attitude resonates with their experience of themselves. The confused drive in some incest survivors to be loved and accepted by a male perpetrator is also often directed toward the paternal deity, thereby obscuring or contaminating the possibility of a truly loving experience of God.

During my adolescence, I was a devout Episcopalian and was sent to an Episcopal boarding school for the last two years of high school. Kneeling on the hard wooden benches, I passionately repeated the prayers, "We do not presume to come to this thy Table, O merciful Lord, trusting in our own righteousness, but in thy manifold and great mercies. We are not worthy so much as to gather up the crumbs under thy Table." Day after day, I stood in the dimly lit chapel pouring my heart into the confession, "Almighty and most merciful Father; We have erred and strayed from thy ways like lost sheep. . . . And we have done those things which we ought not to have done; And there is no health in us. But thou, O Lord, have mercy upon us, miserable offenders."

I felt worthless, scarred, and unrighteous by contrast with Almighty God in heaven. Repeatedly, I recited to myself that in my unworthiness, I lacked any shred of health, thereby negating the hidden healing potential that existed within me. And it all felt just right. It all resonated with and reinforced the profound shame and sense of impurity that, as a victim of incest, I already carried within. I could not resonate with the hymns, "Abide with Me One Hour" or "Oh God, Our Help in Ages Past." As someone who learned early on that I could not depend upon love from those who were powerful and almighty in my life, I could not begin to accept the possibility of love coming from a vague and unseen foreign source. Neither could I hear the words of Jesus, "The kingdom of God is within." If someone had said to me, "God dwells within you as you," as my teacher from India did many years later, I would not have been able to accept that suggestion. I felt too estranged from the positive core of my own being.

Some Western religious attitudes feed into and substantiate a negative, unhealthy view of ourselves as unworthy and even evil. Theologians such as Brother David Steindl-Rast have noted that at the foundation of every major religion are true mystical experience, states of enlightenment in which the full power of divine love, acceptance, unity, and expansiveness is revealed to the spiritual personage. This inner state completely transforms the one to whom it happens. For this reason, there is great similarity at the roots of many traditions. Jesus existed in a state of inner peace, forgiveness, and love. Buddha was enlightened under the Bodhi tree, achieving equanimity, compassion, and freedom from suffering. Muhammad ecstatically received divine revelations that taught him of God's power and goodness.

The later elaborations and interpretations of these original mystical states and the primary teachings that emerged from such powerful revelations generated creeds and dogma that have often brought about separatism and divisiveness. The resulting schisms and partisanship are contrary to the supreme compassion, unity, and eternity that characterized the original event. The focus on the divine as an external force that is separate and removed from humanity is incompatible with the experience of the prophets and saints who transcended their limitations and gained access to their boundless inner capacities.

For the person who is motivated by an intense spiritual thirst, entering a religious arena that focuses on divisive dogma and the image of an external entity is not the way to quench the thirst. In fact, certain religious frameworks might serve only to reinforce the difficulties and damaged self-image that already exist. Inner fulfillment cannot come about through outside sources. Although individuals, communities of people, ideas, and activities can offer guidance, they cannot ultimately bring us the spiritual union we long for. We must find that within ourselves.

Messages from Our Society

We live in a culture that encourages us to look for happiness by directing our energies outward, however. Because most of us would never rely upon our own inner resources to achieve a sense of wholeness, we look for that sense of completion and contentment in the wide variety of enticements around us. Our society tantalizes us with promises, spoken and implied in a multitude of ways. It entices us through advertising, social and intellectual expectations, accepted values, and a general atmosphere of competitiveness: "You will be satisfied and happy if only you look a certain way; earn a college degree; marry the man or woman of your dreams; have two children; buy a powerful, sexy car or two as well as a house in the suburbs; achieve success in the world; make $100,000, $200,000, or $1 million, or $2 million." And on and on it goes.

Everything around us tells us that the only way of satisfying our sense of incompleteness and deficiency is through various external activities or material substances. Since I have been in recovery from my addictions, I have often thought of a story that comes from the writer and philosopher Aldous Huxley: Huxley once overheard a child asking a parent, "Mommy, why are precious stones precious?" The mother had no answer, and moved on. But Huxley was left with the question. Having himself experienced mystical states, he eventually realized that gold and jewels, with their richness of color and splendid radiance, are the closest objects in the material world to the mystical vision. Somehow, people unconsciously recognize this and feel drawn in an irrational way to gold and jewels. They feel an overwhelming need to possess them and are willing to pay outrageous prices to do so.

With this story in mind, I began to look at various advertisements that tempt us to fill our longings in one way or another. I was surprised to see how many of them use specifically spiritual imagery, implying that if we go for a certain product, we will find the sacred connection we are looking for. Not only do such commercials appeal to our vanity or to our sexual desire, but they also summon our mystical craving. Although the advertising industry is not solely responsible for our tendency to seek solutions outside ourselves, it encourages that already present tendency and exemplifies a general attitude held by many in our society.

Let us consider a few of these advertisements. As I describe them, think of some of the religious and spiritual images that employ the same aesthetic ingredients. Beautiful Russian icons, Jewish and Christian holy objects, or Hindu sculptures are often made of precious metals and encrusted with diamonds, sapphires, and emeralds. Native Americans and Tibetans create sacred ornaments and sculptures with silver, turquoise, and coral. Golden Buddhas smile peacefully in shrines and temples all over the world. Aztec and Egyptian artisans formed brilliant images of their gods with gold and jewels. In Persian miniatures, Muhammad bows at the feet of Allah, enveloped by the golden glory of the divine, and travels to a heavenly realm where a splendid bejeweled wish-fulfilling tree grows. Fra Angelico and other artists painted the divine Mother and Child surrounded by golden luminosity. This sacred artistry reflected the highest spiritual vision.

The radiance of priceless metals and jewels also appears frequently in promotions for assorted marketable products, many of them potentially addictive: ice cubes sparkle like diamonds in commercials for alcohol. Crystal glasses are filled with vodka and dazzling chunks of ice and displayed against a luminous silver background. Cognac and whiskey bottles adorned with lustrous gilded labels sit gracefully in the warmth of the late afternoon sun. Human figures in some cigarette and liquor ads are drenched in liquid gold. One picture shows a glass of golden bourbon sitting on a rich wooden table next to a mound of precious gold bars. The message reads: "Order Gold in Bars." Another simply presents a solid gold bottle of vodka. Yet another shows a stream of gin that turns into sapphires as it pours from the bottle into a martini glass.

Merchandisers also consistently use other spiritual or religious symbols to coax us toward their products. Poets and mystics refer to the image of a mountain that represents the spiritual journey and its peak as the ultimate reward; mountains frequently appear on television screens and in the pages of magazines to market cigarettes or beer. Many sacred texts discuss the state of perfection as a goal of the inner life: a perfect couple with perfect bodies sit by a perfectly calm pool on a perfect, cloudless day, smoking cigarettes, and the text reads, "The Perfect Recess." A major vodka company consistently uses the promise of "perfection" in its ads; in one, the artist places a cloudlike halo over a vodka bottle with the words "Absolut Perfection" written underneath. In fact, the very name of the product repeats a name often applied to the divine: the Absolute.

In spiritual art, eternity, heaven, and the mystery of the universe are often represented as a vast blue or star-filled sky. The same images appear in the pages of magazines as a female body smeared with skin cream flows into the sky above. A man wearing name-brand sunglasses or a woman in a popular athletic swimsuit melt into the cosmos. An advertisement for tires pictures an endless road against a dramatic arrangement of clouds in a dark blue sky, saying, "You're Looking at the Inspiration Behind Our Tires." A car company portrays the heavens in a photograph uncomplicated by any other figures, even that of their vehicle. Their product's name simply stretches across the bottom of the page: Infiniti. Other automobiles are offered with rays of light, much like mystical halos or auras, radiating from them.

The peacock, a cross-cultural symbol of spiritual rebirth, stands splendidly behind a bottle of liqueur. A shining gilded eagle, a potent spirit guide in Native traditions, dips its wing into deep blue waters that reflect the luminosity radiating from behind the sparkling cigarette pack. A perfume manufacturer promises wearers they will "Possess the Power" of the moon, which in many traditions represents a goddess or the feminine. Another fragrance pledges it will "release the splendor of you," symbolized by a swan, a Hindu icon for the Supreme Godhead, in flight. These kinds of images peek out at us from every direction, from the weekly newsmagazines in our mailbox, the journals in the doctor's office, nightly television programs, and posters at the local department store. They all urge us to find ourselves, our identity, our greatness, our beauty, our perfection, and our solace in the material world.

The Misdirected Inward Search

We have been concentrating here on the tendency to focus on the external world as a source of satisfaction. We can also misdirect our thirst for wholeness inward, into ways in which we use our minds or abilities. Family members, teachers, and the general atmosphere in our society encourage us to excel, to succeed, to prove our competence in a competitive world. I saw this achievement-oriented attitude in a series of poignant and startling events during my first year of teaching. Freshly graduated from college, I worked in a small private school as an assistant kindergarten teacher with four- and five-year-old children. Sometime during the spring, the principal informed the teachers that we would spend the next few weeks, after-hours, interviewing prospective candidates for the next year's classes.

At the appointed times, parents brought their three-year-old children to meet us and play with us for a while, so we could form an impression of both the child and the adults in the family. I felt dismayed and saddened to discover how many of the parents had prompted their children to perform for us. Tiny girls and boys, rigidly dressed in their finest starched clothing and shiny shoes, automatically spouted numbers, alphabet sequences, and memorized facts without our requesting them to do so. Meanwhile, mothers and fathers related to us their entire educational and career plan for little Tommy or Mary. Getting into a good kindergarten at the age of four would ensure the child of admission into the correct grade school, which would lead to the best high school, a top-notch university, and finally, a respectable, high-paying job and success in the world.

At three years old, these unique, vital, and creative individuals were already being pushed toward someone else's idea of who they should be, with very little apparent consideration of their own needs, motivations, or interests. The same kind of thing often happens with children whom parents, teachers, or coaches prod toward excellence in sports, scholastic achievement, or artistic performance. From a very early age, the child assumes someone else's definition of worth and then works diligently to achieve it—to gain approval and love. The process of finding acceptance from others is endless. Their appreciation remains just out of reach.

The more the child labors, the more pressure he or she feels. And this distinctive, ingenious individual moves further and further away from the possibility of tapping his or her own source of inspiration and unique expression. The desire to reach the unreachable, to finally relax into the ultimate goal that rests at the end of systematic effort, can become amplified by the deep spiritual yearning that already exists. But as long as the individual's efforts to develop certain abilities are misdirected into a relentless drive to achieve approval, he or she will not find fulfillment.

This is not to say that parents and other adults must remove themselves from any responsibility for the development of a child's capacities or that excellence is not desirable. However, the adults' role is in part to guide and support a child toward the discovery of his or her very own talents and passions, not to impose their expectations, insecurities, and hidden desires on an impressionable and dependent child. Excellence will automatically develop if it comes from a genuine place of passion and creativity.

Another way we can misdirect our thirst for wholeness is to confuse that yearning with a desire to know more, to exercise our intellectual capacities, and to develop our curiosity. Ordinarily these skills are useful and necessary in order to function in the world. However, as with anything, mental activity can be misused. The thinking process and intellectual development can become compulsive; when combined with a tendency to escape or avoid pain, it can even become a liability. When individuals who use mental activity compulsively become engaged in the competitive atmosphere of our society, they feel encouraged to use their rational ability to advance themselves in school and in the workplace. But as long as they remain engrossed in excessive intellectual activity and denial, they remain disconnected from the true source of their happiness.

Reaching in Mistaken Directions

We have described the thirst for wholeness and its power in our lives. We have also seen that many of us have lost touch with our spiritual resources through the various layers of protection and denial that we build in order to survive, as well as through our need to escape the pain of reality. Many of us feel so scarred, so unworthy, and so alienated from ourselves that we would never rely on our own resources for guidance or nourishment. Fueled by an unrecognized thirst to return to our divine nature and encouraged by many of the messages in our culture, we easily gravitate toward the complex temptations within and around us. From a relatively early age, we throw ourselves into valiant efforts to somehow find satisfaction in various internal and external activities, relationships, and substances. However, this well-intentioned but misdirected search is ultimately fruitless; it can eventually lead to addiction, to tremendous suffering, and, in many cases, to self-destruction.

With ever-increasing intensity, we reach beyond our limited capacities in order to find happiness and contentment. If we approach them with moderation, many of the things we pursue have the potential to be enjoyable, life-enhancing, even healthy. However, we often bring an urgency and obsessiveness to our pursuits. Our intensity and compulsion carry within them the seeds of addiction, and as we act on them, we meet with increasing pain and frustration.

We vainly try to satisfy the gnawing feelings and fill our inner emptiness with food or sexual partners. We attempt to achieve satisfaction by literally loading ourselves with cookies, potato chips, or hamburgers; as a bonus, the added weight buffers us against our emotions as well as potential external threat. Or perhaps we try to relieve the inner alienation and find unity through repeated erotic encounters, satiate ourselves through intimacy with another person. We consume alcohol, puff on cigarettes, snort cocaine, smoke crack, or inject, drink, inhale, ingest, and swallow an assortment of other drugs. Maybe if we take the perfect amount or find just the right combination, our search will be over, and we will feel gratified.

The perfect relationship will resolve the discomfort. If we find our "other half," "soul mate," the man or woman of our dreams, we will be complete. Romantic images fill our heads as we dream of the supreme union, the wedding of the century, the ideal household. The words of love songs ring true: "You make me feel complete," "I can't live without you." Spurred by our heartfelt hopes, we pursue one possible mate after another.

We abandon ourselves to our careers. We spend most of our time working, hurtling toward some unreachable goal in a job that is never done. If we can just attract the perfect client, obtain the big contract, or make the deal of the century, then maybe we will have made it. We will be happy if only we can do the perfect job. Our work is our life.

We accumulate power, money, or possessions. The more we have, the happier we will be. Amassing a houseful of belongings, a substantial bank account, or an extensive stock portfolio or attaining a coveted promotion on the job is perhaps the way we strive for fulfillment. We achieve elevated social, business, or political status. We conquer, manipulate, control, or influence innumerable others in endless endeavors to achieve greatness. Through our constant efforts, perhaps we will transcend ordinary limitations and accomplish something truly extraordinary.

The more we do, the happier we will be. We maniacally pursue a never-ending education. We become perpetual students, ineffectually striving to quench our thirst through accumulated knowledge or credentials. We retreat into our minds, attempting ever more complex mental gymnastics and aiming toward an impressive array of intellectual accomplishments. We interpret or diagnose the world and those within it, find logical solutions to our problems, create theories, and reflect on philosophical and political judgments. We seek to become experts in our field. We read, collect, and write books. The more sophisticated and comprehensive our thinking, the more satisfied we will be.

We become involved in gambling. If only we can win the sweepstakes or the state lottery, the bet on the big football playoffs, or the poker games on Friday nights. If we try hard enough and invest just a little more, we will achieve the miracle; the odds are in our favor. Or we might travel continuously. We walk, hike, ride, fly, or cruise throughout the world, constantly searching for adventure and new horizons, hoping to find the perfect beach, town, hotel, restaurant, or country.

We decide that if we look the right way, our yearnings will be satisfied. We make innumerable trips to the mall and compulsively dress ourselves in the latest fashions. Perhaps the ideal outfit with the proper accessories or a closet full of the hottest, most expensive clothes will do it. We endlessly search for the guise that will make us feel acceptable, beautiful, or cool. If we drape ourselves with impeccable clothing, we might feel complete.

But in order for the clothes to look right, our bodies need to be flawless. We must look like the supermodels in the latest fashion magazines or the rock stars on television. So we spend hours each day buildi 3 our bodies and years of our lives in search of the perfect diet. We run, jog, climb, row, dance, pedal, and lift our way to perfection. We sweat, strain, bend, and march. We deny ourselves certain foods, limit our intake of others, all the while feeling self-righteous, sacrificial, and miserable. We fill our cupboards with healthy alternatives, forget them, and rediscover them months later. We cleanse our systems, purge our colons, fill ourselves with vitamins, and turn our attention to yet another cure for what ails us.

And we can augment all this by turning to the plastic surgeon. Perhaps a new nose will bring us happiness. What we need is a face-lift, a stronger chin, different eyes, fewer wrinkles, or larger lips. We rearrange our bodies through tummy tucks or liposuction, reduce the size of our breasts or pump them up with silicone. We undergo hair transplants to correct baldness. We pay thousands of dollars as we allow ourselves to be cut, stretched, sewn, and redistributed in our futile search for perfection.

Or we may look for experts to provide us with the wholeness that we crave, in the same way that we depend on a repairperson to fix our television set or automobile. We might find ourselves in a therapist's office with the promise that he or she can fix us, go to EST to "get it," or become workshop junkies. Perhaps the right specialist holds the key that will unlock our possibilities. We blindly put ourselves in other people's hands. We compulsively seek out mentors who can tell us what is wrong with us, what we need, and what to do. With their accumulated knowledge, they can direct us to the secret of our happiness. We search for the seminar, conference, or workshop that will provide the formula or technique to alleviate our difficulties. If we read the right self-help books or get ourselves into the ideal men's, women's, or couple's group, we will feel fulfilled.

We may end up at the feet of some spiritual teacher, shaman, or priest who promises to love us. If we truly give ourselves to our chosen guru and we become good devotees, if we follow the rules and do the correct practices, perhaps we will find liberation and peace. We concentrate on learning every word of foreign prayers and chants. We carefully memorize the principles we are being taught, wear the correct spiritual clothing, adorn ourselves with meaningful symbols, and procure the proper sacred accoutrements. Often ignoring our worldly obligations, we diligently and obediently pursue our prescribed course toward happiness.

Again, many of these activities, relationships, and substances can be valuable, fun, or life-enhancing. What gets us into trouble is our blind compulsion and our clinging. A couple of years ago, my friend Jack Kornfield, a gentle, skilled Buddhist teacher and a psychologist, gave me an article that appeared on the front page of our local newspaper. I chuckled when I read it because it demonstrated the lengths to which human beings will go in the attempt to satisfy our longings and transcend our limitations. In bold, black letters, was a headline: LICK TOADS AT YOUR OWN RISK. Its subtitle: Latest "High" Can Be Fatal. The text begins, "Here we go again. After cheap highs like glue sniffing and mushroom tripping, the latest way to catch a buzz is to lick a toad. Yes, you read that correctly." But, says an expert on reptiles, "if you pick the wrong toad, you won't only get high, you'll get dead."

The article goes on to explain that a certain kind of toad secretes a hallucinogenic chemical called *bufotenine* through its skin when it becomes agitated. With great seriousness, the reporter states that a number of individuals had learned to shake these toads and then lick the chemical from the reptiles' backs, or to boil them and drink the bufotenine-laced liquid. The account warns that only a specific breed of toad is safe, one that is easily confused with poisonous varieties. Consequently, licking toads is a very dangerous activity.

From history I had learned that toad skin was a prime ingredient in the witches' brew of the Middle Ages and that scientists had confirmed that it had hallucinogenic properties. But *who*, I wondered, was the first person to lick a toad, and how did he or she know to do it? What circumstances drove that daring individual to pick up a toad? And was there no other way to achieve the same effect? As a recovering alcoholic, I can understand the immense motivation toward anything that will relieve the pain of existence and perhaps offer a path toward a mystical state—but, toads?

Pseudomystical States

Whatever we reach for as a prospective key to completion might temporarily seem to provide us with the solutions we have been seeking. With the first rush of power, nicotine, or cocaine, the first high of a good orgasm, an amphetamine, a great piece of pie, or of yet another overseas adventure, we become encouraged. We feel hopeful as we enjoy the slow warmth, the melting of boundaries, and the soothing of anxiety after a brandy or two or a couple of Valiums. Perhaps we have found *it* as we lose ourselves in our partner or as the pain dissolves when we fade into the television screen. With the pay raise, the growing bank account, the victorious card game, we feel certain we have come upon the solution to our problems. Maybe we have discovered the path to happiness with the stunning new outfit, the loss of ten pounds, the face-lift.

The activity, substance, or relationship we choose may even simulate the mystical state we yearn for. Our pain seems to be temporarily alleviated. We are infused with a new sense of freedom, and much of our self-consciousness and separateness evaporates. We feel more relaxed within ourselves. Others appear to include and accept us more easily. Imbued with confidence, we feel assured that we can accomplish the impossible. A new sense of strength and purpose washes through us; we no longer feel the pain in our lives or feel bound by our limitations. We seem to be transported out of ourselves, away from everyday anxieties and restrictions. We feel free.

The scholar and psychologist William James acknowledged the role of alcohol in creating what can feel like a spiritual experience.

In *The Varieties of Religious Experience,* he wrote, "The sway of alcohol over mankind is unquestionably due to its power to stimulate the mystical faculties of human nature, usually crushed to earth by the cold facts and dry criticisms of the sober hour. Sobriety diminishes, discriminates, and says no; drunkenness expands, unites, and says yes." Here, James uses the word *sobriety* to mean "everyday consciousness," not the quality of sobriety that alcoholics and addicts discover in recovery.

Bill Wilson wrote the following in a letter:

> *Alcoholics want to know who they are, what life is about, whether they have a divine origin, and whether there is a system of cosmic justice and love. . . . It is the experience of many of us in the early stages of drinking to feel that we have had glimpses of the Absolute and a heightened feeling of identification with the cosmos. While these glimpses and feelings doubtless have a validity, they are deformed and finally swept away in the chemical, spiritual, and emotional damage wrought by alcohol itself.*

James's and Wilson's statements are true not only for alcohol but also for other substances, for some relationships, and for a wide variety of activities. They successfully create for us the illusion that with their help we achieve greater awareness, an expanded identity, and a sense of unity, power, and inner peace.

I have heard many addicts say that when they first discovered the source of their addiction, they felt as though they had come home. They had discovered the solution to their problems, the one thing that gave them purpose and mastery. It was an avenue toward happiness and peace, the best thing that had ever happened to them. It also provided a buffer between them and the painful world in which they lived. It acted to repress difficult emotions and experiences. Their initial introduction to their addiction allowed them, for a brief period, to step out of their state of alienation and discomfort into a window of expansion and relief.

However, as wonderful as it is, this state of pseudofreedom inevitably fades, and we end up with the same incessant craving asking to be satisfied. Or we discover that our endless activity no longer consistently brings us the rewards we originally sought, so we set our sights on increasingly distant and elevated goals. And we go back for more, and more, and more.

The Dark Night of Addiction

Very soon, we become involved in a desperate search for our original experience of well-being and unity. It was available once; it should eventually repeat itself, if we only keep trying. Perhaps we are not taking enough of the right kind of substance. If one pill or cigarette or drink or sexual partner is not enough, maybe two will be better. If two is not enough, then three, or four, or five might do it. If the new suit or the tummy-tuck or the $100,000 does not bring us the happiness it promised, perhaps we need a different outfit, another surgical intervention, or an even bigger bank account. If jogging is not giving us the sense of well-being we are seeking, maybe we should switch to tennis or weight lifting or aerobic dancing. If our therapist or psychic is not providing the peace and joy we had anticipated, perhaps we need another mentor to provide us with a psychological and religious overhaul.

The more the object of our search continues to elude us, the more desperate we are to find this key to fulfillment and release from suffering. The more desperate we become, the more we focus on our goal. Increasingly, our thoughts and actions revolve around trying to re-create our initial taste of joy and freedom. We become progressively preoccupied with the elusive source of our contentment. We think about it incessantly. And we begin to re-arrange our lives in order to accommodate our quest for the "high," the relief, or the sense of belonging. We go to sleep at night and awaken in the morning thinking about the financial deal, the man or woman, the bottle, the drug, the power play, or the new dress that will do it for us. We begin to plan our day around how we will pursue the object of our craving, how we will ingest the food, alcohol, or drug, purchase the object, accomplish the task, or interact with the person of our dreams.

We discover that whatever we are seeking seems increasingly difficult to grasp. Soon, we are caught in a frantic loop of activity: Our level of anxiety starts to rise, and as it does, we become more and more desperate to relieve it. As desperation builds, we throw ourselves even more into the search for the key that will alleviate our ever-growing inner tension. The original thirst for our own wholeness began as a healthy and natural impulse toward personal growth, expansion, and unity with our deeper Self. Now, our divine goal has become obscured by a growing self-destructive and misguided obsession with a substitute. We find ourselves in a terrible dilemma. We have become hopelessly attached or addicted to an activity, a person, or a material substance that is not giving us the satisfaction we long for.

A by-product of our frantic search is the momentary high, surge of energy, or sense of relief that comes from quest itself. Along the way, we have also learned to alter our experience and relieve our pain through obsessive thinking. We move out of the increasing discomfort of reality and into our minds, circling around and around with our thoughts as they spiral into repetitive loops. Our thoughts might sound something like this:

> *This morning I am going to call him. But I wonder whether he's going to be home. Maybe this afternoon will be better. Or tonight. But if I call at night, he'll think I'm trying to start something. On the other hand, he may not be home until tonight. But what if he rejects me? I'm probably not good enough for him. If I could have him in my life, I'd have it made. In fact, I can't imagine living without him. I wonder what he's wearing today. Maybe he doesn't have a girlfriend. Maybe he's not my type. What if I'm the one he's been waiting for? What if all this time, he's been looking for someone just like me? I think I'll call him this morning. Right now. But what if he doesn't want to speak to me? What if . . . ?*

Or like this:

> *I won't take a drink until five this afternoon. By that time, Ann will be home, and we can have a drink together before dinner.*

Maybe she'd like a martini. I wonder if we have enough gin. I'd better go and get some at the store, just in case. I'd better go soon, because I know when I get back I'll be tired. Since I've had the flu, I'll need a nap. Maybe I'll get some orange juice, too. I read that orange juice has a lot of vitamin C, and it's good for flus. If I put a shot of vodka in it, it will help me to sleep, and that will be good for me. I deserve it. I've been sick. I wonder if we have enough vodka. I'd better go check. . . .

This kind of mind-altering activity produces a kind of hypnotic trancelike state that defends us from the reality of our self-destructive behavior. It lifts us out of the everyday stresses of our lives and tucks us safely into our heads, where we swim through our meandering thoughts without being touched by the impact of our actions or our surroundings.

In addition, we discover that the pursuit of our addiction provides a rush of adrenaline. The excitement of putting ourselves in dangerous situations or doing something not socially sanctioned can give us a secondary high. If we live close to the edge, we might find ourselves driving at high speeds or walking down dark alleys in search of drugs or a sexual partner. The preparation for the actual addictive activity becomes part of the addictive behavior itself. All these actions can provide a thrill, a sense of perverse exhilaration: obsessively pursuing a business client; anxiously anticipating the outcome of a bet; racing from store to store in the mall; becoming involved in the great intellectual scheme of the century; or hiding bottles of alcohol in secret places where family members cannot find them and then sneaking drinks.

Often recovering addicts talk about being "drama queens" or "drama kings," people addicted to the melodrama of their lives, to the thrill and importance of the things that happen to them. They experience a form of distorted excitement as they live their lives as a series of theatrical events. One person said, "If there was any kind of a problem, I blew it out of proportion until it became a crisis. I believed that only I had the solution. It was as though I was constantly putting out fires. And when there were no fires, I would light one just so I could put it out." Loosened by the momentary sense of relief provided by the addiction, the addict's emotions flow freely, mounting to great heights and plunging into the depths. Emboldened by grandiosity and propelled by shame, we make histrionic telephone calls, create repeated crises in our relationships, write dramatic poetry, or lose ourselves in television or film dramas that seem to reflect, however inadequately, the spectacle of our existence.

In addition, our original, incredibly creative survival strategies turn against us; our mechanisms for managing our lives become desperate attempts to control ourselves, other people, or our surroundings. However, like a harsh despot, the addiction dictates our reality. As we grapple to maintain some semblance of order in our lives, we increasingly spin out of control until we are completely at the mercy of our addictive behavior. We become progressively subjugated to an unremitting lust for power, money, food, possessions, or sexual encounters. We yield to the perpetual drive toward physical, intellectual, or professional perfection. The terrifying craving for a thimbleful of white powder, a tiny blue pill, a cigarette, or a bottle tyrannizes us.

As time goes on, we slide toward an abyss of shame, fear, and hopelessness. We have become overwhelmed with depression or a deep sense of shame. Although we have tried many times to stop our addictive behavior, we cannot. Each time we return to the compulsive activity, we feel increasingly disgraced. Not only have we let down our family or friends or colleagues again, we have once more betrayed ourselves.

Money, power, sex, other people, alcohol, drugs, or possessions have become our gods, the supreme influences in our lives. And our days revolve around our ever more reckless quest for that ultimate source of fulfillment. We become tragic caricatures of the spiritual ascetic who turns away from everyday demands to focus on his or her service to the Spirit. In our obsession, we neglect or abandon family members, our jobs, our responsibilities, our health, and ourselves as we struggle after the substance, relationship, or activity we have appointed as our Higher Power.

Behind our facades, our bodies and our spirits are sick. We feel fragmented, encased in the traps of our illusions and denials. Our vision is fiercely concentrated on the object of our addiction. Our reality now contains only two principal entities: ourselves and the substance, relationship, or activity that rules our existence. Swaddled in layers of complex denials, rationalizations, and illusions, we alternate between a monumental well of shame, self-degradation, and self-pity and a prodigious stream of grandiosity. We feel, "I am the loser in the center of the universe. Everything revolves around me and my addiction. Nothing else matters."

We become anorexic to life; just as anorexics deny themselves the nourishment of food, we become so constricted that we are unable to take in the bounty of our existence. We cannot love the people who once brought meaning to our lives; we cannot appreciate the natural world around us; we cannot relate to the activities that once stimulated our bodies, minds, and imagination. During the last years of my drinking career, my husband would drive me along the beautiful California coast near our home and I would stare mournfully at the people who were hiking, riding bicycles, or having picnics. As they enjoyed their companionship, the spectacular view, and the warm sunshine, I felt left out and sorry for myself. I told myself that some mysterious and dramatic malady was keeping me from participating in the world the way others were. I fabricated the story that I suffered from some obscure condition, and I genuinely felt depressed; therefore, I was both special and unfortunate. I felt I would never have what they did, and realizing that with a certain dramatic flair, I sank further into the familiar morass of self-pity.

Many of us develop physical problems. Chemical addicts experience a multitude of ailments: weight loss, dehydration, high blood pressure, malnutrition, liver and kidney diseases, to name a few. Those with eating disorders such as bulimia, anorexia, or compulsive overeating exhibit the visible symptoms of obesity, loss of appetite, coronary and circulatory problems, or dental disease. Addictions such as codependency and workaholism that do not necessarily involve the misuse of substances can lead to lack of concern for health, neglect of the need for exercise, a good diet, or sleep, among others. The stress of this kind of addictive lifestyle might result in health problems.

Just as our minds and bodies pay dearly for our addictions, our spirits are also afflicted. As we have increasingly concentrated on the object of our addiction, we have more and more alienated ourselves from the original goal of our thirst. We have become progressively estranged from our deeper Self through the fact of our humanity, through the abusive conditions in our environment, and through the masks and illusions we have created in order to survive. Now, by misdirecting our yearning to reunite with our spiritual selves into addictive behavior, we sever any remaining threads of conscious contact with our divine core. We can no longer reach the source of inspiration and creativity, the peace, joyfulness, and love that was once available to us from within. As we enter the depths of our addiction, we find ourselves in hell.

Religious traditions of all kinds describe hell not only as a place of immense suffering but also as a state of eternal damnation, entirely cut off from any divine influence. These two qualities, that this condition is eternal, and that it means total separation from the influence of a vast benevolent source, appear in many cultures. Though hell might not exist as a concrete geographical location, it certainly exists as a psychological and spiritual state of consciousness. In the depths of our addiction, we are completely out of control. Hidden behind the barriers of our defenses, we are unable to give or receive love. Our addiction has cemented us into a final and extreme state of isolation. No matter what we do, we cannot touch the rewards of the deeper Self. We are alienated from our potential for wholeness. God remains obscured behind the cloud of our addictive behavior and the layers of our false identity.

We feel this experience will never end; it will go on forever. There is no way out. We are doomed. We are stuck in a hopeless, helpless spiral toward destruction. As people who have spent our lives struggling to maintain some sort of control, part of the hell at the bottom of our addiction is the experience of feeling, and often being, totally and desperately out of control. We no longer have any power over the people and the activities in our lives, and try as we might, we cannot even control ourselves. Although we once knew how to survive in the face of abuse or difficult external circumstances, we are now so out of touch with our own resources and so victimized by the ruthless cycle of our addiction that we sink progressively into a quagmire of helplessness.

As they slide toward their demise, many addicts literally lose almost everything in life. Our exasperated families and friends have abandoned us, or we have turned our backs on them. We have been asked to leave our homes, we have been fired from our jobs, and our money has disappeared. Our health is threatened, and we can no longer function as we once did. We are left externally and internally destitute.

Some of us manage to keep our outer world relatively intact, somehow maintaining the semblance of a family life, a career, or a successful lifestyle. However, whatever our circumstances, everyone who gets caught in a helpless, hopeless addictive pattern feels devastated inside. This is the "spiritual bankruptcy" that the Twelve-Step programs describe, a state of severe inner impoverishment. This is the "soul sickness" that comes with an extreme isolation from the deeper Self. We feel forsaken by God. God has forgotten us. We have crumpled into the dark night of addiction.

As we progress toward complete physical, emotional, mental, and spiritual annihilation, we often feel as though we are dying. While our world goes down the drain and our health diminishes, our familiar ways of behaving or of identifying ourselves fade away. Stuck in the seeming eternity of our addiction, some of us find the next step is to contemplate or attempt suicide. We may catch ourselves thinking, "If this is going to go on forever, I don't want to be around for it. If this is all there is to life, I want to die." We translate the undeniable fact of our internal and external bankruptcy into an impulse to act out our complete destruction. Some addicts actually kill themselves, whether they are sex addicts at the mercy of their dangerous activity, gamblers or shopping addicts who are hopelessly in debt, spurned codependents, or drug or alcohol addicts who overdose on chemicals or kill themselves and others in their automobiles. Many of us do not die physically but remain caught between the forceful desperation that tells us we should die and the tremendous fear of death.

Addiction and Culture

Again, much of what we have learned about individual addiction also applies to various cultures and social categories. People who have been denied their heritage and spiritual roots through repression or conquest feel a deepened sense of alienation from themselves, from others, from the world, and from God. They experience what Angeles Arrien calls *soul loss*, which is similar to an individual's state of *spiritual bankruptcy*.

If they have been abused, they learn to violate themselves, members of their families or their community, and others. In the midst of their compromised circumstances, their spiritual thirst pressures them from within, and many seek to remedy their soul loss with alcohol, drugs, and material possessions. As a result, alcoholism and drug addiction are rampant among oppressed groups. Their integrity increasingly fragments as young people move away from their families and communities in search of answers in the commercial world. Because the divine craving is a major factor in addiction, a significant antidote to the serious addiction problems in such groups might be a return to their rich spiritual roots.

The Seeds of Transformation

This chapter has been a dismal one in our story. Unfortunately it represents the grim reality for many, many people. However, there is a bright side to the picture. The depths of spiritual bankruptcy contain within them the potential for tremendous transformation. Immediately on the other side of this hell rests the promise of a new life. The dark night of addiction is often a necessary prelude to the dawn of healing. The experiences of inner dying, of unmitigated surrender, of utter helplessness and hopelessness are essential steps toward the promise of rebirth. Unknowingly, at the very bottom, we have reached the potential turning point. We have arrived at the threshold of a freer, happier, and more loving way of being.

6

Surrendering and Being Surrendered

T HE DAY I hit bottom with my alco-
holism, I was brought to my knees. I did not do it willfully. I did
not intend it to happen. I did not wake up that morning and say to
myself, "Today, I'm going to surrender." The experience of absolute, sheer powerlessness came barreling into my life and flattened
me. I *was surrendered* by a force larger than the part of me that had
been hanging on for years. That day, in the dim rose-colored room
of the chemical dependency treatment center, I let go. As a winter
storm howled outside, I let go of the illusion that I was all right,
that I was different, that I did not have the same kind of problems
as the others around me who were wrestling with their addictions.
I let go of the mirage that told me I did not have a drinking problem, even though every aspect of my life was disintegrating.

My alcoholism stared me directly in the face. *I am an alcoholic.*
I had realized my worst fears: *I am like them.* I felt the pit of my
stomach drop. *I am like those disgusting, smelly, loud, sloppy people I
have always loathed. I am no different from the alcoholics in my life
and in the movies and on the streets that I have judged and hated for
years.* In the depths of intense humiliation, I felt my resistances,
my condemnations, and my defenses begin to fall away as I looked

more clearly than ever before at the reality of my situation. *I am completely and utterly out of control. I have screwed up my life. I am tired and I am sick. I can't continue this way. I give up.*

As I sat sobbing on my bed, knees curled against my chest, my life seemed to slip away. With distinct mental images in full color and a strong outpouring of fluid emotions, I watched and felt myself disappear. All at once, the roles I played in the world, the work I did, the illusions and the games and the denials that had shored up my addictive craziness slid out of reach, down some bottomless black hole. The shell of who I was, was dying, slipping away. I could no longer hang on. I was totally and unequivocally defeated. I wept in the face of this awesome event. I sobbed out of fear and confusion about what would come next. I grieved the loss of an identity that was familiar, the self that had been distinguished as me. And soon, the tears of grief and fear became a flood of relief, relief that I did not have to hold tight to all that anymore. I did not have to continue playing the alcoholic game. I no longer had to pretend.

Within minutes, a nurse appeared at the door to tell me that I had an important telephone call from my husband. Red-faced and sniffling, I took the phone. The warm, loving voice on the other end told me that a good friend of ours had died that day, and before Stan told me the details, I knew he had died as a result of drugs and alcohol. He had died of an accidental overdose. This young man, in his midthirties, had been a drinking buddy of mine, and he had made the tragic mistake I could so easily have made myself. In the fog of his addiction, he had combined the wrong amounts of the wrong substances. And his heart had given up.

The profound experience of defeat, of surrender, had been the first step in my healing process. This timely telephone call was the second. During a long moment of crystalline clarity, I realized I was blessed. In my friend's death, I saw the direction in which I had so recklessly drifted. I knew I could have suffered the same fate: through one casual or unwitting act, or just by staying on the ever more unconscious, destructive spiral toward my own demise. But I had not. I began to feel the quiet presence of a force larger than myself, and I knew it had brought me through the misery and menace of my addiction. I recognized that if left to my own egoistic devices, I would probably have killed myself with alcohol, but I was being given a second chance. The loving and available spiritual source I had been blindly looking for all my life broke through my defenses and revealed itself to me, not on a mountaintop or in some shrine, but in a facility for the treatment of chemical dependency. My recovery had begun.

This process of hitting bottom, of releasing the illusion of control over our situation, is a mandatory step out of the pain of addiction. The experience of surrender is the key to redemption, the gateway to recovery, healing, and the discovery of our spiritual potential. It marks the transition from a limited experience of who we are to an expanded one, and it happens to different people in different ways. Sometimes it is dramatic; sometimes it is relatively subtle. In the dark night of our addiction, our souls become impoverished whether or not we are externally destitute. We find ourselves in a state of spiritual emergency, a crisis that touches us at every level of our being. Whatever our circumstances, when we hit bottom, we are out of control. Caught in the ruinous cycle of our addictive behavior, we arrive at a juncture where our whole being knows that our life is not working. We are at the mercy of a destructive and self-destructive force that is larger than we are. And we are completely powerless against it.

When we surrender, we "let go absolutely," as the book *Alcoholics Anonymous* says. Everything we thought we were—all relationships and reference points, all ego games, defenses, resistances, and denials—collapses. What remains is the essential nature of who we are. The overwhelming power of our addictions, the persons, places, things, or activities we have made into our gods, give way to the healing presence of our true divine source, our deeper Self.

Describing the experience of surrender, a recovering addict said,

> *I felt as though I was in a wrestling match with a strong, monstrous, and brutal opponent. I did not stand a chance. I was on the mat and my antagonist was on my back, hammering away at me and yelling, "Do you give up? Do you give up?" I was battered and bruised, and every part of me hurt. I felt completely whipped, but I kept on struggling. Until I no longer had the strength to continue. Finally, I gave up, and called for help. And from that moment on, my life started changing.*

In the face of the enormity of our addiction, our stubbornness, our fear, and our delusions keep us fighting until there is nothing left to do but admit defeat.

Surrender often occurs in unexpected places at unpredictable times. That moment of resignation might happen at home, in the middle of the cellar steps, in a barroom, in a jail cell, or as we reach for the object of our addiction. One morning, or in the middle of some night, we arrive at the point where we cannot stand it any longer and something within us says, *"Enough! I can't do this anymore! Something has got to change!"*

Maybe we have just finished our third unhappy marriage or walked out of the thousandth strange bedroom. Maybe we are miserable on Christmas Day as we sit in our luxurious home, surrounded by material bounty and feeling empty. Maybe there is a hole in our nose and anxiety in our gut from the endless lines of cocaine, or maybe we have looked down one too many toilet bowls after a night of heavy drinking or an afternoon of bingeing on ice cream. Perhaps, as Joseph Campbell used to say, we get to the top of the ladder and find that it is against the wrong wall. Or perhaps we sit in yet another exotic place, in a hotel room not all that different from the others we have visited, and we feel tired of running.

And somewhere deep within, a small voice whispers, "I give up. . . " and adds, in desperation, "Please help me. . . . I'll do anything." Every recovering addict knows that moment. This is the depths of spiritual bankruptcy. Some say they surrendered. Others admit that the only way they would let go was through the self-destructive addictive cycle that propelled them to a state of absolute defeat: they say, "I *was* surrendered."

The first three Steps of Alcoholics Anonymous address the experience of complete surrender of ego control and the acceptance of help from a Higher Power:

1   We admitted we were powerless over alcohol—that our lives had become unmanageable.

2   Came to believe that a Power greater than ourselves could restore us to sanity.

3   Made a decision to turn our will and our lives over to the care of God *as we understood God.*

Those entering this program of recovery must go through the first Step; it is the initiation into the healing process. The process of admitting personal powerlessness and opening up to our potential resources applies not only to alcoholism but also to any other addiction. In addition, it pertains to any human being who clings to a person, object, idea, activity, or place that gets in the way of effective and creative functioning. Many people who would not define themselves as addicts have had that experience, that moment of truth, of submission.

Surrender as Ego-Death

There are many ways to describe surrender: "admitting defeat," "becoming powerless," "letting go," "hitting bottom," "dying while I am alive," "ego-death." Bill Wilson called it "the shattering of the ego." This experience of *ego-death* is one of the most profound, difficult, but transformative states there is. It is the destruction and metamorphosis of the restricted ego or of limited self-definitions; it must occur in order to make way for the deeper Self to express itself. Surrender opens the door for our Higher Power, *God as we understand God,* to break past the shields and denials that have kept it hidden.

The philosopher and psychotherapist Karlfried Graf Durckheim wrote, "This letting-go of the ego . . . means much more than merely relinquishing all those objects to which during his lifetime a man has become attached. It entails the giving up of the entire life pattern that has revolved around the 'positions' taken by the ego. . . . Only when we have let go of those attitudes wherein we rely solely upon what we 'have, know and can do,' will there arise a new consciousness in which the creative dynamism of life is contained."

The death of old personality structures and of unsuccessful ways of being in the world is necessary in order to advance into a freer, happier, and more loving existence. Ego-death does not mean the disintegration of the healthy ego, the ego we need in order to function in daily life. What dies in this process is the part of us that holds on to the illusion of control, the part of us that thinks we are running the show, that we are in charge. What disintegrates is the false identity that operates as though we are the center of the universe.

The experience of ego-death is the primary stage in a process of death and rebirth. Bill Wilson wrote, "Only through utter defeat are we able to take our first steps toward liberation and strength." Dying to our limitations, to our unhealthy, destructive attitudes and actions, makes way for personal growth, health, and creativity. When we admit defeat, we emerge victorious. On the other side of powerlessness is the limitless potency of our Higher Power. When we let go, we often receive more than we ever dreamed of. By releasing control, whether imagined or real, we realize how much energy we have wasted trying to hold on to something unmanageable. When we hit bottom, there is nowhere to go but up. We can die inwardly and still remain alive; if we die emotionally, psychologically, and spiritually, we are reborn into a new existence. And this is where the work, as well as the joy, of recovery begins.

The novelist and poet D. H. Lawrence poignantly captured the experience of death and rebirth in both poetry and prose. In "New Heaven and Earth," he wrote,

For when it is quite, quite nothing, then it is everything.
When I am trodden quite out, quite, quite out,
every vestige gone, then I am here
risen and setting my foot on another world
risen, accomplishing a resurrection
risen, not born again, but risen, body the same as before,
new beyond knowledge of newness, alive beyond life,
proud beyond inkling or furthest conception of pride,
living where life was never yet dreamed of, nor hinted at,
here, in the other world, still terrestrial
myself, the same as before, yet unaccountably new.

When we surrender, we might feel as though every vestige of who we were is gone, and when we emerge into our new life, it is like stepping into a fresh world. We inhabit the same body, but we are "unaccountably new."

Egocide, Not Suicide

It is well known that addictive behaviors can eventually lead to physical death. Daily newspapers print the grim statistics, and television stations broadcast stories about people with addiction problems and those whom they touch. Addicts can be caught in a self-destructive trajectory toward complete deterioration on every level. And in the process, they may seriously harm or destroy others by projecting this experience of internal and external devastation outward, inflicting it on those within their immediate circle.

With a shift of perception, we can understand this alarming and widespread phenomenon in a hopeful light. In the final paragraphs of the last chapter, I described the slide toward our demise during the dark night of addiction, as well as the loss of health, family, job, possessions, and self-respect that can occur. In this state of spiritual bankruptcy, we often feel as though everything is dying. Our experience seems very real, as though we are actually facing biological extinction. People who overindulge in alcohol use words like "totaled," "wasted," "smashed," "bombed," "polluted," or "blotto" to describe their drunkenness. The same words portray our physical, emotional, mental, and spiritual decay through addictive behavior of any kind. If we do not know there is a safe way out of this terrifying experience of personal annihilation, we might easily make the tragic mistake of attempting to complete it through suicide. In some cases, the pain of our deterioration is so great we act it out toward another individual through violence or even homicide.

The good news is that this process of dying in the grip of an addiction can be completed safely—and with beneficial consequences—*if* it is enacted as a subjective experience. Addicts can avert the danger of physical death if they turn inward and die to their old selves. The dissolution of the unhealthy ego is a crucial step toward profound transformation, toward greater health and wholeness. Rather than translating this essential ego death outward into physical destruction, it can be internalized without damaging the body further. We can turn the impulses toward *suicide,* so familiar to addicts, into *egocide,* or death of the ego. One of the reasons spiritually based recovery programs work so well is that they implicitly recognize the transformative power of surrender; they are able to offer the necessary support and guidance to individuals experiencing egocide.

The Element of Grace

How does surrender occur? When I ask a recovering addict what happened, why she or he surrendered, the answer often is, "I don't know. It certainly wasn't me doing it." Many people maintain that hitting bottom was a reflection of their Higher Power at work. Some simply say they were blessed. A recovering alcoholic declared, "I was struck sober by God. Just like when a person is about to die and their whole life flashes in front of them. . . . That happened to me when I realized I could no longer drink."

Why does an individual hit bottom on a certain day? Some people struggle with their dependency, repeatedly entering and leaving recovery programs, until suddenly something changes so that they no longer feel the need to continue their addictive behavior. What brings about that shift? A number of recovering addicts report, "For a reason I do not understand, my compulsion to use drugs (or to gamble, drink, overeat) was lifted from me. Overnight, it was gone. The obsession that had lasted for years has not returned."

Many people who become involved in recovery programs or in other forms of spiritual or religious life call this experience *grace.* As with other kinds of sacred phenomena, we are incapable of explaining a state of grace. Scholars, theologians, and mystics have tried to describe and interpret it for centuries. My *Webster's Ninth New Collegiate Dictionary* defines grace as "divine assistance given to [human beings] for [their] regeneration or sanctification . . . a virtue coming from God." The psychiatrist and author Gerald May calls it "the active expression of God's love." Part of the reason the experience of grace is so difficult to put into words is that our definition of the divine varies so greatly. For our purposes here, let us use the concept from the Twelve-Step programs "God as we understand God," which allows us to maintain our own unique experience of the deeper Self.

Whatever language and notions we choose, almost all of us have known moments when we received unexpected help or intervention from some unseen force in our lives. This divine assistance may come in the form of a sudden revelation, a release from a problem, or a sense of inner absolution after a mistake. We might be working on a personal predicament, and, from out of nowhere, a breath of clarity and wisdom sweeps through us, offering a solution. For some people who become stuck in addictive patterns, something mysterious and impossible to grasp intercedes. This is the force that brings us to the point at which, on that particular day, we say, *"Enough!"* It is the loving presence that opens the way out of our pain and compulsion.

When we are caught in the throes of our addictions, we disgrace ourselves through our behavior. As our unhealthy egos are progressively shattered, we move toward an experience of surrender. At this point, we are so weakened and so weary that we become open to an intervention by our deeper Self. Our Higher Power, hidden from us for so long by our own defenses and denials, flows into us and offers us liberation. This is a state of grace.

Grace is not something we can strive toward through virtue or good works. We do not achieve it by refining the correct spiritual practices. The expression of grace is not a linear, cause-and-effect phenomenon. Nor is it something that exists separately from our day-to-day existence. Full of mystery, this divine activity transpires in the most ordinary circumstances. Grace simply happens, and although we cannot work for it, we deserve it. If, as our story tells us, we are each composed of a small self and a deeper Self, it is our birthright to become familiar with that deeper Self.

As I write this, I am aware that discussing the redemptive nature of addiction and recovery might appear to be either glorifying or excusing addictive behavior. On the contrary. Addiction and all that it entails is terrifying, perilous, and potentially fatal. I would not wish the hell of this soul sickness on anyone. Hitting bottom and emerging into recovery can be a profoundly transforming death-and-rebirth experience that has life-changing potential, but it is dangerous. There are much less hazardous ways to accomplish the same thing. Too many of us do not make it through the death phase of this heroine's or hero's journey. However, for those of us who find ourselves gripped by addiction, there is hope and the possibility of a physical, emotional, mental, and spiritual renewal with far-reaching consequences.

The Benefits of Surrender

Why should we go through the experience of surrender? Why let go of who we think we are? From one point of view, we may feel we have a lot to lose. However, from a slightly different angle, in disengaging from our limitations, we have everything to gain.

Addiction is a spiritual emergency, a crisis that contains within it the seeds of transformation. Spiritual emergencies can occur in many different ways, and addiction is one of them. When my husband and I came up with the term *spiritual emergency,* we created a play on words, referring both to the *emergency* or *crisis* that may accompany a period of precipitous change and also to *emergence,* suggesting the tremendous opportunity such experiences can offer for personal growth and understanding. The process of hitting bottom and coming into recovery from addictions is a form of spiritual emergency that contains many of the same elements as other kinds of psychospiritual crises.

A central factor in all forms of spiritual emergency is that contained within the crisis, during the experience of ego-death, lies the key to healing and transformation. During our addiction, we have yielded to the bottle, other people, food, cigarettes, or drugs. By fully giving in to our personal powerlessness, we commend ourselves to the care of the deeper Self. Through surrender, we move from hopelessness to hope. We shift from destructiveness to the promise of creativity, from depression to inspiration. From the absolute bottom, we begin to progress toward the possibility of a healthy, fulfilling life.

Some people have dramatic spiritual awakenings in that moment of defeat and demoralization. As they sit on the kitchen floor, pace the jail cell, or hear for the first time the concerns of their family and friends, they relinquish control, often entreating some unknown force to help. Without warning, they may have an experience that sounds like a description from the lives of the mystics. Some people see visions of light or the figure of a benevolent being. Others might hear a voice offering comfort, guidance, and direction. Still others strongly sense the powerful and loving presence of a protective force. These kinds of stunning spiritual episodes can happen to anyone, even to individuals who previously identified themselves as atheists or agnostics. When such people tell their stories, they point to this significant event as the one that shepherded them out of their addictive hell and into recovery.

As we stated earlier, most people do not experience this forceful, obvious form of grace. For many of us, there are no fireworks, no visions, no divine words of guidance. Over time, during the recovery process, we change, and we find ourselves living increasingly happy, honest, loving, and conscious lives. As we do our recovery work, our experience of the deeper Self grows gradually. Our trust and belief in that guiding force evolve slowly. However, each person who has truly surrendered at the bottom of an addictive career knows that experience to be significant, even profound. It is a state of grace that opens us to previously untouched possibilities within.

The Challenges of Surrender

I once heard a recovering addict say, "I feel like a child who is learning to walk. I'm letting go and hanging on at the same time. Why can't I just let go and allow myself to take off?" Her comment reminded me of the Hindu story about surrender. It describes a method used in India that was guaranteed to catch monkeys. Hunters would hollow out a coconut and carve a hole in the shell just big enough to allow a monkey's hand to enter. Then they would secure the coconut to the ground and put some delicious food in it. Upon discovering that day's dinner, the monkey would reach into the opening and grab it. But as soon as the unsuspecting victim clutched the food, its hand would become a fist that was too big to remove from the hole. Rather than release the unexpected treat, the monkey remained with its fist caught in the coconut, easy prey for the hunters.

Like the monkey, some people would rather die than let go. Why is the experience of surrender so difficult for us? Why do so many of us have to be pushed against the wall, beaten into defeat by our addictive behavior, before we let go? One reason is that surrender often requires a change of identity, giving up the idea of who we are. As human beings, most of us firmly identify with the small self, with our ego-existence as an individual with a strong sense of who "I" am. We relate to ourselves as material entities that exist within a limited reality. This is the aspect of us that is necessary for effective functioning in our world.

Going beyond our narrow self-definition can be frightening; it feels as though we are being asked to completely give up our identity. Even though the surrender has the potential for spiritual expansion, many of us are so disconnected from our deeper Self that letting go implies dropping into the unknown. What will we have left if we surrender? Ironically, letting go of who we think we are is essential if we are to change. Just as letting go of one activity is necessary in order for something new to happen, surrendering the small self is necessary in order to know the deeper Self and integrate it into our life experience.

Moreover, many of us build our lives around being in control. We have created strategies for survival in an unstable world, forming a superstructure of defenses, denials, and creative coping devices that give us the illusion of power. In doing this, we have gained a certain sense of mastery over our lives, but eventually our efforts have become rigid. From our positions as individual egos, we begin to assume that we can order and direct every aspect of our lives, including other people.

As we have seen, the construction of our false identity and our involvement in our addictive behavior diminishes or severs the connection with the creative force running the show. After some time, we are left with the illusion that we are in charge and often, that the world revolves around us and our needs. We end up singlehandedly attempting to maneuver our reality, as though we were in the driver's seat of an automobile. Along the way, most of us develop some degree of arrogance, pride, or grandiosity to mask our prevailing sense of shame, fear, and self-consciousness. Our spiritual source remains obscured, and we become too self-absorbed to recognize its existence or its power.

This occurs in all of us to some degree or another. By their very nature, our lives are unpredictable and inconsistent. Someone said, "The only thing we can depend on is change." Every second passes, and the next one is filled with the uncertainty of limitless possibilities. This reality can be both exciting and frightening. Because many of us are afraid of change, we hang on to what we know. Our known reality, even though it might be unpleasant or difficult, offers some degree of perceived safety and personal delineation. When confronted with an alternative to our customary mode of operation, many of us balk. We feel safer if we stay within the confines of our familiar prison than if we risk breaking out.

The natural tenacity of the human ego becomes magnified in someone whose life has been filled with disorder, instability, violence, or abuse. In the face of threatening situations, we draw upon our infinite resources and take charge in an attempt to find some semblance of sanity and safety. If we do not perceive order in our world, we feel crazy; taking control gives us the illusion of normalcy, and letting go of control seems disastrous. After we have spent years building a citadel of (illusory) strength and security, surrendering our false identity is terrifying. If we let go of control, we might feel pain and fear.

For someone with a background of physical, verbal, or sexual abuse, surrender is often equated with violation. Becoming powerless implies being overpowered, defenseless, wounded. Giving up control means *being* controlled by a powerful, brutal force. The idea that surrender provides an entry into benevolence, love, and increased spiritual power seems foreign; it is difficult to comprehend that letting go is transformative and growth-producing. Experience has taught that defenses must be kept intact at any cost; to do otherwise means to be overwhelmed.

In addition, surrender requires humility. It means releasing the facade of false pride and arrogance and allowing our weaknesses to be exposed. Again, this can be very frightening for those who have depended upon their defenses as protection against potential violation. A phrase around addiction recovery groups is, "Through humiliation comes humility." For many of us, this is true. We must feel as though we are reduced to nothing before we give up our defenses. The only way we learn humility is through the reckless, out of control, crazy addictive behavior that propels us to the bottom and destroys our self-respect.

Cultural roles can serve as further obstacles to our experience of surrender. For example, many males in our society are raised with the expectation that they must remain strong, effective, and in control at all times. Families and colleagues depend upon them to maintain a veneer of stability. *Real men don't cry* is the implicit masculine directive. "Real men" do not let down their guard, expose their feelings, or display their vulnerability. Historically, surrender has been associated with losing everything to the opposing force in a war. It means yielding power, possessions, and dignity to an enemy; truly heroic warriors never give up. Admitting to personal powerlessness implies losing the illusion of potency. If men were to do that, they would lose part of the identity that has been assigned to them by our culture.

For racial and cultural minorities, those with unaccepted sexual orientations, women, and others whom society regards as less powerful, the problem is strikingly different. Many of these individuals are already demoralized and out of touch with their own strengths. Others regard powerlessness as something to grow out of; in the struggle for recognition and equal rights, they strive for strength and mastery. Surrender means giving up what they have fought for; it means backsliding into the submission and compliance they already know so well. Power connotes the overbearing political, social, and individual authority that has relegated them to their inequitable position. Even the name "Higher Power" can elicit images of oppressive forces such as these.

However, by becoming powerless, we gain more power. Through the experience of ego-death, we relinquish our ineffective and unauthentic ways of existing and open to the resources of the deeper Self. Whatever our public role, this state of surrender can evoke within us a deep strength that is infinitely more forceful and enduring than the perceived power of our social identity. Unlike the brittle certainty associated with control and influence, this deeper power is vigorous, dependable, and bountiful.

Trying Too Hard to Let Go

There is a difference between surrendering and "being surrendered." If letting go is too intentional, it does not work. Our goal-oriented attitude gets in the way. Surrender is a process, not an event, and the timing is different for different people; it often has nothing to do with our rational expectations and our schedules. One of my spiritual teacher's central themes was surrender to the inner Self, or God. He said, "There are only two ways to live: One is with constant conflict, and the other is with surrender. . . . When someone surrenders . . . his house, hands, and heart become full. His former feeling of emptiness and lack disappears."

That sounds like a wonderful objective. Prompted by our teacher's words, many of his students set about *trying to* surrender in a very goal-oriented fashion. As I settled into meditation or faced a challenge in my life, I would say to myself, "Now I am going to let go. All right. Now I am surrendering. Take me." I sat back and waited, feeling very proud that I had, I thought, achieved my wish. But, inevitably, something would come along that would show me I had not let go. I was still hanging on for dear life to the idea, self-righteous position, person, or activity I had tried to release.

Then, I would say to myself, "OK, this time I am *really* going to let go. All the way." And I would try even harder to surrender. However, the more I focused on it, the more engrossed I became in the idea. The more obsessive my thoughts became, the more difficult it was to detach from them. The harder I tried to surrender, the more important my goal was. The greater the goal became, the more I stretched toward some future promise. As a result, I was completely missing my present experience, the only place where the letting go could occur.

If we try too hard to let go, we become so involved in trying to make it happen that we work against ourselves. Ironically, we try to control an experience that requires *loss* of control. When we are surrendered by a force beyond our influence, whether it is the source of our addiction or challenging circumstances in our lives, we are forced to let go. For some of us, this is the only way we will surrender unconditionally.

Maps of Death and Rebirth

The process of surrender and renewal is not exclusive to the experience of addiction and recovery. We live it each year as we pass through the seasons: we progress from the bounty of summer through autumnal withering and winter's deep sleep into the regeneration of spring. Throughout history, many traditions have acknowledged and celebrated this cycle of death and rebirth. Fortunately for us, our forebears have created maps that describe this process, serving as guides to the ups and downs of our lives. This cyclical death and rebirth model is a very hopeful one, particularly for people who are selectively tuned in to the dark night of inner dying; it offers the promise of renewal on the other side of depths and difficulties.

In reviewing myths and religions from around the world, the mythologist Joseph Campbell realized that the majority of them contained a universal formula that, he believed, reflects a deep aspect of the collective human psyche. The themes in these cross-cultural systems are familiar and represent patterns all of us share. Campbell found that the motif of death and rebirth serves as a central guiding model in both myth and religion.

The Christian story of the crucifixion and resurrection of Jesus provides a powerful and passionate description of death and renewal. During the Easter celebration, images of rebirth abound, as tiny chickens hatch from eggs and baby bunnies are born from mother rabbits, symbols of fertility and plenty. In ancient Egypt, the god Osiris was dismembered by his evil brother, Seth, and brought back to life through the intervention of his sister, Isis. Native cultures worldwide tell tales of heroic female and male figures who descended to the depths, overcame obstacles, and returned to earth transformed.

In his elegantly written book *The Hero with a Thousand Faces,* Campbell describes one form of the death and renewal myth: the hero's journey. The male or female hero leaves his or her familiar dwelling, either intentionally or through a "call to adventure" from some outside force. Following the call to adventure, the heroine or hero enters a realm of unknown and difficult challenges. There, she or he confronts overwhelming forces and trials, finally facing a supreme ordeal. Emerging victorious, the heroine or hero meets the spiritual Self, an encounter that can take any of several forms. The final task, often the most difficult, is to return home, transformed and with new gifts to share with others.

The Greek myth of Odysseus, who ventures forth into unknown realms and faces life-threatening challenges, reflects the encounter with death and renewal of the hero. In a myth that provides an allegory for the movement of the seasons, the Greek goddess Persephone is abducted into the underworld and, through the intervention of Zeus, returned to her home for part of the year.

The three stages of the hero's or heroine's journey—*separation, initiation,* and *return*—characterize the stages in the journey of addiction and recovery. We separate ourselves from our known, if unhappy, worlds with the initial taste of our addiction. The first drink, drug, sexual encounter, eating binge, or taste of power is our call to adventure. It is a seductive whisper or a resounding reverberation that beckons us into unknown, wondrous, and terrifying territories. As we become further entangled with our substance, relationship, or activity of choice, our challenges increase until we meet the ultimate ordeal: surrender. Surrender is our initiation. If we let go absolutely, if we release our ego control, we emerge from the underworld and begin our journey home. We return to the familiar territory where we started, but we are different. Having passed through many lessons, we are transformed. And we have the wisdom gained from our experience to offer others who need help.

In his discussion of the hero's journey, Joseph Campbell drew in part upon the formula of separation, initiation, and return that is essential to rituals called rites of passage in many cultures. Our own lives are hero's or heroine's journeys, composed of a series of cycles. We grow from the extreme dependence of infancy into childhood, from childhood through adolescence to adulthood, from life as young adults often into marriage and then to middle age, from middle age to our elder years, through old age to death. We die to one period of our life and emerge into a new one. Each one of these transitions introduces important changes within and produces its own set of physical, emotional, mental, and spiritual challenges.

Because of the importance of life transitions, numerous cultures have created rites of passage in order to mark an individual's progression from one stage of the life cycle to the next. Rites of passage facilitate the process of surrender and renewal. They provide an opportunity to face emotional and experiential limitations and to move beyond them. Participants often go through a "second birth": they die to one phase of their lives and the roles, attitudes, and patterns associated with that period and leave it behind for a new stage with a new identity.

Initiates are honored by their community and supported and guided by those who have gone before them. Through the ceremonial form, those in transition are accorded a designated position within the community. They gain a firm and clear definition of their identities, social roles, and personal boundaries. They know where they fit. In addition, wise members of the community assist each initiate in integrating the changes into his or her being.

Initiates also have an opportunity to experience their own creativity, the source of inner strength, love, or spiritual potential, through the powerful transformative methods within the ritual. Often through a symbolic confrontation with death and rebirth, initiates are propelled beyond their mortal limitations. They experience the mystical or spiritual domains that provide guidance, inspiration, and an expanded sense of self. Contact with these spiritual states is necessary in order for healing to take place.

If we have the courage to face both the dark and the light in our psyches, we no longer feel unconsciously motivated to turn them against ourselves or project them onto others and onto our surroundings in a harmful way. Instead, we have the chance to transform ourselves and to contribute to the world without the influence of disturbing unconscious material.

Unfortunately, our modern culture, by abandoning such sanctioned rites of passage, has lost a major tool for transformation. The well-known anthropologist Margaret Mead believed that modern society's movement away from sanctioned rites of passage is a critical factor in the increase of various forms of social pathology. On the basis of her cross-cultural studies, she concluded that we carry intense emotions and impulses in our personality structure that, if we do not deal with them internally, we project into our everyday life. We create our own pseudo–rites of passage, usually without knowing it.

A glaring example is the adolescent gang activity that is sweeping American cities. A 1991 article from the *New York Times* described ritualistic components of a gang that included, as part of its initiation, the demand that potential members shoot someone in order to prove their worth. This requirement has an obvious and horrifying similarity to that of the young African who must kill his first lion or the Eskimo boy who shoots his first seal as a way of demonstrating manhood. Gang activity and rites of passage share other similar elements: wearing of certain symbolic clothes, hairdos, or other accoutrements; danger and competition; confrontation of fear and other limitations; an encounter with death; separation from the daily life of the culture; and experience of nonordinary states of consciousness. None of these elements is harmful in itself; each can be used in positive ways. Of prime importance are the context in which they occur and the intention that motivates them. If we were to provide an accepting and loving context in which individuals could confront and integrate their inner impulses and emotions, it might prevent some destructive and self-destructive acting out, including addictive behavior.

A good addictions treatment center is one of the only sanctioned frameworks in this culture where a powerful form of rite of passage takes place. There, in a loving and supportive atmosphere, an individual in the dying phase of a profound, life-transforming process of death and rebirth is allowed to hit bottom and move into regeneration and healing. The therapists are like midwives who know they are not in control of the process but have the skills and understanding necessary to help it along if it gets stuck. Many of the staff members have been through their own initiation into recovery; it is well known that, because of their own experiences, people who are stable and committed to their own recovery from addictions are the most effective facilitators in the treatment world.

Once the passage has taken place, the initiate is given educational instruction and practical tools that will allow him or her to develop tender, fledgling awarenesses and integrate them into a new, spiritual way of being. And he or she receives guidance in developing means to regularly contact a personal Higher Power, Self, or God.

When You Think You've Hit Bottom, Just Look Down

In the first few weeks of my recovery from alcoholism, I thought that perhaps I had finally been blessed with *the* experience of surrender. My life changed substantially immediately after hitting bottom, and as my head began to clear, the world suddenly came alive. After several years of disconnection from everything but the bleak reality of my addiction, the riches around me and within me began to flood into awareness. The natural world sparkled with welcome, food tasted wonderful, and the warm water in my bathtub enveloped and nourished me. I felt long periods of peace and a new crystalline stream of grace and creativity percolated within me. "Could this be it?" I dared to ask myself. "Has this been the experience of ego-death I have been waiting for?" And then someone said, "When you think you have hit bottom, just look down."

Since that time, I have learned what many recovering addicts already know: the experience of hitting bottom with our primary addiction is just the beginning. There are many more bottoms to come within the recovery process and as part of life itself. The initial experience of surrender is a major turning point that often feels dramatic, mystical, and revolutionary. However, this important moment also marks the beginning of a great deal of hard, but rewarding, work. No matter how profound and enlightening it might be, if we do not follow up this step of letting go by making a continued effort at recovery, it will become only one in a number of forgotten experiences.

The process of surrender offers a blueprint that is beneficial as a practice and a life strategy. Living our lives is like riding a wave on a surfboard; we consistently face ups and downs, times when we feel challenged and times when everything seems to be going our way. Many deaths and rebirths occur in the course of our lifetimes, the endings of phases, relationships, projects, or roles and the beginnings of new ones. Change is inherent in our existence, and we have limited control over it. As a result, we inevitably confront many minor and major situations in which we must decide whether to fight, hang on, or let go.

In certain instances, we can change through our own efforts. However, we often discover that our ability to influence the events and people in our lives is limited. Many circumstances exist beyond our control; try as we might to modify them, we cannot. Those of us who have spent our lives trying to maintain control realize that this has been the wrong strategy. Our firm commitment to the illusion that the world's events should unfold according to our plan leaves us exhausted and miserable. We have been fighting our way upstream in a rushing river. Gradually, we learn to stop struggling and allow its current to carry us. Ultimately, we can only transform ourselves, and that transformation is necessary for our strength and well-being. During early recovery, we find that our lives often offer us a choice: we can either suffer the pain of hanging on or feel the relief and equanimity of letting go. We can cling to something, or we can practice surrender. The words of the Serenity Prayer provide a useful formula:

> *God, Grant me the Serenity*
> *To accept the things I cannot change,*
> *Courage to change the things I can,*
> *And the Wisdom to know the difference.*

We can surrender to the things in our lives we can do nothing about, change those we can, and work toward developing the wisdom to know the difference. The practice of letting go becomes a way of facing challenges. We learn to step back and allow our deeper resources to guide us, even though we do not do it completely and perfectly each time. We begin to recognize when it is time to gracefully acquiesce. And as we continue, we realize that there are many layers of surrender that occur in stages. We might release what feels like a significant amount of ego control, only to discover that there are many more subtle and not so subtle levels of the same experience. With the guidance of others who have gone before us, we continue to practice letting go until we can increasingly allow the river of life to carry us.

7

Addiction and Attachment

Iɴ ᴛʜᴇ ꜰʟᴜsʜ of early recovery, I felt tremendous relief. Released from years of painful, reckless obsession with alcohol, I discovered a new sense of freedom. I thought that now that I was no longer drinking, I would be free to live my life unfettered, with the help of an ongoing recovery program. I had cleaned up my act, and therefore I had become liberated from addiction. But very rapidly, I found I was not as emancipated as I thought I was. I noticed that, as the chemical craving disappeared, the familiar inner thirst remained. And because of the new, almost raw state in which I found myself, I felt the elemental yearning in a purer form than ever before.

I became aware of the times when I felt the internal restlessness I know so well, and I learned to observe my response to it. It often coincided with an uncomfortable or painful situation in my life. Writing at the computer, I would sometimes feel stuck; the ideas stopped flowing, and the words seemed awkward. Suddenly, I would catch myself thinking about the bag of pretzels in the kitchen cupboard, a new skirt at the local clothing store, or the flowers I wanted to plant in the garden. During a difficult interaction with someone, the promise of a friendly telephone conversation beckoned, the refrigerator would call to me, the image of a new pair of earrings would flash through my mind, or I would become mesmerized by plans for the next day. As I went about my daily activities, the unfulfilled discontent in my soul would ask for satisfaction through extra hugs, a visit to a neighborhood restaurant, or a new item for the house.

Whether or not I acted on these tempting urges and images, I soon realized that they seemed to offer both the promise of inner satisfaction and an escape from the discomfort I was feeling. If I submitted to the tantalizing possibilities around me, perhaps the internal void would be filled and I would finally be happy and free from pain. Soon I discovered that the various enticements were threatening to fill the same role alcohol once played, although to a much lesser extent and with much different consequences.

I began to see that I was facing two different phenomena: there are some things I do in my life that are definitely addictive, that can lead to severe repercussions if I do not stop them, and there are others that have similar characteristics but will not cause me or other people obvious harm. Some of them even bring genuine pleasure and enjoyment. However, just as with alcohol, these activities, substances, or relationships *do* bring pain, however mild. When I do not have them, I feel pain. If I want them but cannot reach them, I feel pain. If I get them and realize they will not last very long, I feel pain. If I have had them and want them again, I feel pain.

At first, I thought I was merely a hopeless addict who would become addicted to anything that came my way. But then I realized that, although I felt lured by many of the world's offerings, they did not have the out-of-control power of true addictions. Then, what were these enticements? I remembered a central theme in Buddhist teachings: the root of all suffering is attachment or clinging to other people, places, objects, or behaviors. The Four Noble Truths, a major teaching in Theravada Buddhism, says, simply stated, that life contains suffering; the cause of suffering is attachment or craving; it is possible to alleviate attachment; and there are means to the cessation of attachment.

Perhaps, I thought, attachment and addiction are two aspects of the same phenomenon. Could it be that much of our understanding of addiction also applies to the problem of attachment, and vice versa? Although I had stopped drinking, I still was mistakenly trying to express the familiar spiritual yearning through external or internal substitutes for the spiritual completeness I craved. The temptations around me represented the lure of the plentiful attachments that exist in our world. As we will see, attachments have the potential to become addictions but do not do so inevitably. Let us explore this notion further.

Spiritual and religious traditions address the subject of *attachment* in various ways, and because of their different attitudes about and treatment of this subject, there is no unanimous definition of it. *Clinging, craving, grasping, clutching, holding on,* and *wanting* are other words for this universal human experience. We can become attached to almost anything: to our roles in life, to our attitudes and prejudices, to the goals we set for ourselves. Many of us become tenaciously attached to our denial systems.

We might cling to significant relationships: to our children, our mates, our friends, or our colleagues. We may hold tightly to our roles as influential contributors to society, as parents, as members of an exclusive group. As miserable as we might feel, we hang on to our familiar identities as superior or downtrodden, as victims or aggressors. We grasp at the intensity and drama in our lives, at the suffering or the joy, at the pain or the pleasure. We clutch our material wealth, possessions, pleasures, escapes, personal or professional recognition, or success.

This tendency to become attached is not exclusive to individuals. Entire racial, religious, or national groups have hung on to their identities as exclusive and superior to others. Throughout history, diverse communities have engaged in bitter wars over land, borders, and ideologies they believed to be theirs. Religious groups have battled one another, fueled by the conviction that God sides with them because they are the righteous. Within religious institutions, differing factions have clashed. The human race has even set itself apart from the rest of the animal kingdom, clinging to a sense of superiority over other life forms.

Various spiritual or religious traditions understand attachment in different ways. Many of the Eastern religions treat attachment as something to be conquered, overcome, dissolved, or transcended. Spiritual seekers must train, eliminate, or detach from their grasping, which is recognized as a source of pain, grief, bondage, fear, and hatred. A Buddhist aphorism states, "The creeper of craving grows everywhere," and during spiritual practice, the seeker must "cut off its roots by the power of wisdom." As we let go of our clinging, we find happiness and freedom. By abolishing our attachments, we eradicate suffering and foster serenity. Craving is the flip side of love. If we can eliminate the negative constraints of craving, we discover the generous bounty of love within us.

Occidental religions often regard attachment as something seekers can harness, transform, channel, and integrate into their lives. If we cling to lowly, earthbound temptations, we submit to the snares and transgressions of the world. The craving for sexual pleasure can become the sin of lust. Grasping at material wealth often leads to greed. If we hang on to ego gratification or a need for fame, we become bound by pride. However, if we redirect our attachments toward God, we demonstrate our devotion to the divine and become open to its influence and power. Our desire to be happy and free or to belong to God is a natural component of human life. Our attachment to the divine cultivates our love and benevolence. Through faith and spiritual practice, we learn to direct our attachments into a vital and productive desire for spiritual well-being.

In both Eastern and Occidental systems, not all attachments are seen as negative or potentially harmful. There are positive and useful desires, both within our daily lives and in relation to the divine or transpersonal realms. We will discuss healthy desire more extensively in another chapter. In the broadest sense, we can say that the Eastern view of attachment is useful in describing the human predicaments of attachment and addiction, and that both the Eastern insights about surrender and the Occidental notions of transforming attachments are useful for the process of recovery and spiritual growth.

Addiction and Attachment

Blending the wisdom from many traditions, let us look at the universal human reality of attachment and its relation to addiction. Here, we will look at the notion that the root of suffering is attachment. In the next section of the book, "Healing and the Path to the Self," we will explore ways we can work with and transform our desires. Addiction and attachment exist on a continuum. At one end are mild attachments, momentary diversions that, if removed from our lives, leave us with only faint feelings of discomfort. At the other end is true addiction. And in between the extremes of severe addiction and mild attachment are many conditions that contain characteristics of each.

From an experiential perspective, the differences between addiction and attachment have only to do with their quality and intensity. All of us have attachments, but not everyone can be identified as a true addict. A central component of *addiction* is absolute personal powerlessness and lack of control. True addicts surrender themselves completely to a substance, activity, or relationship. Addiction is progressive in nature; it builds momentum as it advances.

As the addictive process continues, addicts become compulsively harnessed to the object of their addiction as well as to the destructive and self-destructive behavior implicit in it. Increasingly fortified by a misleading denial system, they continue engaging in addictive activity in spite of increasingly harmful consequences. Over time, addicts develop a tolerance for their addiction, need more and more to obtain the same effect, and experience severe withdrawal if it is removed.

Attachments have the potential to become addictions if we follow them too far, but not all our attachments are addictions. We can hold on to a point of view or to our roles in the world and feel pain as a result of our unyielding attitudes; however, the quality of that experience is less intense than a total commitment to drugs, alcohol, food, sex, power, or another addiction. Addictions take precedence over all else, even life itself. Attachment and the suffering that comes with it are part of the human dilemma. But addicts experience a qualitative difference between the craving that manifests as attachment and the craving that becomes addiction. Attachments are part of life, but a severe addiction is usually life-threatening.

If we all have problems with attachments, then we can understand addiction as an extreme version of attachment. We become addicts when we spin out of control with our attachments. A father who is attached to his son faces a dilemma all parents share to some degree: What is the fine line between loving and guiding our children and allowing them to develop as unique individuals without interference? When do we step in and offer direction, and when do we let them go? How and when do we release them into the world to make it on their own, without us? However, if the same father becomes so wrapped up in his child that he loses his own identity, his attachment slips over the line into addiction. If he cannot stay out of his son's affairs, controls and manipulates him because of his own needs, or depends upon his adulation for his well-being, then his attachment develops a compulsive quality.

Addiction is attachment amplified, and addicts are simply caricatures of the rest of humanity as we wrestle with our attachments. Addiction and attachment cause varying degrees of suffering. The extreme physical, emotional, mental, and spiritual anguish sustained by addicts is a magnified version of the discomfort or pain experienced by someone who is attached. The amount of suffering we inflict upon ourselves and others is equal to the force with which we hang on to our attachments or addictions. Chemical dependency and other forms of obsessive addiction result in a forced suffering from which it is difficult to detach.

An extremely evocative image from Tibetan Buddhism is the realm of the hungry ghosts or *pretas*. Beautiful Tibetan paintings of the Wheel of Life depict the various inner heavens and hells that we can experientially visit during our lifetimes or at death. One of the hells is populated by the hungry ghosts, beings with bellies as big as mountains, mouths the size of pinholes, exceptionally thin necks, and insatiable appetites. They are never satisfied. Eternally, the banquet table is just out of reach, fruit trees turn to thorny timber, and the world around them appears to be barren.

These unappeasable creatures are wonderfully appropriate representations of our struggle with attachments and addictions. We, too, are often insatiable as we act out our cravings. We want something or someone, and when we get it, it loses its allure, in the way that the thrill of a new romance eventually dissipates with time. The very energy of the pursuit holds excitement, but when we finally possess the object of our search, it is no longer enjoyable. Yet, we have difficulty letting it go. So we hang on to it and keep looking for something more satisfying. This process, whether it relates to sex, food, power, money, alcohol, drugs, people, or the myriad of other possibilities in our life, repeats itself over and over. If the repetition continues past a certain point, the initial attachment acquires the obsessive quality of an addiction. In the case of chemical addicts and alcoholics, once a cucumber becomes a pickle, once we have crossed the line into addiction, there is no going back to mere attachment.

A friend once mused,

> My husband and I used to live in the country, in a big house with lots of space around it for gardens and grass. Eventually, we decided that it was too big for us and that we were spending too much time taking care of the place. So we moved to a lovely, small condominium right near the city, and at first, I felt delighted. It was perfect for the two of us. We had the advantage of being able to see the

trees without having to maintain them, and we had time to devote ourselves to other things. But after a few months, I found myself thinking more and more about the place in the country. I began to wish that I could walk in the grass and work in the garden. The strange thing is that I know that if I were to move again, I wouldn't be happy either. It all boils down to the problem that it is difficult for me to relax and enjoy where I am.

This sort of mental meandering and sense of dissatisfaction are common as we respond to our attachments. Who has not had the feeling that the grass is greener on the other side of the fence? A different job would be preferable to the one we have. Perhaps a new car would bring us the satisfaction we seek. Or during a period of marital conflict, who has not entertained the thought that somewhere, there has to be someone who will understand and treat us better? No matter what we achieve or accumulate, the initial excitement wears off, and we once again become dissatisfied. We cannot enjoy what we have, so we set our sights on something else.

The recognition of attachment as a problem in our lives does not come solely from the East. In *Man and Superman*, George Bernard Shaw wrote, "There are two tragedies in life. One is to lose your heart's desire. The other is to gain it." Samuel Johnson said it this way, "Life is a progression from want to want, not from enjoyment to enjoyment." Benjamin Franklin stated, "If you desire many things, many things will seem like a few." All these reflections point to the human dilemma of attachment and our hungry-ghost nature. Often, we become so dominated by our desires that we lose the ability to be happy in the present moment.

Why Do We Become Attached?

If addiction and attachment exist as extremes on the same continuum, then it makes sense that some of the deeper roots of attachment and addiction are also similar. We cling to relationships, roles, activities, or material objects for many reasons. Sometimes we hang on out of fear or to try to escape the pain in our lives. In an attempt to satisfy our genuine unfulfilled need to be loved and accepted, we attach ourselves to other people, to animals, or to social and professional roles that promise to bring us what we long for. Perhaps we are filled with shame and constantly look outside ourselves for something to make us feel better. Or perhaps we try to create a sense of security and meaning by defining ourselves in terms of our points of view or opinions. Our spiritual thirst propels us to seek fulfillment, and we make the mistake of trying to quench it in the wrong direction.

Attachment is also very closely linked to our attempts to control a transitory and unpredictable world. Have you ever been enjoying an ice cream cone and suddenly become aware of an undercurrent of ambivalent feelings? On a hot afternoon, a scoop of cool sweetness is delectable at first taste. Then it starts to melt, and you realize that your pleasure is time-limited. There is no way of holding on to your enjoyment because of the nature of the ice cream and the ticking of the clock. A slight feeling of sadness and dissatisfaction begins to overshadow your delight. As the ice cream melts, you lick it faster, and it disappears even more quickly. You find yourself mourning the end of this experience before it is even over.

Within seconds, you start thinking about replacing this cone with another one. You envision yourself buying it, and you can almost taste what flavor it will be. You become so involved in the fantasy of the next treat that you completely miss the experience of finishing the first one. And then, before you realize it, the ice cream is gone, and you once again feel dissatisfied. It has all happened too fast, and you did not find the pleasure you thought you would. At the same time, your stomach tells you that you are full.

Now, your mind tries to talk you into another cone. Either you know you would not enjoy it and decide against it, or you go for another one. As you plunge into the second one, it does not meet your expectations. There is a good chance that the initial taste placates your craving, but almost immediately, the craving recurs. In any case, you are left annoyed and discontented.

The unhappiness that accompanies an ice cream cone is minimal compared to the intense suffering of a chemical addict, but it illustrates the ongoing influence of our cravings and the power of our fear of change. A myriad of potential attachments faces us every day. As we have said previously, the only thing we can depend on is change. Our cravings combined with the transitory nature of our life lead to pain. And our discontent keeps us from participating fully in our lives. By yearning for something in the future, we lose our experience of the present. When we grasp it and hold on, it changes. In projecting ourselves into the future or dwelling in the past, we forfeit the only real experience we can count on: the present moment.

In addition, our satisfaction does not last. We attain the object of our desire and taste a fleeting moment of enjoyment and relief from craving, and then, within a short time, the thirst begins again. The pleasure comes not in finally achieving the experience or gaining the object we have been seeking but in the cessation of the desire, that brief period before the next craving. As that instant fades, we attempt to hold on to it or replicate it. If we have a need to control our reality, our efforts increase. Eventually, we become so focused on repeating that taste of satisfaction that we become obsessed. Our attachment slides toward addiction.

Although we enjoy times of happiness, we also feel varying degrees of discomfort brought about by our constant craving and our inability to appreciate what comes our way. In the face of the ephemeral nature of existence, we try to stay in control. We have expectations about our lives, our goals, and our wishes. When we achieve an objective or satisfy a desire, it shifts. The change causes fear and pain, and we hold on even tighter to whatever we have accumulated as we continue our search for satisfaction. Some of us become rigid or even greedy as we increasingly pursue immediate pleasures.

There are times when we cannot allow our life to flow. We become temporarily blocked from enjoyment of the present moment because we fear we will lose what we have gained. We may even develop a sense of guilt about what we accomplish, perhaps feeling we do not deserve it. We do not want to move out of the limitations we have established for ourselves. Our restricted and painful life is what we know, and we are afraid to let go of it. As we hang on to our known identity, we further remove ourselves from contact with the deeper Self.

Does this sound familiar? Here again, the dynamics of attachment and the dark night of addiction are similar, although they reflect different levels of intensity. We mistakenly direct the underlying search for wholeness toward internal and external activities, substances, and relationships that neither give us the answers we crave nor fill our spiritual emptiness. The continual problem of attachment and the resultant pain keep us separated from potential joy and freedom.

The present moment is a window into the divine. The mystics tell us that the object of our spiritual search is right here, right now, but that most of the time we cannot see it because of the barriers within. Some of those barriers have to do with our attachments and with the rigidity and fear associated with them. Because we cannot enjoy the present wholeheartedly, we cannot fully connect with our vital, creative, loving, and inspirational source. Our attachments keep us separate from the divine.

We All Share a Common Ground with True Addicts

This statement, "We all share a common ground with true addicts," might come as a surprise to someone who has never identified himself or herself as an addict. But if we think about the human dilemma of attachment and suffering, we will see that we all face some version of it whether or not we call ourselves addicts. The discussions in this book about craving, the small self and the deeper Self, alienation and abuse, survival mechanisms, the dark night of addiction, and surrender apply not only to addicts but to all of us to a greater or lesser degree as we encounter our attachments.

This notion certainly does not fit with the depiction of the addict or the alcoholic many of us are accustomed to. When I was growing up, there was a standard image of an alcoholic: the one the adults discussed with patronizing words and hushed voices as we passed a bum staggering along the street, bottle in hand. Addicts were thin, gaunt figures with transparent skin and stringy hair, slumping in alleyways. Track marks from multiple injections of heroin scarred their arms. Dirt and grime and empty needles surrounded them where they lay. These people were separate and different from us. We kept them at arm's length because they were bad and morally corrupt. They had no self-control, and they were mean and less honorable than we were.

Hollywood bolstered this perception of the addict: In the movies, we saw Jack Lemmon in *The Days of Wine and Roses* sitting cross-eyed and unshaven in an insane asylum, wrapped up in a straitjacket because of his alcoholic behavior. *Reefer Madness* portrayed marijuana users as perverted monsters. There was no possibility that these people were struggling with a solvable problem. There was no understanding that alcoholics and addicts are intense seekers who have made the mistake of looking for answers in the wrong places. Addicts felt the tremendous fear and shame associated with the cultural stigma of addiction.

This conception of addiction began to change when the American Medical Association recognized alcoholism as a disease in the 1950s. Still, it was more acceptable to be identified as the long-suffering wife or child of someone with a drinking or drug problem than to be recognized as an alcoholic or addict. When challenged to do so, family members found it difficult to admit to their attachments and the addictive behavior that naturally occurs in the tangle of an addictive family system.

Perhaps part of the reason we have historically set those we call addicts apart from the rest of society is that they are caricatures of our own dilemma of attachment. Maybe we have imposed taboos on them, incarcerated them in institutions, labeled them as "bad people," and even considered sterilizing them because their condition reminds us of our painful cravings. When we pass demoralized drunks or drug addicts on the street, their very existence brazenly confronts us with our own tendencies toward addictions and attachments. We do not want to admit that we have that much suffering in our own lives; it is much easier for us to judge or hate an addict than to realize that, to some extent, we are all in the same boat.

Serious addicts have something to teach us about ourselves. By recognizing that as human beings, we share the common dilemma of attachment, but to different degrees, we open the way for understanding and compassion toward ourselves and others. We can even discover a sense of relief and liberation as we recognize the reality of our mutual dilemma. Once we honestly identify the problem, we can do something about it.

Besides defining the condition of attachment and its symptoms, Buddhism's Four Noble Truths give us a recipe for treating and becoming free of it. They tell us that it is possible to alleviate the suffering caused by attachments and that there are tools available to accomplish this task. The realization that we are dealing with an all-human predicament changes our perspective toward those with addiction problems. We are able to feel more kindness and love, not only toward people who are severely addicted, but also toward those who are subject to less extreme forms of attachment. As a result, we become willing to look more honestly at the suffering brought by attachments and work together toward releasing them.

Although there are still many places in the world that treat addicts like criminals, there has been a tremendous change in cultural attitudes toward addicts during the past few years. Partially due to the courageous work of those recovering from addictions, our society is shifting from prejudice to growing acceptance. More and more people are addressing the addictions and attachments that keep them stuck in unhappy lives and are speaking honestly about their addictive behavior. As they do, recovery programs have grown in number. There are now well over a hundred

Twelve-Step fellowships, based on the program of Alcoholics Anonymous and addressing issues of all descriptions. We can go to Twelve-Step meetings to work on our problems with gambling, relationships, cigarettes and other drugs, food, sex, romance, incest, debt, and many more.

As these recovery programs have proliferated, they have been criticized as representing just another fad or narcissistic obsession, or as being an American form of pop psychology designed solely to line the pockets of the writers and seminar leaders who articulate the problem and suggest solutions. Perhaps in some cases this description is true. However, I prefer to see the phenomenon in a different way. I believe we are waking up to the reality of our attachments and the pain they create and are attempting to do something about them. As we all know, our world is struggling with the suffering created by our attachments to power, territory, money, and prestige, to name a few. At the same time, all over the globe, people are sitting in church basements and community meeting rooms addressing their cravings, attachments, and addictions in the context of an inspired spiritual program.

For over half a century, the Twelve-Step format has proven that it works well with people facing chemical dependency problems. It is not at all surprising that this structure is now being transposed to address the widespread and multiple forms of addiction *and* attachment. I find great hope in the fact that this effective tool, among others, is available to those who choose to use it.

Attachments and the Lessons of Mortality

We have an opportunity to learn many valuable lessons about our attachments if we look at them against the background of our eventual death. Rather than treating our inevitable physical demise as a morbid prospect, we can approach it as a valuable teacher. The fact of death surrounds us constantly. Living through the San Francisco earthquake of 1989, I once again learned that the future is only a promise that might not be kept. On a warm, sparkling afternoon, the earth suddenly began to shudder without warning. Within fifteen seconds, everything had changed. There was no damage to our house and, although I was shaking inside, I escaped physical injury. But some people in neighboring areas died. Their names and the stories of their misfortune repeatedly circulated through newspapers and news broadcasts. How many of those individuals knew when they awoke that morning that this would be their last day alive?

The day President John F. Kennedy was assassinated and during the weeks that followed, residents of the United States, as well as many others in the world, shared a wrenching confrontation with the reality of death. The nobility of the First Lady and the power of the ceremonies during that period brought the archetypal atmosphere of a Greek tragedy to the issue of human mortality. In our sadness, we found ourselves asking, "Why?" and "What if . . . ?" or lamenting, "If only he had not gone to Dallas that day." But the moment had come and gone. The deed was done. There was no going back; it was impossible to regain the past.

We all eventually learn the lessons of mortality, of the reality that someday, we will die. We learn about death in many ways. Some people first confront our fragility as human beings when they are children and a favorite pet dies. Others face the loss of someone close: a parent, grandparent, friend, or neighbor. The possibility that we are not immortal begins to creep into our awareness and continues to develop in some form as we grow older. Many individuals taste their own death through near-fatal accidents, illnesses, violence, or addictive activity. As we confront the ultimate gateway, we learn that, with the exception of suicide, we have no control over how and when death will occur.

Many native cultures treat death as part of the life cycle. They acknowledge it as a passage from one state to another. When people die, they are still included within the daily routine of the family and the community. Families do not isolate those who are sick or aging, putting them into inhospitable institutions with other infirm persons; instead they include them in the community. Elders are revered and respected for their life wisdom, and death is regarded as a sacred time. As individuals are dying, they are guided and supported by those around them as they complete their journey through the material world and enter the realms of the afterlife. Spiritual traditions such as those of the Egyptians, the Tibetans, the medieval Christians, and the Aztecs created elaborate "books of the dead" to assist in this important transition.

However, the reality that we will eventually die can be extremely frightening to someone who has not come to terms with death as a chapter of life. Largely because of our own unwillingness to accept our mortality, much of our society has sanitized and hidden the notion of death. Individuals often die in institutions, separated and concealed from the living. Morticians whisk their corpses away and cosmetically revamp them to simulate their appearance when alive. As a result of this cultural denial of death, many of us grew up with an intense fear of it. Death was the grim reaper, a great mystery, a dreadful prospect. Through the glorification of violence, films and television have accentuated this image of dying as a terrifying prospect.

In the past couple of decades, the work of Elisabeth Kübler-Ross, Steven and Ondrea Levine, Ram Dass, and others has begun to return us to a more honest approach to this inevitable fact of existence. Compassionate individuals recognized that we needed an alternative to dying in hospital settings. They began to build and operate hospices, comfortable, homelike settings that offer medical care if necessary but refrain from treating death as a pathological condition. Convincing studies of near-death experiences and the numerous books written on the subject have led us from fear-based denial of death to curiosity about it and even to some feeling of comfort. Because of this expanded acceptance of death, coupled with a renewed interest in spiritual systems, many people have entertained for the first time the possibility that death may not mean total extinction.

Whatever our belief about the continuity of consciousness after death, this universal human experience is a powerful reference point that enables us to acknowledge our attachments. If we accept that someday our physical bodies will die, then at a certain point we realize we will not be able to hold on to our possessions, roles, or relationships forever. We may be startled by the insight that we do not *have* our children; they are on loan to us. The marriage vows in which we promise to love, honor, and cherish mention that death will someday part us from our spouses. Any relationship we enter will eventually end, whenever the first person dies, if not before. We occupy our corner of the world temporarily. The piece of land we own and the property line that is a source of conflict with our neighbor will succeed us. Our bodies will eventually grow old and die. The social and professional roles with which we identify ourselves will become obsolete, and others will replace us.

Realizing all this can be devastating for someone who is attached to his or her identity as a parent, mate, landowner, socialite, or job holder. Individuals who have put a great deal of time, effort, and money into their professional image, their athletic achievements, or their material possessions often focus so intently on their goals that they lose sight of the fact that it is all temporary. Those who spend years amassing a fortune or accumulating power realize with alarm that they cannot take it with them through the portals of death. Our attachments are restrictions if we are afraid of losing them.

The fear of death and our unwillingness to acknowledge and accept it is often a motivating factor in our attachments and addictions. If we are already uneasy because our life involves change, the fact that someday our lives will end is the utmost lesson in the transitory nature of existence. Whether or not we allow ourselves to consciously accept this reality, the underlying knowledge of our mortal limitations and the fear that death evokes adds a frenetic, covetous flavor to our lives. We feel driven to accomplish, achieve, or acquire before it is too late. If we attain one goal, we reach for the next.

If we hold on to our wealth, status, families, or possessions, we gain an illusion that we are immortal, that this temporary sense of security will last forever. But somewhere beneath the fantasy stirs the uncertain feeling that nothing is permanent. This evokes even more pain within us, and in order to escape the pain, we feel impelled to accumulate or strive for more and more. When our mirage eventually fades, either before death or during our last breath, we must painfully let go of the identity we have created for ourselves. Those who work with the dying know that, very often, individuals with the strongest attachments are also the ones who experience the most difficulty letting go into death.

The way out of this predicament is to recognize that ultimately we do not own anything. Everything associated with our identity as the small self is temporary. The only permanent element in our lives is the deeper Self, the part of us that, as many religious and spiritual traditions believe, continues beyond physical death. Many people who confront death during illnesses, accidents, or suicide attempts report experiences that convince them that some immaterial aspect of them continues to exist after their physical demise. They may call it their *spirit* or their *soul.* The ancient Indian text, the Bhagavad Gita, says,

> *Even as a person casts off worn-out clothes and puts on others that are new, so the embodied Self casts off worn-out bodies and enters into others that are new. Weapons cut It not; fire burns It not; water wets It not; the wind does not wither It. This Self cannot be cut nor burnt not wetted nor withered. Eternal, all-pervading, unchanging, immovable, the Self is the same for ever.*

The encounter with death and the discovery of the deeper Self often opens us up to the mystical dimensions of our lives. Those who had not previously identified themselves as spiritual or religious discover they are more than they thought they were. Many people who had strongly identified with their small selves, with their physical bodies and their ego-centered activities, glimpse a larger reality and embark on a path of further self-discovery. In addition, many people who have come close to biological death realize not only the transitory nature of their lives but also how valuable they are. They recognize how many qualities they take for granted, and their gratitude increases.

Once we come to terms with the impermanence in the world, we can be free to enjoy what we have without being engulfed by the fear of losing it. If we do the necessary work to emotionally let go of our relationships, roles, and possessions, we can relax into the present and savor its diversity. This attitude does not mean we need to adopt the "eat, drink, and be merry, for tomorrow we die" approach to life. Rather than becoming nonchalant and reckless, we approach each day with enhanced awareness and appreciation. When we try to live each moment as though it is our last, it is not because we fear death. Instead, our awareness of the impermanence of our limited existence provides a backdrop against which the riches of our lives seem more valuable.

The following is a revealing exercise designed to teach us about our attachments and the importance of letting them go, as well as to enhance the appreciation for our relationships, roles, and possessions: Take a piece of paper and write down as many attachments as you can think of, in order of value. When you have done so, imagine yourself during your own dying process letting them go, one by one. Start with the easiest item, and work your way up the list. You may discover that surrendering the first few attachments is relatively easy—butter on your bread, a favorite book, the new vase in the living room, your computer. But as you continue, you might discover that the process becomes more difficult—a favorite dog, your job, sunsets, your sight, friends, your children, your partner, your own life.

You might ask, "Why should we occupy ourselves with such a morbid exercise? We have our lives to live; we will have plenty of time to think about death when the time comes." Maybe and maybe not. Of course, it is possible to become stuck in a macabre preoccupation with death. But awareness of its presence in our life can open us to the value of our existence and to the dimensions of ourselves that exist beyond our physical reality.

Many spiritual practices include a confrontation with death as a central exercise necessary to transformation. Medieval Christianity, Hinduism, Buddhism, and the school of Tibetan Vajrayana, among others, all included contemplative practices on the cycle of life and death or on the decay of human bodies as a lesson in the acceptance of our own impermanence and the release of desires. Buddha's encounter with disease and death was the turning point that directed him from his existence as a wealthy prince to a life of devotion to the spirit.

In addition, these systems recognize the value of the process of death and rebirth. We can die while we are still alive and be reborn into a spiritually oriented way of being. Jesus said, "That which is born of the flesh is flesh, and that which is born of the Spirit is spirit. Do not marvel that I said to you, 'You must be born again'" (John 3:5–6). Moreover, if we die to our attachments during our lives, our inevitable death will be easier. Abraham a Sancta Clara, a seventeenth-century Augustinian monk, wrote, "A man who dies before he dies does not die when he dies."

As we surrender our attachments, we let go of our limitations and open ourselves to our spiritual possibilities. During experiential psychotherapy, meditation, and other approaches to self-exploration, we can confront the reality of our mortality, our fear of death, and our cravings. In this process, we discover we have defined ourselves by our attachments, thereby restricting our understanding of our nature. Emotionally surrendering our clinging does not mean that we automatically turn our backs on the relationships, roles, opinions, or material objects in our lives; it means we release our need to hang on to them.

Attachment and Surrender

Attachment, addiction, and surrender are closely linked. Everything we have said about surrender in relation to addiction applies to the problem of attachment. Just as recovery from addiction demands a first step of surrender, so freedom from attachments requires surrender. It is a useful practice to notice this process in daily life. If we become stuck in traffic, we have two choices: we can hang on to the notion that we have to be somewhere by five o'clock, thereby creating stress and frustration for ourselves, or we can relax and surrender our deadline with the knowledge that we will get there eventually. As we let go, we are free to really listen to the music on the radio and to notice the beautiful day, the brightly colored flowers growing along the side of the road, and the winsome child in the next car.

This approach is increasingly difficult to implement when it involves more consequential aspects of our lives. If, during a divorce proceeding, the court awards your former spouse custody of your children, you face the challenge of surrendering your role as a parent. This does not mean that at that point you stop being a mother or father; however, in order to alleviate the intense suffering caused by the separation, you need to let go of your notion of what a parent should be. If you hold tightly to the concept that good mothers or fathers live with their children and see them every day, then you will only become consumed by your hurt, sorrow, and anger. You may even find yourself so constricted by your point of view and by your painful emotions that whenever you are with your children, you cannot freely enjoy your time together.

Obviously, the issue of separation is complex and multifaceted, and we are here focusing on only one aspect of it. However, we can do a great deal by letting go of the position we have taken, addressing the emotions involved, and allowing our deeper Self to lead us through our pain. When we begin to experience the influence of that larger, wiser force in our lives, we start to develop trust in its benevolence and guidance. Gradually, we surrender more and more easily, knowing that the deeper Self will be there when we do. In the community of individuals recovering from addictions, many people use the saying "Let Go and Let God" as a reminder that we are not in charge of our lives.

Before we learn to surrender, we may think in terms of *my* role as a parent, *my* job, *my* point of view, *my* children, *my* husband or wife. By letting go of our attachments, we relinquish the restrictions of the small self and increase our access to the deeper Self. Once again, we have the opportunity to move beyond our mortal limitations into the blessings within and around us. As we confront our limited self-definition, we are more able to appreciate the world and those within it, as well as an expanded sense of ourselves. We are increasingly able to enjoy the process of eating the ice cream cone for what it is, including the twinge of dissatisfaction at its fleeting nature. And we are much more willing to allow and trust the wisdom of the life process as it unfolds.

A metaphor for the freedom and sense of connection that comes from letting go of attachments is a story that comes from the United States astronaut Rusty Schweickart. When he talks about the 1969 Apollo 9 lunar module flight, he describes a profound experience he had during the return to Earth. The first part of the flight kept the crew members so busy with a multitude of tasks and tests they were assigned to perform that they did not have any spare time to look out the window. Only as they were orbiting the globe in preparation for their return did Schweickart allow himself to gaze at the view below.

He describes waking up over the Middle East and Africa, eating breakfast above the Mediterranean and imagining the civilizations that originated there, continuing past India and Southeast Asia, the Pacific Ocean, the United States, and farther. From sunrise to sunset, they repeatedly circled the entire planet in an hour and a half each time. And as they did so, Schweickart found himself at first identifying with each region, thinking about its unique history and contributions. After a while, something began to change:

> *You begin to recognize that your identity is with the whole thing. . . . You look down and you can't imagine how many borders and boundaries you cross . . . hundreds of people are killing each*

other over some imaginary line that you are not even aware of, you can't even see it. From where you are, the planet is a whole and it's so beautiful and you wish you could take each individual by the hand and say, "Look at it from this perspective. Look at what is important."

I always feel moved when I read this account because it speaks so directly of the human condition. Because of our attachments and the fear, greed, and pain that arise out of them, we remain limited, and we impose our own emotional suffering on others. As long as we remain imprisoned by our desires, we stifle our creative and compassionate possibilities and keep ourselves separate and hidden. By releasing our attachments, whether we are individuals, communities, or nations, we reduce our limitations and rigidity. We move toward our identity with "the whole thing."

6

Healing and the Path to the Self

8

The Promise of Healing and Spiritual Maturity

Dᴜʀɪɴɢ ᴛʜᴇ ᴘʀᴇᴠɪᴏᴜs chapters, we have traveled through some of the most dramatic periods of our story, beginning with our divine roots, and moving through increased separation, into the dark night of addiction and attachment, all the way to the bottom and a humiliating state of surrender. In this final section of the book, we will explore life after such an essential defeat. Having passed through the supreme ordeal of our hero's or heroine's journey, we arrive at a crossroads. One road beckons us back into the darkness, back into the suffering, alienation, and limitations of our false, addicted identity. The other offers us a rich, blessed path of healing, recovery, and self-discovery that promises to lead us to the source of our wholeness. If we choose the latter, we choose the way toward unlimited possibilities. This path will provide us with the next clues in the treasure hunt that will ultimately lead us to the key to the heaven within and around us.

Many people who go through a profound experience of surrender or an encounter with death automatically open to the spiritual dimension. It is the next step. The state of inner dying has led to rebirth. Now, they face a very different way of existing. The old self has perished, and as they tentatively emerge into their new lives, they often feel gentle inner guidance from the deeper Self. And they might find themselves peeking at some untapped qualities within, perhaps even getting a glimpse of their divine core. They become interested in developing their spirituality and begin to sense the direction in which they would like to grow: toward a more conscious, committed life of healing and personal growth.

There are others for whom the early vestiges of recovery are difficult and confusing. They are plagued by physiological cravings for their drug of choice, reluctant to leave their former life, or bewildered by the references to spirituality and God in their recovery programs. As we will discuss later, the path of recovery does not always entail inspiration and incentive toward transformation. It is often challenging, painful, or discouraging. However, someone who has truly surrendered at the bottom of an addictive career is automatically launched over the threshold into a new way of living. Whether or not they name as "divine intervention" that moment of clarity that propels them into recovery, addicts at this point tap into previously forgotten or unknown resources beyond their ego-based selves.

In early recovery there is often a stage many people call *the pink cloud.* This is the period of days, weeks, or even months when the world looks wonderful and we feel reborn and free. Not everyone experiences the pink cloud, but those who do feel tremendous relief at not having to continue their addictive activity, at finally receiving the help they need and realizing there is a way out of their misery. As we become more willing and able to accept the reality of our addictions, we become increasingly aware of avenues toward healing and well-being that were previously obscured by our self-centered addictive behavior.

Chemical addicts feel their heads beginning to clear, and those who were addicted to activities or relationships redirect their attention to include a wider spectrum of experience. Some people experience what they describe as a state of grace, a period of unmerited divine benevolence. As a result, their perception of the world becomes brighter and more distinct. Some proclaim that they feel "high on life," happier than ever before, blessed, or grateful for what they have. They feel lucky to have been given another chance at life, often recognizing for the first time the perilous trajectory on which they had been stuck. Others actually had life-changing spiritual experiences when they hit bottom and are bathing in the afterglow as they integrate their new awarenesses and expanded self-concept.

Like many phases in recovery, the pink cloud is temporary. Eventually, the obvious reality of everyday life reappears, accompanied by the challenges and the dedicated work of healing. Without our addictive behavior, buffers and escapes that allowed us to repress or avoid difficult emotions or painful situations no longer protect us. We descend from our oasis of clarity and insight into a raw state of vulnerability. When the pink cloud fades, some people are apologetic about it. Because it is not permanent, it was not real. Because they are unable to maintain the original intensity and clarity, they consider their insights and perceptions during that time to be invalid. In addition, they may feel angry and let down because they could not hang on to that blessed state.

The pink cloud is an important experience that must not be ignored nor diminished. For many people, it is a sacred interlude, although they might not call it that. It is a period of spiritual awakening, a glimpse into the realm of possibilities. It is a long look with clearer eyes at the wonders of existence. When I hear people describing the pink cloud, I think about tiny birds who have spent their formative weeks within the enclosed, contained system of the egg. All at once, having pecked through the shell, these fledglings find themselves in a vast new world that contains opportunities that, in their former state, were beyond their comprehension. Or I am reminded of the beautiful German Renaissance woodcut that portrays the prophet Ezekiel pushing past the limits of the sky and breaking through to the mystery of previously unknown realms. "The doors of perception [are] cleansed," as the poet William Blake put it. Or we might regard the pink cloud as a return to a childlike awareness of the world that is fresh, innocent, and uncontaminated.

A similar kind of expanded glimpse and sense of freedom also often occurs when we release an attachment. While we remain attached, we direct our attention and energy toward the object of our desire. We become so focused in one direction that we wear blinders that keep us from envisioning other options. When we let go of the activity, substance, or relationship, we suddenly perceive many previously unavailable choices. When we leave the unsatisfactory job and step into the unknown, we become aware of jobs we had never considered because we concentrated so intensely on one possibility. If we finally give up a destructive relationship, fearing we will never find another one, we become open to the attentions of someone we had not even noticed.

The important period of the pink cloud points us toward a more fulfilled life. It introduces us to wider options and gives us a view of potential goals for our healing process. When the doors of perception or childlike awareness once again become clouded by the reality of our limitations, we begin to understand that we have some work to do.

Another period many people in early recovery experience is an interval of grieving and remorse. Those who have focused solely on a substance, activity, or relationship mourn its loss. As painful and difficult as it may have been, the object of our addiction or attachment has in many ways been our best friend or our Higher Power. As addicts, we have given ourselves completely to alcohol, food, gambling, drugs, or a quest for power. The move away from it is a major event in our lives, and we grieve its loss as we would mourn the death of a lover. As relieved as we might be not to continue our addictive behavior, we also feel a void. On the most mundane level, we are suddenly left with a lot of time on our hands, time we used to devote to the object of our addiction.

In addition, all our priorities change. In order to grow toward health, happiness, and freedom, we discover we must put ourselves and our recovery at the top of the list instead of drugs, alcohol, food, sexual activity, or relationships. It becomes clear to us that if we do not maintain our own health and sense of well-being, we cannot begin to successfully engage in daily activities or interactions with others. For some time, we may not even have a clear idea of who we are. If we have identified ourselves with our addiction or attachment and the behavior implicit in it, we face a complete shift in our self-definition. Who are we becoming?

We also begin to realize how limited and self-destructive our lives have been, how many opportunities we have missed because of our addictions or attachments, how many people we have hurt or ignored, how insular we have been, how much money we have spent. We count the years and months of wasted, unproductive time. We realize how unconscious and self-serving we have been. Again, addicts serve as extreme caricatures of this kind of behavior, but the insights from such actions apply to all of us as we confront our attachments. An alcoholic becomes aware of the timeless eternity spent on a bar stool in the same dingy dive or passed out in bed with the curtains drawn and the telephone turned off. A bulimic enumerates the hours each day that she focused on obtaining, hiding, eating, and purging food. A gambler recognizes the enormous effort that he dedicated toward finding the winning combination or the big payoff. A sex addict chronicles the frantic, continuous search for the perfect partner who will satisfy the emptiness.

The dilemma of these addicts differs only in intensity from the dilemma of those who struggle with attachments. After leaving the unfulfilling job or the unhappy marriage, we may feel deep regret that we put so much time and energy into our unrewarding position or relationship. We might say, "I gave them the best years of my life." Whether we are letting go of an attachment or an addiction, we become tempted to beat up on ourselves: "I was so stupid. Why did I let myself get involved in the first place? I should have seen how crazy it was!" Or we become angry at the circumstances and the people involved: "Tom was basically an obnoxious, selfish person. It was all his fault. He seduced me into a relationship and then betrayed me."

This phase of recognition and mourning is part of the natural progression away from addictions or attachments. For many people, it is an essential stage of recovery, one to be fully experienced and lived through. However, it is important not to become stuck in the grief, self-reproach, or anger. They can only bog us down, even become obsessive and self-destructive. Certainly, they can impede us from moving forward with our recovery and healing.

The next stage for many people is the recognition that each step until this point has been important in a larger process. Even our years of unconscious and clumsy participation in life were essential ingredients in our development. Our painful detours have tempered us, and we have gained with experience a wisdom that would not have come any other way. How can we wake up without having been asleep? Those years in which we forgot who we really were are an absolutely necessary part of the plot, a background against which the miracle of personal and spiritual discovery is even more potent. We can regret the pain of our previous destructive and self-destructive lifestyle and do what we can to repair and heal our misdeeds, but if we are to continue growing, we cannot afford to dwell on them.

The Promises of Healing

When we come into recovery or the spiritual life, we are in need of healing on every level. Our bodies have often been sick, our emotions and our minds are in turmoil, and we are in a state of spiritual bankruptcy. To heal literally means to become whole again, to restore the health we once had and lost. When we hit bottom, we gave up control. We admitted our personal powerlessness and let go. Surprisingly, we not only lived through it but also began to become aware of some of our inner resources. When we surrendered, when we let go of our perceived control and limitations, we did not spin off into some undefined void; as we slipped into the unknown, a power greater than our small selves caught, embraced, and supported us, whether or not we recognized it at the time. It guided us toward a greater source of power as well as a new, expanded identity.

During the pink cloud and the mourning phases, we glimpse the avenue toward wholeness. We may also begin to develop faith in the deeper Self, familiarity with the surrender process, and a connection with other people. As we feel the influence of that force within and around us, we begin to trust it and its potential role in our lives. The second Step of the Twelve-Step programs expresses that faith: "Came to believe that a power greater than ourselves could restore us to sanity." The term *sanity* comes from the Latin word for *health;* the promise of the second Step is literally that we will regain our health, our wholeness. The insanity of our addictive activity has been caused by our own willful and destructive behavior; once we can step back and allow the deeper Self to take over, our state of mind and our lives become increasingly sound. If we have surrendered once and felt the support of our spiritual source, perhaps it will work the second time, and the third. Soon, we begin to realize the potential of a general life strategy of surrender.

We become able to take the next step: "Made a decision to turn our will and our lives over to the care of God *as we understood God*" (italics in original). The phrase *as we understood God* allows us the latitude to create our own personal definition of the spiritual presence in our lives. Remembering that there are many names for the sacred, we can engender our own concept of it, experience of it, and relationship with it. Whether or not we practice them in a program, these Twelve Steps describe the attitude of surrender and acceptance that is essential for spiritual growth in general and recovery in particular. As we have said, many spiritual traditions incorporate surrender to a force larger than ourselves as an essential component of their practice.

Through surrender of our ego control, we begin to develop a relationship with the deeper Self that brings us increased inspiration, health, and wholeness. A joke around recovery groups is, "Religion is for those who do not want to go to hell. Spirituality is for those who have been to hell and don't want to go back." In order to stay free of the hell of our addictions, we progress toward a direct experience of the divine and its influence in our daily lives. Again, Jung's formula, *spiritus contra spiritum,* the recognition and utilization of the Spirit against the ravages of addiction, is relevant here.

As we touch our deeper Self, our experience of alienation slowly disappears. More and more, we feel as though we belong, often for the first time in our lives. As our separateness melts, we feel increasingly connected with other people and the world at large, at times experiencing a sense of deep unity with them. When I was in treatment for my alcoholism, I spent the first ten days telling myself how different I was from the other patients. At first, I was different because, from my position of denial, they all had trouble with addictions and I did not. But even as I began to accept that I might have a "drinking problem," I was still better than they were because I was only an alcoholic, and that was not as bad or severe as a cocaine or heroin addict. In addition, I was special because I had a spiritual life and a spiritual teacher, and I practiced yoga and meditation.

Wise individuals in the community of people recovering from addictions call this kind of attitude "terminal uniqueness." Hanging on to the illusion that "I am special" can be lethal because it can keep us from seeing the reality of our condition. Before going into treatment, I had read and reread the section on alcoholism in the *Merrick Manual,* a reference book for medical professionals. I had only seen the reasons that the life-threatening symptoms did not apply to me. This attitude was deadly.

During the humiliating experience of hitting bottom, that self-centered posture melted, and I began to see the similarities rather than the differences. That afternoon, when I walked into the group therapy session, the distinctions between the others and myself disappeared. Income, education, race, drug of choice, vocation: those apparent distinctions became inconsequential through my new eyes. I felt a profound recognition that we were all survivors on the same lifeboat, no matter what our individual stories were. We were all in this dilemma together, wrestling with similar demons and aspiring toward similar goals. I began to feel the power of the support and love we had to offer one another. Since that time, I have heard many people who are involved in anonymous recovery groups describe comparable experiences: leaving their worldly identities at the door of a meeting and, for a while, entering a domain in which everyone shares a common ground and speaks the same language.

The healing power of the community is well known in many spiritual and religious traditions, including the Twelve-Step fellowships. Although they differ in function and importance, almost all spiritual situations incorporate some form of community. There are organized orders or associations that focus on certain moral and ethical principles, tradition and ritual, an inspirational leader, or religious attitudes. In addition, there are looser, more spontaneous constellations of caring people who come together naturally out of common need. Through the examples of other people, whether or not they are identified with a group, individuals can discover commonalities that validate their own experience, as well as love, understanding, support, and camaraderie.

In addition, becoming part of a large network of sympathetic human beings is often a major step for someone who has felt separate or different for most of her or his life. We slowly learn to trust others and to allow them into our isolated world. We feel less solitary and lonely as we realize that their stories are similar to ours. And we learn that our own suffering diminishes when we offer to help another person. If life events have taught us that people are not safe, contacting others and feeling the power of their love, as well as the love that is evoked within us, can be a revelation.

Soon, we begin to meet other people who manifest qualities we would like to build within ourselves. Perhaps they radiate a sense of freedom, joy, kindness, and serenity that inspires us. They seem to be comfortable with themselves in a way we are not. They find genuine pleasure being alive, and they often embody the kind of wisdom that comes with living consciously. Usually, they have spent some time in recovery or on another journey of self-discovery, healing, or the accumulation of life wisdom, and we want what they have. Often, their stories tell us they have experienced challenges and difficulties that were not very different from ours. We automatically develop relationships with those of like mind, and their guidance and example help us.

In addition, we observe and benefit from the changes we see in others as they continue their healing. As they grow, they provide motivation for us. We find hope in someone who shares a similar history and manifests qualities we would like to see in ourselves. We might feel, "If he can do it, so can I." Gradually, sometimes without realizing it, we move away from our former associations with people who are as constricted as we were. They are currently at a different stage in their development, one in which we no longer want to participate.

Many people in recovery describe as wondrous the seemingly small as well as the major transformations in themselves and others. As we hear others tell their stories, describing the demoralization and the depths of their addictions and their path of healing, we feel inspired. Watching their ease, confidence, emotional availability, and sense of humor, we find it difficult to imagine the despair and degradation from which they came. A popular automobile bumper sticker reads, "Expect a Miracle." The metamorphoses that we see and experience regularly during the healing process are indeed miracles.

The Qualities of Spiritual Maturity

Motivated by the glimmers of increased possibilities within us and by the examples of other people, we begin to want to develop certain qualities that will take us toward a life of sobriety and spiritual maturity. In this context, *sobriety* connotes freedom not only from alcohol, drugs, food, or other addictions but also from compulsive, excessive behavior. It signifies increased physical, emotional, mental, and spiritual health. Spiritual maturity, or becoming "spiritually fit," as *Alcoholics Anonymous* calls it, occurs through a lifelong cultivation of certain health-promoting attributes and actions. Once we become aware of their existence, their potential influence on our lives, and the possibility of attaining them, we become interested in pursuing them.

What are the qualities of spiritual maturity? As we explore some of them, let us keep in mind that these are ideals toward which we can grow, one step at a time, not characteristics we can expect to perfect overnight. Although each one takes time to develop and practice more fully, we will see that many of them already exist within us.

LOVE AND COMPASSION

Love and compassion lead to the ability to engage in honest intimacy with ourselves, other people, the world, and God. They are central to most sacred traditions. The opening of the heart, the birth of compassion and love from within, is often the beginning of the true spiritual life. From that initial awakening, it becomes essential to further develop these qualities throughout our lives. We have all heard phrases such as "Love is eternal" or "God is love." Love is a limitless state of being that expresses itself in many ways: from erotic enjoyment, through deep caring and reverence for others, to a perfect state of divine grace. In order to know love and realize its significance, we must experience it directly. It dissolves confusion and fear and elicits kindness, openness, and respect. Unless we love and trust ourselves, we cannot love others. As we increasingly open to our own capacities, we replace shame, self-pity, and hatred with a sense of self-regard and understanding. Our ability to accept ourselves is reflected in the way we treat those close to us. We learn how to give to others without expectations, conditions, or demands.

And we gain a deep commitment and loyalty to ourselves and others.

Compassion exists beyond a personal form of love. It is the love for all of creation. Some call it "cosmic love" or "the love for all beings." It has to do with a generous, expanded way in which we relate to ourselves and others, without a sense of doing it for someone else, without the division between "them" and "me." Compassion is a pure, rich state of being that does not have anything to do with competition or accomplishment. It is often elicited through the awareness of suffering and is expressed out of concern for the welfare of ourselves, others, and the world around us.

HONESTY AND AUTHENTICITY

Addicts are known for dishonesty and deception during active addiction. We lie to ourselves and others about what we are doing, how much, and what the consequences are. Although some of these fabrications are conscious, many of them come about as a result of our denials and defenses. Over years, we have built layers of protection that shield us from the truth. We delude ourselves about the reality of our history and our present situation, selfhood, and behaviors. We create a counterfeit identity that has very little to do with our actual nature.

In recovery, our first step toward regaining honesty is our experience of surrender to the fact of our addiction and our lack of control. Gradually, we begin to realize how deceitful and insincere we have been, not only toward other individuals, but also toward ourselves. Friends, family members, or colleagues were aware of our addictive activity before we were. We are often the last to know. Now, we more honestly confront the truth of our behavior. This kind of forthright attitude reaches beyond "cash register honesty," which is lawful, fair, and credible conduct in society; it also involves self-honesty, a genuine and truthful acknowledgment of the patterns, behaviors, and strengths that shape and motivate us. Through a more open and direct contact with ourselves, we become able to conduct increasingly straightforward relationships with others.

PHYSICAL, EMOTIONAL, MENTAL, AND SPIRITUAL CLARITY

Emerging from a relatively muddled and unconscious relationship with life, we learn that we can be more aware of ourselves and our surroundings. This means developing a sharp, discerning manner free from confusion or deluded thinking. It involves mental lucidity that dispels illusion and ambiguity. Other people understand our communication, and our lives reflect a general uncluttered simplicity.

Our mental and emotional clarity increases as we work on our feelings. Identifying and expressing unacknowledged emotions is a foundation of healing; it entails a willingness to address the anger, fear, grief, guilt, shame, and other difficult feelings that keep us stuck and unhappy, as well as to recognize and accept happiness, joy, serenity, and love. Physical clarity has to do with attention to the body's health through diet, exercise, freedom from intoxicants, and adequate rest. Many spiritual disciplines describe the body as a temple for the divine, one that deserves the same devotion and reverence that we might give a sacred structure. They offer specific practices that lead toward increased bodily clarity, the removal of toxins and physical blockages, and the release of trapped energy.

Spiritual clarity encompasses all other forms of clarity. It may come about through grace, but it often involves a regular and committed effort toward healing all aspects of ourselves. As we achieve greater physical, emotional, and mental clarity, we are able to more lucidly perceive the spiritual dimension.

RESPONSIBILITY AND DISCIPLINE

After a period of disorganization and recklessness, we begin to value ways in which we can redirect and shape ourselves, including our moral character. Responsibility includes the ability and willingness to fulfill obligations and daily tasks reliably. It also means that we begin to define our personal limits, becoming accountable for ourselves and separating ourselves from other people.

Individuals with a history of abuse usually lack internal boundaries: the knowledge of where they end and the world begins. They become confused about which emotions or actions they are responsible for and which belong to other people. They may blame themselves for things they did not do, or they may hold someone else accountable when, in fact, they themselves are at fault. In spiritual maturity, we disentangle ourselves from others and take responsibility for ourselves instead of feeling excessively responsible for others.

Discipline is related to order. It is necessary for the dependable completion of responsibilities. We establish a certain degree of structure within and around us through which we determine our boundaries and directions. This is different from obsessive rule-bound systems that are limiting and oppressive. Discipline is like a foundation from which we can expand in creative directions. Without it, we might not even be able to recognize the possibilities because of mental confusion and laxity. If we have been subject to procrastination, we learn to enjoy the satisfaction of steady effort and attention.

SERENITY

Serenity is an attribute that is much discussed in recovery from addictions, as well as in many spiritual disciplines. When we become caught in a life of attachment or addiction, many of us become easily agitated by our own drama. We are thrown around by unruly emotions, feel easily overwhelmed, or become dependent upon intensity. Another way we respond to the rich chaos of the world is to deny it. As we shrink into the protection of our defenses, we feel agitated and unhappy.

Serene individuals do not feel easily disturbed or perturbed. They enjoy an experience of physical, emotional, mental, and spiritual balance in the face of the fluctuations and challenges of the transitory world. Serenity is a state of equanimity or evenness of mind. The faces of holy personages in every tradition radiate this inner tranquility and peacefulness. Poetry and spiritual metaphor represent serenity as a clear, calm lake on a windless day that is unthreatened by storms or unpleasant change.

PERSONAL FREEDOM

Personal freedom is different from the impulse to seek emancipation from the dictates of external authority. It is what the spiritual disciplines call *inner liberation,* and it stems from the ability to face life's challenges without drama, escape, or avoidance. Freedom means learning to "accept life on life's terms," in the words of the Twelve-Step programs. It implies a state of surrender, an ability to flow with the ups and downs of existence without resistance, denial, or compulsion. Liberation requires letting go of attachments and constrictions, releasing the suffering that accompanies them. Someone who is free is flexible and expansive in choice and action, not rigid and limited.

TOLERANCE AND PATIENCE

Tolerance is the opposite of judgmentalism and bigotry, and it involves acceptance and sympathy. And as with all the other attributes, it applies both to ourselves and to others. It is the ability to embrace our own faults and weaknesses, as well as our gifts and strengths. This does not mean that we must condone or like them, but that we accept them as they exist in the present. Externally, tolerance signifies the ability to allow and indulge other people, beliefs, or activities that may differ from our own, to make room for them as part of a complex, varied, and dynamic world, rather than judging and excluding them.

Patience exists beyond ambition. The old adage "All good things come to he who waits" applies to our journey of rediscovery. Patience means the capacity to take events and experiences as they come without complaint or expectation. We cannot push the river, but instead, must flow with its rhythm. Patience requires that we live one day at a time. We learn to put one foot in front of the other and attend to whatever is in front of us. Where we were once compulsively busy and impetuous, we become willing to wait. Patience is related to trust.

FAITH, TRUST, AND INNER SECURITY

Faith is described as "the assurance of things hoped for, the conviction of things not seen." Although this quote comes from the New Testament, it applies not only to other spiritual systems but to life in general. It is the ability to participate in our present reality without anxiety or doubt. Faith, trust, and security all involve feelings of confidence. Each one develops over time and with experience, whether it relates to oneself, another person, a group, the mechanics of our existence, or God.

Many of us have heard the currently popular advice "Trust the process," but although trusting the process means abandoning expectations and ego control, it does not imply blind dependence. Faith emerges as a response to a direct experience of the divine. Trust and faith are creative and positive attitudes of the human mind and spirit. After learning from experience that "this too shall pass," that difficulties as well as times of ecstatic delight eventually fade to make room for the next experience, we develop a sense of confidence in the cadence of existence and faith in the force that guides it. Out of faith and trust grow a certain inner security and relief from fear and deprivation.

WISDOM AND UNDERSTANDING

Wisdom is different from intellectual knowledge, and understanding is more than accumulated information. Wisdom is gained through experience, through learning and integrating the daily lessons presented to each of us, and understanding comes when we grasp their meaning. The Indo-European root of the word *wisdom* means "perceiving" or "seeing." A person's wisdom is the result of what he or she has seen and, consequently, learned.

Sages say that all of existence is a classroom, and that our task is to be students of life. Many cultures revere and honor elderly people because of the deep insight that has grown within them over time. In spiritual arenas, however, someone can be mature without necessarily being old. Through spiritual practice or revelation the seeker can develop a profound and far-reaching understanding of the connections in humanity and the world. Wisdom is manifested as a way of being that evolves out of insight expressed through everyday action.

GRATITUDE, HUMILITY, AND WILLINGNESS

Gratitude comes from the heart as appreciation for the gifts and benefits that come our way. It dispels fear, anger, and resentment. Individuals who survive an encounter with death, hit bottom with an addiction, or suddenly open to the blessings in their lives often feel grateful. Gratitude is necessary in order to recognize miracles that, although they exist around and within us, often remain unseen. People who emerge from the dark night of addiction often feel they are being given the gift of a second chance and are deeply grateful.

Humility is the opposite of pride, which many spiritual traditions see as a major impediment to spiritual development. Humility is the ability to move beyond arrogance and grandiosity toward an honest acceptance of ourselves, with all our limitations and faults. An act of surrender is an act of humility. The first step of Alcoholics Anonymous, admitting that we do not ultimately control our lives, is a step of humility.

Willingness involves the surrender of pride. It means moving beyond stubbornness and self-will and becoming open and ready to respond. Even though we do not know what the next step might be, we move forward without reluctance. Bill Wilson wrote, "The willingness to grow is the essence of all spiritual development."

HOPE, HAPPINESS, JOY, AND HUMOR

Hope is the opposite of despair. It is an expansive state of being, an attitude rather than a goal. We can feel hope without hoping for something specific. Happiness is a state of well-being and contentment; people who have been caught in suffering and fear often have trouble accepting it. Though happiness is often the result of something that happens to us, joy exists independent of everyday events or deeds. Joy grows from gratitude. It emanates from a deep feeling of inner wealth that is unaffected by the fluctuations of daily life. Hope, happiness, and joy are all associated with an open heart.

Humor in this context refers to the ability to laugh lovingly at ourselves, at our humanness, at the entire cosmic game. Emanating from a pervasive sense of joy, it is the capacity to recognize life's drama as not only extremely serious but also exquisitely funny. If we are rigid, we cannot feel amusement. There is a wonderful turning point in recovery from addictions where we can laugh at some of the things we did during our addictive careers. This compassionate recognition of the comedy within tragedy can be very healing.

A BASIC CONNECTION WITH THE EARTH
AND WITH DAILY LIFE

The life of a spiritually mature person is not about leaving the world; instead, his or her every action is itself an expression of the divine. Even though we might find great inspiration in sacred systems or transcendent experiences, we recognize the sacredness of daily activities, of our own bodies, other people, other life forms, inanimate matter, and nature. Rather than remaining aloof, spaced-out, or self-serving, we acknowledge the richness and beauty of our everyday reality and live with a conscious awareness and respect for it. We actively participate in our humanity with reverence for the earth and the environment.

THE ABILITY TO LIVE IN THE PRESENT MOMENT

An individual who exists in the present moment is here, rather than somewhere else. Most of us spend much of our lives dwelling in the past or projecting into the future. Or we might dissociate or move into compulsive thinking in order to alter our experience of the here and now. Many spiritual systems have developed specific practices that will encourage the student to be present for whatever this instant offers. The Twelve-Step programs encourage us to "live one day at a time." This is all we really have. Living in the present means that we must be able to continually let go and start afresh. Again, surrendering unnecessary or bothersome emotions and experiences or our attachments is the focus of many spiritual practices.

A MYSTICAL WORLDVIEW

Although we are in touch with our daily lives, we can also maintain a cosmic perspective that comes from direct spiritual experiences, rather than from just reading or hearing about God. A mystical worldview is inclusive, unitive, and expansive. It involves an awareness of the interconnectedness of all of creation. If we do something to someone else, we also do it to ourselves. If we harm the earth, we also harm ourselves. From this perspective, there is no room for exclusivity, prejudice, or divisiveness. This spiritual outlook acknowledges that we are more than our material identity. The deeper Self and the small self coexist, and we are cognizant that both are essential and important aspects of our nature.

The Strategy of Healing

The qualities of spiritual fitness on our list are only some of the common but essential attributes that become available during spiritual transformation and healing. A specific spiritual or religious interpretation may emphasize one or another. It is important to remember that, although these qualities all exist as possibilities within each of us, we only get in our own way when we try to force them or attempt too hard to achieve them. If we adopt a comprehensive strategy of inner growth and healing, and if we continue to do our work with the support of others, we will automatically discover these attributes and integrate them into our lives.

What is this strategy? In order to describe it, we must return to the image of human beings as comprised of both the small self and the deeper Self and to the story that portrays us as individuals who are separated from our divine source. Earlier, we explored the role of abuse, survival mechanisms, and the dark night of addiction. All serve to remove us from the deeper Self. However, no matter how concealed our spiritual identity remained during addiction, it was always there; we simply were not able to see it. It was shielded not only by the fact of our humanness but also by our behavior and our physical, emotional, mental, and spiritual wounds. Bill Wilson wrote, "Deep down in every man, woman, and child is the fundamental idea of God. It may be obscured by calamity, by pomp, by worship of other things, but in some form or other, it is there."

To heal means to rediscover that divine idea, that place of wholeness within each of us. Our task in recovery or in the spiritual journey is to peel away the layers between us and the deeper Self. We can use the image of a vast ocean that is barricaded away by a dam that keeps us from knowing it exists. Even though our intellect may learn there is an ocean, we cannot conceive of it because we have never directly experienced it. And then, for an instant, we transcend the barrier, and we see and feel the ocean directly. Once this has happened, we become strongly motivated to experience it again, for a longer time. How can we do this?

The dam between us and our source is made up of the unresolved emotions, experiences, and memories that keep us stuck and cause suffering and constriction in our lives. Over time, during the healing process, we remove this barrier between the small self and the deeper Self. This is not a linear process. We do not eradicate fear, then anger, then memories of abuse, and then shame in a neat, ordered sequence. Rather, during our spiritual practice, recovery work, or therapy, we chip away at chunks of the barrier until it is eliminated altogether. With every blow, a little more of the deeper Self becomes available to us, in the way that rivulets of water trickle through tiny holes in a dam. When we eliminate enough of the dam, the water flows freely. Not only do we get to swim in the vast expanse of our possibilities, but we also taste, savor, and use its resources. On a practical level, as we increasingly work through the obstacles within us, we become more conscious of the readily available qualities of spiritual maturity.

This notion is very different from some of the earlier theories in psychology that taught that the deeper we go into the human psyche, the worse it gets. The further we delve into ourselves, the more we discover the negativity and disharmony within us, the base instincts and destructive tendencies. In our healing model, the deeper we go, the more we discover our potential: the positive, light, joyous, grateful, passionate, and loving qualities that were previously hidden. On the way, we run into the spectrum of emotions, impulses, and behaviors so eloquently described by the father of psychoanalysis, Sigmund Freud, and others, but they must not be confused with our true identity. They are only materials that have built the dam that walls us off from our true nature.

This approach is also substantially different from the rigid disease model that prevails in much of psychiatry and psychotherapy. I discuss this at some length, because I feel it has great relevance to the understanding and treatment of addictions. The disease concept of addictions and recovery revolutionized the addictions field, and I am grateful for it. For decades alcoholics were regarded as third-rate, degenerate individuals with no self-control or ethical standards, but the image began to change when alcoholism was recognized as a disease.

As alcoholics and later chemical addicts became accepted as *sick* rather than *bad,* many people felt relief. A tremendous personal burden was lifted as they discovered they were dealing, in part, with a biochemical, genetically based problem rather than moral depravity. Instead of being identified as social outcasts, those suffering from chemical dependency were recognized as once functional people who had developed a disease. This model allowed addicts and their addictions to reenter society and be treated humanely instead of punished. A broad revolution took place in the understanding and treatment of addictions. Within this new climate of acceptance, even Betty Ford, the wife of a president of the United States, could admit to her addictions, in the same way that she later disclosed her breast cancer. Someone with that stature was no longer in danger of being treated as a "bad" person. Instead, she was regarded as a strong, courageous woman who was admired and lauded because she had recognized and confronted her illness. Her courage made it possible for her to effect tremendous changes, especially in the understanding and acceptance of women's addiction problems.

The new concept also offered an important step in recovery: the stage at which addicts could separate themselves from their disease, could realize that they were more than their behavior or their self-concept. "I am not my disease. I *have* a disease. My self-definition is broader than my identity as an addict."

However, when our awareness of addiction shifted to include addictions other than chemical dependency, we began to run into trouble. Addictions that involved activities and relationships included behavior similar to that of chemical addicts, as well as an intergenerational history. They lacked the chemical or genetic components of alcoholism and drug addiction, however, and still they were referred to as diseases. As time has gone by, more and more people have questioned whether the "disease model" of addiction is really appropriate when applied to addictions such as shopping, religion, or codependency. It is easier to label as a disease an addiction that directly affects the body, such as bulimia, anorexia, and some extreme forms of codependency, or behavior that is obviously pathological or socially unacceptable, as in some types of sex addiction or obsessive thinking.

If addiction is an exaggerated attachment, and if we all struggle with attachments, then generously applying the disease model to every kind of addictive behavior paints a picture of humanity as being universally sick. This judgment reflects the outdated psychiatric or psychological attitude that the deeper we go into ourselves, the darker view we must have of our human nature.

Certainly, our addictive behavior creates enormous dis-ease or suffering. But I cannot believe that we are all sick. In addition, this attitude can be detrimental to those who already feel constricted, isolated, and filled with shame. The disease model works well for a linear mind. It offers a handle on which to hang the complexities of our addictive behavior and the resultant suffering. However, it also labels as pathological those who are, at their core, healthy and whole.

I propose a somewhat different perspective that is much more in keeping with the ideas and attitudes put forth by transpersonal psychology and spiritual approaches. This viewpoint includes the notion that we can define addiction as a disease, where that definition is truly applicable. But addiction is broader than that. I would like to see a wellness model for the understanding and treatment of addictions rather than a sickness model. Within the wellness model, human beings contain a vast, divine potential that may be hidden. In our attached, addicted existence, we live in the illusion of the limited, small self. We think that is all we are. We exist in a state of mistaken identity. We have forgotten who we really are.

During the healing process, we seek to rediscover ourselves. It is a process of remembering, of reconnecting with our wholeness. Recovery is really rediscovery. The original definition of the word *recovery* extends beyond implications for pathology. To recover means "to get back, to find or identify again." In our recovery, we *get back* our wholeness. We bring our small self together with our deeper Self, and make a whole. Recovery applies to the process of healing from illness, but it also can be used to describe the retrieval of our true nature. It is clear to me that part of what I am involved in is healing from the physical, emotional, and mental pathology related to my alcoholism and other aspects of my history. I am also aware that it is larger than that. Behind and beyond my "recovery" is a deeper process; it is a path of transformation that is profound and deeply influential to my whole being. It is healing on every level, but it is also a quest for the divine that has been part of humanity, no matter what the cultural and ethnic distinctions, from the beginning of history. An essential component of this process of spiritual growth is the release or transformation of attachments and addictions.

In true recovery, we work to remove the barriers between our small self and the deeper Self. In this process, we become acquainted with the miraculous healing power within each of us. This "inner healer," as it is known in various holistic and transpersonally oriented medical and therapeutic approaches, is the deep wisdom and profound power of our spiritual identity. The inner healer knows what to do if we give it room and encouragement. Instead of relying on outside forces for our healing, instead of automatically depending upon techniques, medications, or the directives of professionals, we learn that we have the resources within us. This does not mean we must go through recovery alone—just the opposite. We need the valuable support, love, and guidance of well-trained professionals and teachers and the community of fellow seekers. However, within this framework of support, the healing ultimately happens within ourselves.

In traditional Western medicine, if people get sick, they go to a physician, receive treatment, and then pay a fee. In ancient Chinese medicine, patients paid the doctor as long as they stayed healthy. If someone became ill, the doctor had to pay him or her. It was the doctor's job to teach and to help people live in a state of health, balance, and well-being, by employing their own resources. I believe this is the promise of addiction recovery. Many of us begin to break through the dam that keeps us from knowing our true identity when we hit bottom with our addictive behavior. From then on, we have the opportunity to embark on the journey of personal recovery and rediscovery that ultimately leads to wholeness and equilibrium.

9

Recovery, Rediscovery, and the Spiritual Path

Freshly released from our help-less, unmanageable struggle, we emerge raw, unsteady, and vulnerable like a newborn fawn. After we drink in the wonder of our new world, the reality of old emotions, experiences, and personal patterns, as well as the challenges of the external world, begin to close in. Floating in our pink cloud, even as we relish our new existence, we may be aware of an undercurrent stirring within. Beneath the relief, gratitude, and enthusiasm for our second chance, we feel the pull of all-too-familiar feelings. But we cling to our grace-filled oasis, resting there as long as we can and filling ourselves with its nourishment. As the pink cloud fades, we continue to feel thankful and relieved that the cycle of addiction has been broken. But we also discover that life is not automatically easy just because we are in recovery.

Tugging at our awareness are our unaddressed physical, emotional, mental, and spiritual issues. For years, most addicts repress, escape, or deny painful or unacceptable emotions, memories, and experiences. Food, gambling, sex, alcohol, drugs, or a drive toward power buffer the real issues and contribute to the compulsive search for relief. Use of these means of external or internal escape does not eradicate the pain, anger, guilt, or shame. These escapes do not make the troublesome memories or low self-esteem go away; they simply hide them temporarily. When we eliminate the addictions, we remove the insulation that worked so well to shield us from our distress, and all the emotions, experiences, and memories that we repressed during our addictive behavior come flooding to the surface.

Moreover, we have surrendered at the bottom. We have become powerless. As self-centered, egotistical individuals, we have relinquished control and weakened our defenses. As a result, we become more easily aware of the deep inner reservoir of previously unseen material. If we do not find some way of working with and eliminating these emotions and experiences, they will directly affect or even control our behavior.

I remember meeting Glenn, a vital, darkly handsome man in his early thirties who was in the first months of recovery from alcoholism and cocaine addiction. When Glenn talked about his wife and baby daughter, his eyes lit up with pride and obvious affection. He also felt deeply committed to his recovery. He had been to hell, and he did not want to return. He was willing to do anything to hang on to his newly discovered clean and sober life. However, he had a major problem that was causing great distress to his family and to himself and severely threatening his marriage. Glenn was subject to violent rages.

He described the horrible dilemma of going to Twelve-Step meetings, where he was a regular member, talking about his former addiction and rededicating himself to recovery, then going home to fight with his wife. Sometimes, his verbal and emotional barrages escalated to the physical level. He knew he could not continue this behavior without dire consequences for himself and the people he loved, yet he could not control his fury. He had talked with an aftercare counselor who advised him to go to a "men's rage support group," where he discussed his tendencies. The group helped him to rationally understand some of the causes of the problem, but the emotional storms persisted.

Eventually, Glenn received the help he needed through participating in a form of experiential therapy during which he could actively express the tremendous anger he had bottled up during years of childhood abuse. As he continued, he was able to discover and work with the roots of his rage. He said, "Talking about it was not enough. I had a hurricane brewing inside me, and I did not have any way of containing it. When I finally discovered I could vent my anger during a therapy session, it was like letting steam out of a pressure cooker. If I did that enough times during therapy, I didn't have to take it home with me."

Although Glenn's story is somewhat more dramatic than many, it speaks to the predicament faced by most newly sober individuals, whatever their addictions have been. Confronted suddenly by powerful, formerly latent, numbed, or exaggerated emotions, memories, and experiences, we have a choice: either we can allow them to overpower and control us, or we can work with them. Now that our heads are clearer, we may look back on our addictive career and realize the destructive as well as self-destructive ways this undercurrent of unresolved material influenced us and others.

Our own pain, our own wounds, may have caused us to strike out at other people whom we love and who love us. Perhaps our lack of control or feelings of inadequacy have driven us to overpower, control, or abuse other people and ourselves. Our feelings of loneliness and mistrust may have forced us to withdraw from and alienate our spouses, families, and friends. For example, someone who has suffered childhood sexual abuse may not be able to touch or be touched without fear, confusion, shame, and anger contaminating the love we might feel. This is a painful way to be, and the anguish is all the more intense simply because, in our recovery, we can no longer run away so easily.

In addition, many of us have been so wrapped up in our addictive behavior and so well defended by our false identity that we have not fully participated in our lives. Some of us learned early in childhood that the world is not a good place to be and that we must flee whenever possible. Now, here we are, plunked down in the middle of our daily routines without our usual defense mechanisms and escapes. In this unguarded and often fragile state, we must pick ourselves up and learn to live in the world, often for the first time.

During the first few years of my recovery from alcoholism, I went through periods that mimicked a child's development from infancy into adolescence. On the rainy afternoon I stepped out of the treatment center, my immediate environment seemed exceptionally busy and complex. In my raw and vulnerable state, crossing the street that day seemed like a new experience, as though I was learning to walk for the first time. After a while, I progressed into the "terrible twos," a stage that mirrored a child's exploration of boundaries and her place in her surroundings. Where did I end, and where did the world begin? How should I define this new self? Where do I fit? I learned to say "No!" and "Mine!" but with a vehemence that revealed the unacknowledged anger circulating through my system. Of course, my stubborn and resentful manner did not play well in my relationships.

Next there was a phase in which I learned to talk, in which I began to delve into the ongoing issues of communication. How do I relate to myself, to others, and to my surroundings without the denials and defenses so ingrained in my being? How do I discover and verbalize my own needs? How do I learn to listen? And there are other questions. After maintaining a viselike grip on the lifeboat of my recovery methods, how do I develop enough trust in that newly rediscovered deeper Self to relax a little and allow it to assist me? And how do I accept the help of other people?

In early recovery, I would adamantly shut myself away in my room to read my meditation books and pray with a vengeance or sweat through my hour of daily exercise. If anyone interrupted me, I would become indignant. Although this was a necessary stage during which I was familiarizing myself with the mechanics of recovery, the ensuing inflexibility eventually provided more stress than comfort or healing. After some time, I learned I could still maintain these health-promoting activities without being rigid and defensive about them.

During the pink cloud, we might have realized that the world can be nourishing, beautiful, and even miraculous. However, this perception is often so new to us that we need time to gain trust in ourselves, in other people, and our surroundings. We need time to develop faith in the rhythm of our lives. Issues such as these, as well as previously unconscious emotions, experiences, and memories, bombard us in the first months and years of freedom from addiction. Fortunately, there are many ways to work with them and incorporate them productively and creatively into the process of healing.

Recovery as a Spiritual Path

Bill Wilson wrote, "Is sobriety all that we are to expect of a spiritual awakening? No, sobriety is only a bare beginning; it is only the first gift of the first awakening. If more gifts are to be received, our awakening has to go on." He goes on to discuss the process of gradually discarding our old life, piece by piece, and replacing it with a new life that can and does work under any circumstances. In order to do this, we must be willing to do the much-needed work of healing. The first Step of the Twelve-Step programs, "We admitted that we were powerless over alcohol [or whatever the addiction is] and that our lives had become unmanageable," is the only one of the Twelve Steps that mentions the addiction. The rest of the program is about creating a life of quality that includes the attributes of spiritual maturity.

Recovery requires commitment, courage, and patience. It is not something that happens overnight; it is a lifelong spiritual path. This fact may seem daunting at first. Recovery may sometimes feel tedious. However, if we return to the slogan "One day at a time" so often heard in the recovering community, then we learn to restrain our minds from wandering into the "what ifs" and "I can'ts" that bubble up when we project into the future. As we put one foot in front of the other and do what each moment requires, we may not find the gratification of instant change within us; however, we will begin to be aware of accumulating important and necessary steps toward growth.

Our journey of transformation is like stringing a precious necklace: with each small miracle, with each step toward growth, we add another pearl to the strand until, over time, we have created a magnificent piece of art. After we have been at it for a while, we will begin to realize that, even though our efforts sometimes feel tedious or difficult, the results are cumulative. All the moments in our path of rediscovery add up to produce a blessed and creative life.

Those who continue in recovery realize over time that they are not the same people who first embarked on this journey of rediscovery. Have you ever pulled a new shirt out of its plastic wrapping, unfolded it, and then tried carefully to replace it the same way? Recovery or any kind of personal transformation is like this: once we start to unfold, it is difficult to return to the way we were. I like to sew, and I think about this when I pull a pattern out of its envelope. Suddenly, I find myself handling several diaphanous sheets of paper that outline a map for my new project. But at the end of the day, when I try to fold it back to its original size and shape, I end up with a crumpled bundle instead. The moment I began to undo the package and spread out the pattern, its nature changed. There is no going back to the way it was.

This theme is a familiar one in recovery. Even though during a challenging moment in sobriety, we might want to return to the relative surity of our former life, we cannot. Even if we slide back into our addictive behavior, it is not the same. My counselor in treatment once said, "Even if you relapse, treatment and recovery will have ruined your drinking." Each time we eradicate a layer or two of denial, we become increasingly aware of our actions and their consequences. We take another step toward our new identity.

The Tools of Recovery

Fortunately, there are many approaches to therapy, spiritual practice, and other forms of self-exploration that will help us to resolve unaddressed issues and open us to expanded identity. Some people have never become interested in any form of introspection. They might feel, "Life is just fine, thank you. Why meddle with it? Besides, those people who get into that stuff end up gazing at their navels and never amount to much." During the process of hitting bottom and coming into recovery, however, these same individuals often realize they need to make some major personal changes. For the first time, they become open to working on themselves.

Others are already involved in therapy or spiritual practice when they enter recovery. They discover that familiar tools can become even more useful and beneficial. A friend told me, "I dabbled in psychotherapy and workshops on different subjects. I learned some t'ai chi and played with meditation before I got sober, but they did little good while I was still drinking." Whether or not we have ever felt interested in self-examination and personal growth, in recovery we face the challenge of doing the inner work we need to do in order to grow into happier, more fulfilled lives.

What are these tools for recovery? I will mention some general categories, many of which are compatible with one another. Although we may prefer a particular approach, it need not be the only one we use during our healing and transformation. There are so many effective therapeutic and spiritual resources available that we can creatively combine the ones that work for us. A method that seems appropriate for one stage or area of growth may not be the best one for the next.

Because recovery and the spiritual path are about reclaiming our true nature, the approaches we choose need to include a broad understanding of the mechanics of the human psyche. This means a definition of each person that is comprehensive and accommodates not only our identity as the small self but also our expanded spiritual identity. If we become involved in a course of self-exploration that focuses solely on our role as materially oriented individuals and our biography as the sole source of our difficulties, we are limiting ourselves. Approaches from various spiritual systems and transpersonal psychology, among others, provide a holistic view of human beings that includes our physical, emotional, mental, and spiritual qualities and our expanded potential.

Twelve-Step Programs

The Twelve-Step programs offer an inspired spiritual practice to anyone who chooses to use them. They have proven their effectiveness for over fifty years, since the founding of Alcoholics Anonymous in 1935, and millions of people have benefited from them. The authors of the Twelve Steps put together a comprehensive blueprint, not only for dealing with addictions, but also for building a life that is, in their words, "Happy, joyous, and free." Some people have difficulty with the male-oriented, Christian language that dates from the time when the program was created and the text, *Alcoholics Anonymous,* was written. However, if we take the time to look past the words at the broader concepts and suggestions for healing within the Twelve Steps, we find an approach that contains many of the ideas inherent in time-tested spiritual systems.

For example, many forms of Buddhism emphasize the importance of the *dharma,* the *sangha,* and the *Buddha,* or the *path* (or *truth*), the *community,* and *our divine nature.* Among native peoples, the extended family, the community, or the tribe are essential components of daily life and spiritual activities. In Christianity, Jesus emphasizes the need for community by saying, "Where two or three are gathered together in my name, I am there also." The same essential ingredients appear in the Twelve Steps. The community, the *sangha,* or the fellowship, as the Twelve-Step group is called, is a cornerstone of the program. During Twelve-Step meetings, members receive the wisdom, love, and support of others who share a similar history and speak a familiar language. They also select and regularly communicate and work with sponsors—people in the program who have been in recovery longer than they have and can offer guidance. A sponsor also serves as a regular touchstone, someone with whom an individual maintains a consistent relationship.

Loneliness dissolves as, in an atmosphere of acceptance and understanding, those in recovery realize that their problems are not unique. The Twelve Steps also offer a prescribed path or *dharma* through the Steps, which promises to lead the practitioner to a spiritual awakening, a relationship with God (as one understands God), and a "road to happy destiny."

In Buddhist practice, the pathway out of attachment begins through the experience of surrender that is so essential to recovery and is explicated in the first three steps of the Twelve Steps. Many of the other components of the Twelve-Step programs are also fundamental in diverse spiritual approaches: the confession of wrongdoing, the healing of harmful or selfish transgressions from the past, working to reduce or eliminate "character defects," and developing positive attributes, regular prayer and meditation, and the practice of service to others.

In order to benefit from the Twelve Steps, participants need to consistently work at the Steps and incorporate the principles of the program into their daily lives. Over time, with serious effort and through the loving human contact of an accepting community, they decrease or overcome their self-destructive and destructive emotions and patterns, gradually quenching their spiritual thirst.

Spiritual and Religious Practice

Because recovery is a spiritual path, many people find it useful to participate in a specific spiritual practice or religious tradition, in addition to a program directed specifically toward their addictions. The eleventh Step of the Twelve Steps addresses the necessity of "conscious contact with God *as we understand God*" through prayer and meditation. This is an applied effort to communicate with the deeper Self, to open ourselves to the guidance and wisdom of the divine influence. There are many ways we can do this. I once heard it said, "Prayer is when we talk with God; meditation is when we listen for the answers"; through some sort of regular religious or spiritual practice, we open the lines of communication between ourselves and the deeper Self, or God.

There are as many styles of prayer and meditation as there are individuals who pray and meditate. Each of us has her or his own voice. A religious or spiritual framework offers structure, discipline, and guidance for those who want it. In choosing a path, it is important to look for one that allows us to maintain our own personal contact with our Higher Power. The healing through the Spirit, *spiritus contra spiritum,* cannot happen through simply learning about God from books, lectures, and sermons; it must come through an immediate encounter with that spiritual force. Some people find themselves returning to the religion of their youth, after abandoning it earlier in their lives. Having experienced a profound surrender, they can now enter a religious context, receiving true guidance and inspiration beyond the confines of the dogma that formerly troubled them. They find deep meaning in reconnecting with the tradition of their roots, and within that sacred structure, they engage in a genuine relationship with the spiritual force.

Other individuals become involved in some form of spiritual practice that, although it may have originated in another cultural context, provides significant meaning for their spiritual lives and offers them methods for growth and for accessing the deeper Self. We live at a time when many spiritual disciplines, some of them hidden or isolated for centuries, have become available. Various forms of yoga, Sufism, Buddhist meditation, Jewish and Christian mysticism, Native American practices, and shamanism are a few of the spiritual approaches that have gained prominence in recent years.

Mythologists, transpersonal psychologists, and consciousness researchers have described the sacred and mythological themes and symbols from many traditions that exist within the rich pool of the human psyche or, as Jung called it, the *collective unconscious.* Someone from a Christian background may suddenly have dreams that involve intricate Hindu or Native American images along with insights into the meaning of specific rituals. Another person raised as a Buddhist may encounter the figure of Christ during meditation. As a result of such experiences, these individuals may find themselves drawn toward the wisdom of a culture that is externally foreign to their own but that resonates with them internally.

One of the most important guidelines in choosing a practice is to ask whether this path feeds and exercises our hearts. Does it include the discovery and expression of kindness and love as a central teaching? What is the motivating principle behind it? Do its teachers focus mostly on spreading the word, protecting an exclusive doctrine, or raising money to build expensive temples? Or is it a compassionate, inclusive tradition that emphasizes humility, gratitude, and love, as well as the practice of its principles in daily life?

Therapy

In addition to spiritual or religious pursuits, many people undertake some form of therapy. The role of therapy is to help us identify and address the repressed emotions, memories, and experiences that stand in the way of a healthy and happy life. As we do so, we heal the wounds and, piece by piece, remove the dam between our individual identities and our deeper Self. The human psyche is complex and multidimensional, and as psychologists, psychiatrists, and other professionals have seen, no one method of therapy provides the answers for everyone. Fortunately, there are many choices to suit many needs and tastes. And different therapeutic approaches may be appropriate for different stages or issues in the healing process of a single individual.

One-on-one or couples work with a reliable and caring therapist may be essential in order to work on the past and to discard emotional barriers and defenses, gradually increasing the ability to trust. However, if the issues revolve around unexpressed physical and emotional experiences or problems with intense feelings, a more active, experiential approach such as anger work, Gestalt practice, Reichian therapy, or Holotropic Breathwork™ are useful. An individual who becomes interested in discovering deeper dimensions within him- or herself might benefit from methods that use nonordinary states as a pathway toward healing, such as guided imagery, work with dreams, rebirthing, or Holotropic Breathwork™.

Whatever methods we choose, they must include certain ingredients. First, a client needs to resonate personally with the therapist. The therapy will be as good as the therapist. This may mean interviewing several candidates to find the person who feels right, with whom one has the right personal chemistry. A prospective therapist may have impressive credentials or glowing recommendations, but if we do not feel a certain level of comfort, trust, and safety, the work will not be effective.

Second, the therapist must operate within a theoretical framework broad enough to incorporate all aspects of human beings, including the spiritual dimension. With that understanding, the professional must be willing to follow clients wherever they need to go within themselves. This means that if a person delves into memories from childhood, the therapist focuses on the biographical history. If the individual encounters experiences from birth or prenatal life, the professional is willing to take them seriously and support them. If the client becomes aware of mythological, archetypal, or spiritual influences, he or she acknowledges them as important and works with them.

Third, a good therapist knows that we are our own healers. A therapist open to the spiritual dimension knows that we each contain a deep source of wisdom, creativity, and healing within us. The professional's job is to create a safe, supportive setting in which clients can effect their own growth and evolution. A good therapist stays away from the position that as a trained professional, she or he has the ultimate answers and techniques to fix other people. Instead, the therapist points the way to the clients' own resources, throws them back on their own innate healing power, and allows them to discover their own solutions.

Finally, the therapist must be ethically sound and clear about his or her boundaries as being separate from the client. A therapist without strong ethics can cause additional damage to a client who already carries wounds from the past. Although recently the news media have brought to public attention a number of cases of client abuse by therapists, the majority of professionals are skilled and morally sound. Their work has had a positive affect on many people.

Regular Time in Nature

The restorative power of nature is well known. Many of us need to "get our feet back on the ground," particularly if we have been compulsively preoccupied with our addictions or attachments. A walk through a meadow, a hike in the mountains, or a day at the beach exposes us to fresh air and sunshine. We also enjoy a respite away from our regular routines during which we can relax and appreciate the rhythms and cycles of the outdoors. As we take time to notice the variety of plants, animals and insects, the cloud formations, and the beauty of the day, we grow to appreciate the miraculous ingenuity of creation. We may also feel a deep recognition of our place within the natural order.

All over the world, native peoples regard the earth, sun, moon, fire, water, trees, mountains, and other forms in nature as gods. Birds and animals act as heavenly messengers or spirit guides who link us to the divine realms. Watching the dancing flames of the campfire on a starless night, reflecting on the majesty of a snow-capped mountain or the grace of a soaring eagle, or becoming absorbed in the splendor of the sky as the sun makes its way into the heavens, we can directly experience the sacredness of the natural world. Our time in nature not only regenerates the body but also stirs the soul. Even those who live in urban areas can find ways to spend time outdoors, lying on the grass in a local park, walking to work in the early morning, or taking a picnic up to the rooftop.

Creative Expression

Recovery allows us to touch our creativity and passion, often for the first time. Many people discover an impulse toward creativity that was previously hidden by the chaos and confusion of an addictive life. Artists who formerly used drugs or alcohol to stimulate their music, poetry, or painting often realize that their attempts at creative expression were muddled by the influence of these substances. But creative expression is not limited to those who are identified as artists; it is available to everyone.

In recovery, as our heads clear and our perception becomes sharper, we may feel stimulated by waves of inspiration. We might find ourselves drawn to activities such as painting, dancing, writing, or composing poetry or songs, playing a musical instrument, or implementing innovative projects in our professions. These artistic endeavors may emerge as ways to communicate experiences and discoveries that are difficult to capture in daily conversation, or they may be spontaneous responses to a previously unrecognized unconscious impetus.

Creative expression can be fun, therapeutic, and a way to step out of mental activities and engage a more intuitive part of ourselves. If you have ever, even for a short time, abandoned yourself to the movement of a dance, the puzzle of a science project, the production of a delicious meal, or the planting of tiny seeds in the garden, you know the joy and regenerative power of creative activity.

In many people, the spiritual impulse and the creative force are similar, if not the same. Yogic systems call the creative force *shakti*. Feminine in nature, the shakti is the spiritual spark that initiates creation. In their book *Higher Creativity,* Willis Harman and Howard Rheingold include quotes from many famous artists and scientists stating that their inspiration came directly from the divine. The great composer Johannes Brahms told a biographer, "Straightaway the ideas flow in upon me, directly from God. . . . Measure by measure the finished product is revealed to me when I am in those rare, inspired moods." Puccini described writing his most popular opera, *Madame Butterfly:* "The music of the opera was dictated to me by God." The English poet Shelley said, "One after another the greatest writers, poets, and artists confirm the fact that their work comes to them from beyond the threshold of consciousness."

Of course, this kind of divine inspiration does not happen all the time. We bring to our creative endeavors all of our self-consciousness and feelings of inadequacy. When I taught art to children, I used to see the moments when a crestfallen child would turn off access to that creative flow, usually when a parent or teacher walked into the room and criticized his or her newly created project. Later in my career, when I worked with adults using Holotropic Breathwork™, we incorporated drawing and painting into the process. In almost every group, some people would panic when they found themselves staring at a blank piece of paper. Their immediate reaction was "I can't" or "I won't". Then they would tell me about childhood incidents like the one I just described. I believe that, just as we all have the potential to experience our deeper Selves, every one of us has the ability to tap our source of creativity. Activities geared specifically in that direction help to open the doors to that possibility.

Attention to Diet, Exercise, Rest

Most individuals enter recovery in dire need of physical attention. Some of us have abused our bodies with drugs, alcohol, too much or too little food, purging methods, sexual misconduct, or simple disregard for basic physical maintenance. Chemical addicts have literally and willingly intoxicated themselves, filling their bodies with toxins or poisons. Codependents may have been so focused on others or so preoccupied with trying to control an uncontrollable world that their personal needs have been ignored. Workaholics have often stretched their physical resources beyond reasonable limits, resulting in problems such as high blood pressure, excess weight, ulcers, or colitis. Because regeneration in recovery must involve all aspects of the individual, attention to physical requirements such as diet, exercise, and rest is essential.

So many of us learned long ago to leave or disregard our bodies. We may hate our bodies, feel critical of them, or mistreat them. In recovery, we gradually confront the events that happened when we were not "there" to participate. In this process, we may begin to feel compassion for all that this physical self has endured. If our addiction has brought us close to death, we often recognize the miracle of our lives and of how much physical stamina we have in spite of great odds. At this point, we realize that we are fortunate to be here and that we deserve to take care of ourselves.

Around Twelve-Step programs, we hear the watchword H.A.L.T. These initials stand for Hungry, Angry, Lonely, and Tired, and they caution us to watch for these warning lights that indicate possible relapse into addictive behavior. Two of them apply to our physical condition and two to our emotional well-being. When we recognize them in ourselves, it is time to halt: to stop and pay attention to them.

Attention to our physical needs is simple, and it pays off. Not only does it involve specific healing from the ravages of our addiction, but it also includes daily attention to adequate sleep, a healthy diet (vitamins when indicated), and moderate exercise. The many forms of physical exercise offer stimulating and beneficial ways to reintroduce ourselves to our bodies, to befriend and enjoy their miraculous capabilities. We learn to receive regular medical checkups (something many of us avoided or dismissed in the past) and treatment when necessary. Some people benefit from approaches such as acupuncture, chiropractic, and nutritional counseling, when offered by well-trained, able practitioners. Body work, such as Rolfing or massage therapy, can help to relieve physical blockages and somatized traumas. And we may simply enjoy the nurturing and comfort of hot baths, saunas, or other sustaining physical indulgences.

The Practice of Surrender and the Relief from Suffering

Earlier in the book, we devoted a whole chapter to the issue of surrender—defining it and exploring its essential role in spiritual practice and, more specifically, in recovery. Now, let us return to this fundamental ingredient in our healing journey and discuss how we can implement it in our daily lives. In the most general sense, our attachments are what underlie our unhappiness and feelings of constriction. We see them everywhere we turn. We are attached to emotions, such as anger or pride. We cling to people: our spouses or our children. We stubbornly harbor a point of view, "I am right and you are not," or protect a social role, such as our identity as the perfect wife or the star athlete. We hang on to expectations, "All my children will get good grades," or goals, " I will finish this project by four o'clock." There is nothing wrong with our identity as parents or athletes, and we all need goals and dreams. What gets us in trouble is our *attachment* to them.

If something happens to obstruct the fulfillment of our roles or expectations, how do we react? If the athlete breaks an arm just before the big game, the creative child does poorly in math, or an electrical failure keeps us from completing a project, can we be flexible enough to let go? Or do we cling to our desire to be in control and feel miserable as a result? How many times have we held on to our opinions so tightly that there is no room for any creative solution to a dispute with another person? We know we have the answers, and our partner, sibling, or friend is wrong. Even though we may be right at the outset, we cling to our emotional stance with such a vengeance that we cannot possibly hear the other person's side. We further complicate matters with the self-righteousness, stubbornness, pride, and increasing anger that we heap onto the issue, until it has nothing to do with the original problem. Both people suffer as a result.

During our recovery program or on our spiritual path, we learn that when we are in pain, we are attached. When we notice suffering, we are hanging on to something. Our level of pain becomes an indicator of the degree to which we are attached. The quickest way out of the suffering is to surrender. "Let go and let God," as the AA slogan says. "God grant me the serenity to accept the things I cannot change," entreats the Serenity Prayer. We are trapped by our attachments, and the way to become free and happy is to learn to let go. For this reason, our recovery program or spiritual path must have, at its core, the regular practice of surrender.

Recently, I took my first ride on a roller coaster. I waited until I was well into the middle of my life until I had enough trust to step onto the ride. And once it started moving, I knew why. As we sped around the curves and careened down from the heights, I could hear the people around me screaming with delight, their bodies swaying with the movement of the cars. I sat rigidly in silence. I held my breath and gripped the safety bar in front of me until my knuckles turned from pink to white. I could feel my back begin to protest in pain as I fought every movement with my unyielding position. Midway though the ride, I noticed what I was doing, and exhaled.

All my issues about control and the fear that accompanies them had rocketed to the surface. I was in a situation over which I had no authority. Someone else was at the controls, and no matter how diligently I held on and how much I helplessly tried to maneuver my vehicle, it was part of a larger system that was uninfluenced by me. I realized that I had a choice: I could continue trying to run the show and stay stuck in fear and anguish, or I could say a small prayer, relax, breathe, and go with the roller coaster. When I started breathing again, I even laughed out loud. My terror became pleasure, and I stepped off the ride vowing to repeat it.

For years, I had heard the adage, "Life is a roller coaster," and I had always thought it meant that life has its ups and downs. But that day, the old saying took on a new meaning. It became a metaphor for the necessity of surrender in the midst of the inevitable daily fluctuations. During my existence, I am on someone else's ride. The deeper Self, the Higher Power, or God is at the controls. I cannot control the twists and turns of my life. However, this does not mean I have no choices. I can choose to fight whatever happens in my life, or I can surrender and, in that process, become open to the guidance of the divine force. By letting go of ego control, I discover gifts and abilities I may not have noticed. I find my role in life, my own form of creative expression, or my *bliss*, as Joseph Campbell called it. As I *follow my bliss*, do whatever inspires and energizes me, with an attitude of honesty and surrender, I am directed where I need to go. I can make an effort to achieve my goals. I will realize some of them, and not others. However, if I do not enjoy getting there, I have lost touch with the creative spirit that propels me.

In his book *God*, the theologian Alan Watts tells the story of Mary Magdalene, who, upon seeing Jesus after the resurrection, tried to cling to him in devotion. He responds by saying, "Do not touch me!" Watts interpreted this to mean, "Do not cling to me! Do not hold on to the spirit." He writes, "Don't cling to your breath, you'll get purple in the face and suffocate. You have to let your breath out. That's an act of faith, to breathe out and it will come back. The Buddhist word *nirvana* actually means to breathe out; letting go is the fundamental attitude of faith."

The practice of surrender opens the doorway to faith and trust in ourselves, other people, and God. We cannot enjoy faith without surrendering. Turning our will and our lives over to the care of God, as the third Step of the Twelve Steps says, requires some degree of faith that we will not be dropped into a vacuum. When we surrender, we find that our suffering is alleviated and we feel the guidance of the deeper Self. Once we have surrendered a few times, we begin to incorporate the attitude of "letting go" into our daily lives.

However, turning it over is not always easy. After a life of imagined control, we need time to build trust that someone else *is* running the show and that this deep force is ultimately benevolent. We discover that surrender comes about in increments, little by little. Over time, we gradually relax our grip on an issue, person, emotion, or denial pattern in our lives. We let go in layers, one day at a time, one moment at a time. Whenever we let go, a little more faith emerges, and as a result, we relinquish control more easily the next time. This is the path of surrender.

If we incorporate into our everyday routine the practice of letting go, we become increasingly open to the beauty, joy, and creativity within and around us. But as our lives become more pleasurable, they can also become more painful and difficult; with heightened awareness of the beauty and pleasure in the world, we also feel less protected from its pain and ugliness. When we surrender, we gradually dismantle the solid fortress of denial and defenses that kept us from truly perceiving the intensity of our existence. We may have actively protected ourselves from the truth, and when the truth reveals itself, it often hurts.

For example, a child who suffers physical or sexual abuse locks those memories securely away and constructs illusions to replace them so that he or she can survive. At the time, the pain of this overwhelming event is too much for a vulnerable, dependent child to handle. Perhaps a little girl cannot remember her childhood or has told herself that Daddy was a hero or a god and she was a bad person by comparison. A growing boy may believe the prevailing myth that his violent family was superior to others in the neighborhood or that Uncle Jake was expressing love toward him when he touched him in secret places. These illusions are easier to accept than the truth of what actually happened.

Our spiritual path of recovery teaches us that when we feel pain, we have some work to do on an attachment. Our suffering ultimately becomes an opportunity for increased freedom. We suffer greatly as we hang on to our justifications and rationalizations, perhaps developing difficulties such as health and relationship problems, low self-esteem, or the inability to find an appropriate place for ourselves in the world. Many people find that the level of pain increases until they become willing to explore the issues behind it. As adults, we have become strong enough to begin—in safety, with support and guidance—to peel away the many layers of protection that have shielded us from the reality of our history, emotions, and behavior.

As we actively work on ourselves, we continue to remove the veils hiding our true identity. We confront the physical, emotional, mental, and spiritual barriers we all carry with us, which are in large part the result of the events in our past and the destructive and self-destructive behaviors we developed in response to them. Through our Twelve-Step practice, our therapy, prayer, meditation, or other forms of self-exploration, we gradually discover and remove the underlying causes of our attachments. With the guidance of others, we begin to honestly confront the memories, emotions, and responses that have kept us constricted and unhappy. Gradually, we release the protective layers of denial about ourselves and our past. We work at stripping away the masks of illusion between us and the world, discarding the layers of the false self.

Using regressive approaches, we might relive birth and realize its effect on our lives. We recapture emotions we may have locked away, buffered with our addictions, or allowed to rage out of control. We recognize and express our grief and our anger, our shame and our fear. Accepting that even the so-called negative emotions are part of the human repertoire, we discover how to experience and communicate them in healthy ways. We no longer need to treat feelings such as anger, fear, and sadness as unacceptable or uncontrollable but understand them now as normal, healthy responses to some situations.

We discover ways to become responsible for our feelings, rather than ventilating them on others or allowing them to seethe within. Fury becomes transformed into strength. Survivors of abuse know that behind the anger, fear, shame, and sense of betrayal is an enormous sense of personal power waiting to be released. We begin to act rather than react, to function through our own volition rather than constantly opposing or responding to external situations and people.

As we more fully experience previously unacceptable or "negative" emotions, with support from others, we also gain access to the "positive" ones: joy, happiness, gratitude, and love. We become aware of the aspects of our character that keep us stuck in suffering. The practice of a personal inventory is an integral component of the Twelve-Steps as well as other approaches: keeping track of our shortcomings, such as self-pity, hatred, or selfishness; recognizing them when they occur; and correcting them. Many of these shortcomings (all of them universal human feelings and traits) are opposites to the qualities of spiritual maturity: dishonesty, false pride, intolerance, procrastination, or selfishness. As we learn to monitor them and work daily to discard them, they have less and less influence on our lives.

We also begin to come to terms with the state of our relationships. When someone in a relationship enters recovery or therapy or embarks on a spiritual path, the dynamics of his or her relationships almost certainly change. When one person within a friendship, marriage, family, or community begins to grow, the whole structure shifts. That structure may have been founded on unhealthy assumptions or may have revolved around dysfunctional behavior patterns that are no longer appropriate for a person in the process of personal transformation and healing.

Inevitably, these relationship changes present problems. No matter how glad our family or friends may be that we are finally doing something about our problems, almost everyone tends to hang on to the safety of what was. No matter how miserable our former lives were, at least we existed within certain familiar parameters. Now our active involvement in personal development seems to require others in our lives to follow us into unknown territory. This can be threatening, even scary, to people who had convinced themselves that we were the problem in *their* lives.

What we learn very quickly is that ultimately we cannot affect another person's behavior. Some friends, spouses, or other family members have already become involved in their own transformation process and are happy to welcome a new companion in the adventure of self-exploration. Others feel inspired by the changes they see in us, accepting the shifts in the relationship as opportunities for their own growth. Still others remain firmly embedded in their own ways of doing things, their own behaviors and points of view. They may actively or unobtrusively resist, judge, or become angry with our efforts. We realize that the only person we can change is ourselves and that, even though it might threaten the security of our relationships, our newfound path of healing and rediscovery is worth it.

As we continue our work, we begin to examine and change our unhealthy contributions to relationships. If we have been demanding and needy, we discover how to let go and trust our own resources. If we feel easily trapped, overwhelmed, or lost, we learn to distinguish the reality of our situation from our inner state of distress. Has our marriage or friendship really ensnared us, or have we felt that way all our lives, regardless of circumstances? Do we feel useless because someone else treats us as expendable, or because, deep within, we feel insignificant? If our answers to such questions suggest that something is wrong in our external situation, we summon the courage to change it. If the problem is with our self-image, we find an opportunity to explore ourselves further.

We might be afraid of commitment; others have hurt or abandoned us too many times. Or we keep those we love at a distance or behind an emotional wall through anger, judgments, or criticism.

Perhaps we place our parents, partners, or children on pedestals and lose ourselves in the process. The moment we become aware of these and other relationship issues, we are on our way to changing them. Although the temptation to "fix" or change our partner or friend may draw us out of our own healing process, we learn to consistently return to our own self-exploration. As we continue to grow, we become more open to trust, intimacy, and love toward ourselves and others. We may even notice subtle and perhaps unexpected changes in the people around us.

Surrender means "dismantling, undoing, opening, giving up," as the Tibetan teacher Chögyam Trungpa wrote. It means "taking off our clothes, our skin, nerves, heart, brains, until we are exposed to the universe. Nothing will be left." Nothing will be left of the protections and restrictions that keep us from fully participating in our lives. During the healing process, we are not fighting our addictions or forcefully avoiding temptation but neutralizing and transforming our cravings. We also learn to recognize the spiritual thirst when it appears and to quench it in nourishing and fulfilling ways.

As we let go, we more easily embrace the whole of life's drama, the joy as well as the suffering, the beauty as well as the ugliness, the pleasure as well as the pain. Without escaping or denying any aspect of the roller coaster ride, without selectively focusing on or clinging to the suffering or the joy, we become increasingly free. We can relax and enjoy the ride with a sense of gratitude, humility, and deep love for ourselves, for others, and for the one at the controls. Eventually, the uncovering process and the practice of surrender become exciting—sometimes miraculous. Even though our recovery is excruciating at times, we persist because the dam between us and the deeper Self is disintegrating and our lives are changing significantly.

Sometimes, working on recovery is like getting into a tub of hot water. First, I test the temperature with my little toe and make the decision whether to continue. Gradually, I dip a few more toes, pull back for a while, and then proceed, until I immerse the whole foot. So it goes, dipping and pulling back, dipping a little further, retreating, and resting, until I submerge more and more and resist less and less. As this experiment continues, things happen along the way that let me know I am on the right track. Sometimes I experience synchronicities, those wonderful coincidences that remind me I am not in charge, or periods of grace in which I feel guided. During a rest period or a plateau on the path, suddenly a new piece of the puzzle, a forgotten memory or unclaimed emotion, presents itself, and I inch my way toward the edge once more or, summoning my faith, plunge in headfirst.

The Ego and the Mind

Many spiritual traditions consider the mind to be one of our greatest assets as well as our worst enemy. In the Twelve-Step community, people often refer to "the committee," the legion of inner voices that are constantly advising or directing us, reminding us of our fears and inadequacies, projecting into the future or dwelling in the past. The mind is very tenacious and very creative.

The way some Eastern traditions describe the mind is very close to the Western description of the ego or the small self. It encompasses not only our cognition but also our senses, emotions, and sense of personal identity. At the core of its function is the process of thinking. We often define ourselves by our thoughts, and we only have to sit still or turn inward to notice the constant parade of ideas, opinions, and fantasies that march through. Much of Eastern spiritual practice involves quieting, controlling, or taming the mind in order to transcend it. From a position behind or above the mind, we can witness its gymnastics. This "witness" is the force beyond the ego. It is the deeper Self that is free and separate from the dynamics of the mind.

The late Swami Muktananda, a contemporary master in the Siddha Yoga tradition, used to tell a story about a poor man who, one fine day, found himself in a celestial garden, sitting under a wish-fulfilling tree. This splendid tree would grant the wishes of anyone who sat beneath it. (But, "no matter where we go, the mind goes with us. We can never leave it behind, and it never leaves us alone," said Muktananda.)

As he sat in that lovely garden, the man began to think. "I would enjoy this place even more if I had the ideal woman with me." Suddenly, the ideal woman appeared. The magical tree had granted his wish. The man felt momentarily delighted, but as his new companion settled down beside him, he thought, "This is wonderful, but it would be even better if we had a big house with luxurious furniture." Immediately, a beautiful house appeared, containing all the man and the woman would need.

This continued until the man had wished for and received a staff of servants who cooked the couple a delicious meal that they served at the grand table. Just as he was about to take the first bite, the man had another thought. ("This is the nature of the mind," said Muktananda. "It always doubts.")

"What is happening here? I thought of a woman, and she materialized. I thought of a house and furniture, and they appeared. I thought of servants and a lavish meal, and here I am sitting in the midst of them. This must be the work of a demon!" Instantly, a demon loomed before him, mouth opened wide. "Alas! He's going to eat me up!" the man cried. And the demon devoured him.

This story points to the tremendous power of the mind to influence experience. We consistently use our minds to talk ourselves out of positive or pleasant states or activities. How many times have we been in an ideal situation, only to be hounded by our thoughts? Perhaps it is a beautiful Sunday afternoon stroll in the park, a day with a favorite friend, or a long-awaited vacation. There we are, in the perfect setting, alone or with the perfect company, and our minds begin to churn. We find ourselves thinking about the unfinished projects at work, guilt-tripping ourselves about things we should be doing, or creating a scenario in which the person we are with secretly dislikes us and is planning to leave. If we were happy when we started the day, the mood gradually sours, and we end up completely unable to enjoy ourselves.

This is what many spiritual systems call the "monkey mind." Like a monkey, the undisciplined mind frantically bounds into the past and the future, into fantasies and illusions, until we have no hope of enjoying the present. It can also successfully talk us into believing its misperceptions, denials, and rationalizations. Before becoming a full-blown alcoholic, I became familiar with meditation practices designed in large part to quiet and control the mind. I also thought that I understood a little bit about how strong and authoritative it can be.

However, it was not until I entered recovery that I had any inkling of the power of the mind. During my drinking days, as I was destroying myself on every level with alcohol, my mind told me time and again that I was just fine. It effectively concealed from me the reality of my situation and convinced me of many reasons, other than alcohol intake, that my life was not working. When, in recovery, I realized the extent of the airtight denial system I had created around my alcoholism, I began to feel a new reverence for this potent force.

Work with the mind or "the committee" is an essential component of recovery or of any spiritual path. We notice its games and become aware of its tendency to hide, dissuade, or stray; we use tools such as meditation to quiet it. Many meditative practices include essential techniques that encourage the student to control the mind, to diminish or stop the mental chatter, or to detach from thoughts in order to witness them. Because the mind is closely connected with the ego, it is essential to quiet or transcend it as a way of moving beyond the small self. This quieting opens us to the experience of the deeper Self, to have the "spiritual awakening" that the twelfth Step promises. It also cultivates the serenity so central to recovery, increasingly allowing us to remain present for our daily experience.

Healthy Desires and Preferences

Perennial wisdom has given us two major recipes for confronting our attachments, thereby curing the dis-ease in our lives. In very general terms, one approach is to relinquish our attachment to the world as we think it is so that we can see it as it really is. The other focuses on ways we can convert our attachments into healthy desire and devotion to God. As author Ken Keyes suggests, we can reprogram our addictions to become preferences. Both these approaches to the problem of addiction or attachment, surrendering them and transforming them, are applicable to our path of recovery. One strategy may be pertinent at one moment; the other, at the next. I have discussed the practice of surrender. Let us explore the metamorphosis of our attachments and addictions into healthy desires and preferences.

The flip side of attachment is love. How many times have we confused the two? Is there any way to transmute our attachments and addictions into love? Let us return to the idea that the force behind our addictions is the thirst for wholeness, for union with the divine. At its origins, our spiritual yearning is a natural and healthy impulse. When we misdirect that craving into attachments and addictions, we obscure its positive potential. By redirecting this thirst toward the deeper Self, we move in the direction of healing or wholeness. In opening to the Spirit, we dispel the power of our addiction. *Spiritus contra spiritum.* We tap the source of love and divine creativity. We replace our craving for food, alcohol, gambling, drugs, or sex with love. We realize that the divine was not hiding from us, but that in our blind attachments and addictions, we had turned away from God.

When we misdirected our thirst for wholeness into attachments or addictions, we experienced pain, constriction, and decay. When we redirect it toward the divine source, it becomes potentially expansive, unifying, and creative. During our addictive career, our addictions took the place of our Higher Power. When we hit bottom, the strength of that distorted devotion gives way to the true, even more potent force of the divine.

There is a story from India about an opium addict. In the depths of his addiction, the addict went to a famous guru, asking him for help. The next day, the wise teacher gave the man a scale and a piece of chalk, along with a treatment for gradual withdrawal from his drug. He told him to weigh the chalk each afternoon. Whatever the chalk weighed, the addict could eat the same amount of opium and no more. But, the teacher instructed him, before he put the chalk on the scale each day, he had to write the name of God on a blackboard. The man followed the guru's advice, and with each name of God, the chalk decreased in size until it disappeared altogether. By this time, the craving for opium had also vanished, and the addict had become so concentrated on God that he had transformed his addiction to the drug into intoxication with God.

As we talk about addiction to God, let us remember two things: first, intoxication with God in this context does not mean spiritual or religious addiction, and second, God is not some detached foreign entity that is unavailable to us. We will talk about attachment and addiction to spirituality and religion in more depth in the next chapter. Briefly, when we discuss transforming our addictions into a healthy desire for spirituality, we are not recommending that we switch one addiction for another, that we become compulsively, humorlessly attached to a concept of God. Faith does not mean blind dependence on anything.

In transforming our addictions and attachments into an impulse toward the divine, we are redirecting our craving for wholeness toward its original goal. We are opening ourselves to the direct experience of something larger than our small selves, becoming devoted to the force at the controls. We are turning our wills and our lives over to the source of all health and creativity, whether we name this force the Great Spirit, the Christ, love, the creative energy, the Great Mother, our Buddha nature, the deeper Self, or Higher Power. Though we can devote ourselves to the transcendent divine, or the sacred force that is beyond our reality, we also include the immanent divine, or the God within and around us.

In addition to the healthy drive toward the spirit, mystics and poets have spoken of the beneficial and enjoyable worldly desires, such as the desire to act out of kindness, love, or understanding. Out of our deep compassion for the suffering in the world, we want to assist others, to help alleviate misery. We wish to care for and nourish ourselves, our family, our friends, community members, and the earth. We desire to be honest and respectful, to remain sensitive to our needs and the needs of others. We desire to participate in the bounty of the world around us and to enjoy its complexity. With enthusiasm, we want to get up early on Saturday morning to take a walk in the springtime freshness. When our children take their first steps, we desire to be there to hold their hands, or we wish to be present when someone close to us dies, in order to ease their transition. These are all healthy preferences that naturally emerge as we clear away the underbrush around them. They have been there all along, but often, our addictive patterns and unrecognized personality issues have hidden or contaminated them.

In this chapter, we have surveyed some of the attributes and tools of recovery or the spiritual path. Any description of this process of rediscovery, including this one, will be, by its very nature, incomplete. Each person entering this path is unique, with her or his own array of needs, characteristics, and discoveries. For this reason, each chronicle will be personal and different. However, I believe that everyone on this journey needs some degree of courage, commitment, humor, and a willingness to do the work.

IO

The Challenges and Pitfalls of the Path

Now our spiritual journey or recovery takes a new turn; it becomes an active spiritual quest. We have a sense of the goal, and we are exploring ways of getting there. Savoring the initial benefits of our healing, we commit ourselves to continuing to do more, one day at a time. We experience the quiet miracles and awesome changes in ourselves and in our lives. Our minds enjoy moments of crystalline clarity, and we relish the ever-expanding hints of serenity that bubble up from within. Sometimes our hearts overflow with love for other people or swell with gratitude for our new lives. However, in spite of all the blessings, we discover that life is not suddenly all sweetness and light and inspiration and bliss, just because we are on *the path*.

Although the spiritual path is rewarding and wondrous, by its very nature it also entails challenges and pitfalls. Like any other aspect of our daily existence, it has its shadow side, as the Jungians would say. The shadow is a common, natural part of the experience. Some people who are just beginning to test the waters of their spirituality for the first time become distressed when they recognize this fact. They might have read books that describe splendid transcendent states, heard tales of divine intervention and compassionate action, and responded to the allure of notions such as "enlightenment," "love," "ecstasy," "peace," or "grace." To their dismay, they discover that, although the spiritual life can include all these experiences and more, it is not exclusively luminous, gentle, or easy. It can be extremely demanding and difficult at times.

The shadow is a wonderful image. Imagine yourself strolling down a tree-lined country lane on a bright summer morning. As you glance down, you notice that patterns of sunlight and shade dapple the road, configurations that move and shift with the breeze. You continue to walk, through the sunny spots and through the shadows, regarding the variations along the way as part of your total experience. The spiritual path and the entire journey through our lives are no different. They, too, are composed of patches of light and dark. We feel tempted to put value judgments on these contrasting elements, often because we are attracted to ease rather than discomfort, to joy instead of pain. We designate some aspects of our lives as *good* and others *bad*, or we use words such as *positive* and *negative* to describe a feeling, an experience, a person, or an event.

Of course we would rather be comfortable than uncomfortable, and we do not have to like everything that comes in our direction. Yet many people discover that judgments and labels can get in the way. If we cling only to the "positive," light-filled segments of our lives, we are denying a very real, very vital part of our experience. Spiritual teachers, theologians, and philosophers have wrestled for centuries with the question of opposites: good and evil, light and dark, yin and yang, higher and lower, the positive and the negative. They all exist as part of the human drama. The questions remain, How do we make sense of them? What do we do with them? How do we respond?

One suggestion that makes sense to me is to somehow treat them as a whole, as integral ingredients that add dynamism to our lives. The "negative" occurrences will not go away. They are part of the game. Rather than fighting or resisting them, perhaps we can change our relationship to them. We can honestly acknowledge both the difficulties and the beauty in our lives, pass through them, learn lessons from them, and integrate them into who we are. This is a challenge. Can we learn to embrace "the contrasts and patchwork" of life, as Ralph Waldo Emerson called it? Can we include the passion of our grief as well as the rapture of our delight? This attitude does not mean we must blindly accept our pain or the suffering of others. This does not mean that, by accepting the reality of a painful history, a survivor of childhood abuse must believe that the devastating experiences were good or necessary. Rather, we become willing to recognize *what is,* the dark as well as the light.

Aurobindo, the late poet, philosopher, and spiritual leader from India, is said to have mused, "The spiritual journey is one of continually falling on your face, getting up, brushing yourself off, looking sheepishly at God, and taking another step." The pitfalls and confusions of the spiritual path are natural developmental stages for many of us as we open to our new capacities. Some people get stuck in one or another of them because of their character structure or because of fear, immaturity, or a sense of spiritual neediness. We all stumble and fall. This is inevitable and appropriate.

For one thing, we take with us on the path a large bundle of our unaddressed personality issues. We carry our unresolved self-esteem problems, our guilt and shame, our projections, denials, and rationalizations. We lug along our tendencies to project or to idealize, our need to control, our unhealed wounds. If we have hit bottom or experienced a profound surrender, we become more naked than ever before, stripped of some of our masks, props, and escapes. As a result, we find ourselves face to face with the reality of everyday feelings and events without our familiar buffers and avoidances. Our egos are still alive and well, and they are very cunning as they struggle for survival. Life still has its ups and downs, tremendous pain as well as joy.

We discuss the pitfalls of the path because they are often be-wildering and troublesome. Moreover, they are part of the road map: dips and bumps, curves and detours that are useful to know about. I recognize them from my own life, and I have seen them in many other people, whether they participate in Twelve-Step re-covery programs, Buddhist meditation, various forms of yoga, the Christian or Jewish faith, or other kinds of spiritual practice. There are as many variations as there are paths and individuals on the paths. As we look at some of these turns in the road, let us maintain a sense of humor and a touch of humility. In writing about *them*, I am also talking about myself.

Confusions Along the Way

Let us begin by identifying a few of the challenges that serve to confuse us. The first one is the *confusion between spirituality and religion*. We can see this confusion in many spiritual contexts, in-cluding the Twelve-Step fellowships. Many people who enter a recovery program grew up in families or communities that pro-moted a formal religious structure. As they grew older, they moved away from religious participation and became involved with other activities, including their addictions. When they hit bottom with drugs, alcohol, food, or relationships, they have a powerful death and rebirth experience that frequently opens them to the spiritual dimension. Then, suddenly, they find themselves sitting in Twelve-Step meetings, listening to language about God that is reminiscent of their upbringing. Or they hear prayers and terminology that are unfamiliar, that represent a tradition foreign to them. And they do not know how to put it all together.

I have already referred to the distinction between spirituality and religion in an earlier chapter. In general, spirituality pertains to the direct encounter with mystical or transpersonal realms, real-ities that give our lives meaning by adding a sacred dimension. Spirituality does not require any mediation by a religious authority. It is our own intimate, personal contact with God and not someone else's account of the divine.

Spirituality does not have to do with blind faith, doctrine, or belief. When a reporter from *Time* magazine interviewed C. G. Jung toward the end of his life, the journalist asked the wise psychiatrist whether he believed in God. Jung replied, "I could not say that I believe. I know! I had the experience of being gripped by something that is stronger than myself, something that people call God."

Although the great religions of the world originated with direct mystical experiences, over time they have often become rigid, entangled in dogma, hierarchies, and politics. Organized religious groups may or may not have anything to do with spirituality. Many people experience true contact with their Higher Power in churches, synagogues, and other religious frameworks. Others, like Jung, find deep connections with God as they understand God outside an organized theological context.

Another common confusion is that *God or the Higher Power is outside us.* Again, many of us grow up in religions that point to a God *out there* and even use language such as "Our Father who art in heaven." As children, many of us assume that heaven is somewhere in the sky, and we wonder, if we stare long enough, will we see God? Many of us become confused because we never find that very masculine presence out there, yet the priests and the texts tell us that only he will provide salvation. We gain the impression that God is not only separate from us but unreachable. We attribute the miracles of our lives or of our recovery as addicts to some vague force we cannot touch. This attitude might even prevent an intimate and immediate relationship with the divine within us and surrounding us.

In this age of highly visible religious leaders, spiritual teachers, and gurus, this confusion can lead to serious problems. Many people become addicted to the priest, the evangelist, or the master. The notion that the divine exists externally makes supreme sense because of our own reservoir of shame. Along comes someone whose principal identity is as a representative of God, and we grab ahold. Particularly if the practices and teachings stir a place of inspiration within us, we begin to feel we have found the answer. And we go back for more. The teacher may even offer guidance such as, "Discover the God within," or "When you bow to the guru, you are bowing to your Higher Self." But we miss the point.

Even in relation to the most illumined and moral teachers, our attachment can eventually bring us great suffering. We cling so intently to the messenger that we miss the point of the message. We confuse the signpost with the destination. We become so wrapped up in the presence of the other person that we lose our own integrity. A wise and ethically sound teacher will recognize this as an inevitable stage in our spiritual growth and will gently help us turn our outward devotion and love inward, toward ourselves. A spiritual or religious leader who is unprincipled and corrupt can use this confusion to his or her advantage, to gain financial support, sexual contact, or power—with devastating consequences.

According to the story I have been telling in these pages, the key is within each of us. God is present in the room in which I am writing this book as well as in the place where you are reading it. We are each divine, and so is the world in which we live. A few years ago, I had the opportunity to meet Mother Teresa of Calcutta and to see her do her work in India. I witnessed her quietly and lovingly making her morning rounds, through rows of lepers, children with amputated limbs, the dying, the mentally ill. As I watched and later, as I listened to her speak, I asked myself, How is she able to do her work in such apparently difficult circumstances? After some time, I began to understand not only that she was aware of herself as God's instrument but also that she was able to see God through the visible exteriors of those around her. She was able to look past the disease, disintegration, and death and contact what she termed "the Christ" within each person.

Another confusion on the path is the *confusion between the small self and the deeper Self.* We have discussed the distinction between the two throughout the book. The small self is the egoistic self that is limited by a material form, an individual personality, and a lifetime that goes from conception to death. The deeper Self is that creative, boundless, eternal, free, and unitive core we all share. The confusion occurs when we inappropriately mix these two aspects of ourselves. I will give you a couple of examples.

In the past decade, it has been popular to say, "You create your own reality." I have heard many variations of that theme: "You created your relationship problems or your difficult childhood history so that you could learn from them." "You chose your family." "You created your illness." My friend Anne had just turned fifty when she discovered she had breast cancer. In hope of gaining their support and counsel, she openly discussed her disease with the people close to her. One well-meaning friend told Anne that, according to a book she had recently read, Anne had created her own disease. Anne felt outraged at the thought, but as time went by, the comment stuck with her. Gradually feelings of shame seeped into her already shaky self-confidence as she accepted that—just maybe—she was directly responsible for her life-threatening condition. Perhaps she had done something very wrong. Maybe she had worked too hard, eaten improperly, or thought too many negative thoughts. The pain of her situation became intensified as she heaped large doses of guilt and shame on herself.

What became clear was that the woman who made the comment confused two aspects of Anne. She suggested that Anne, as the small self or the ego, had generated her cancer in the way she might produce a hand-knitted sweater. Although researchers are addressing the emotional and psychological factors in disease, as well as the contributions of stressful or unhealthy lifestyles, this does not mean that any individual single-handedly brings about her or his illness. This implies cause-and-effect logic that does not apply to a situation no one completely understands.

The idea that "we create our own reality" may have originated from an expansive experience of the deeper Self and then been inappropriately transformed into an ego-based statement. During a transpersonal or spiritual state, we may have the insight that we are part of a divine field of consciousness out of which everything emanates. The Creator and the creation are one. From that perspective, we feel we have a role in the creative process. However, if we reduce this insight to everyday life and try to squeeze it into a statement about our behavior in the material world, it can only produce unnecessary confusion.

Related to the confusion between the small self and the deeper Self is *the issue of powerlessness,* which is central to the Twelve-Step format as well as to any practice of surrender. Some people in my lectures have focused on this issue as they question the widespread interest in Twelve-Step recovery programs. I can understand their concern. "Isn't there a danger," they sometimes ask, "of creating a generation of powerless, helpless people who cannot make decisions or care for themselves? Aren't they prime candidates for submission to the dictates of a higher order? Isn't there a danger that, in their helpless state, they will blindly succumb to some spiritual or political mandate, or fall in, lockstep, behind some dictatorial leader?"

As we have seen, the first three steps of the Twelve-Step programs are about admitting powerlessness over our addictions and our lives and putting ourselves in the hands of a Higher Power. I once heard a recovering drug addict say, "I have been taught all my life that, as a male, I should be strong and in control of my life. I have been trying to do that for forty-four years, and now this program is telling me that I should become *powerless?*"

The irony is that when the ego or the small self steps aside, it creates room for the deeper Self to express itself. This divine reservoir within us is literally our Higher *Power,* that boundless, creative, and benevolent force that is more potent than our individual strength. By releasing our grip on our limited self-definition, we tap the reserves of a larger one. We discover that we are not ultimately in control of the course of our lives: who knows what is waiting for us around the next curve? When we submit to a higher order, it is not an external one.

Fueled by the guidance, vitality, and wisdom of the deeper Self, we become more effective as we live a day at a time, doing what is in front of us. We learn to accept the things we cannot change, discover the courage to change the things we can, and develop the wisdom to know the difference. As we make the choices and decisions in our lives, we learn to evoke and employ the Higher Power within us to strengthen and guide us. Mother Teresa describes herself as "a pencil in the hand of God writing a love letter to the world." As she moves effectively and forcefully in the world, she is no weakling. Yet she embodies the state of surrender, which is much more powerful than the perceived force of any controlling ego.

Many people become confused by thinking that *the spiritual life is different or separate from everyday life* or that *spirituality is about "getting high."* There are those who regard much of secular existence as low level, second rate, or something to escape from. There is spiritual or religious practice, and then there is the rest of daily life. Some people go to their meditation groups, churches and temples, workshops, or Twelve-Step meetings with the idea that if they do just that, they will be spiritual; it is a kind of holy insurance. And then, they go home and beat up the kids.

Some individuals regularly abandon their families and friends in order to frequent religious services or Twelve-Step meetings. These gatherings become the focus of their lives, to the exclusion of other people or activities. Yet they become so caught up in their frenetic participation that they cannot integrate into their daily interactions the lessons they are learning. This single-pointed commitment makes sense for some people in the early stages of recovery; their recovery program is their lifeline, and they hang on to it tightly for fear of returning to their addictive career. As time goes by, however, they are in danger of using any tool of self-exploration, including the Twelve Steps, as an escape from the everyday routine.

There are also those who begin spiritual practice with the illusion that it involves only love and light and great heights that are separate from the rest of life. Often these individuals focus on and idealize the positive components of human experience as they ignore or deny the dark or difficult ones. I have met a number of angry yogis who have all the props that tell themselves and the world that they are deeply mystical. They labor to keep themselves from looking at anything that reminds them of their own discomfort or negativity. As they do so, they automatically deny a large part of the creation.

Some people treat spiritual life as a very mental process. Through religious study, extensive reading, or travel, they amass an intricate and sophisticated knowledge of various systems and their goals. Their minds often comprehend complex historical and theological concepts, but their hearts are relatively underdeveloped. Others collect an assortment of varied experiences, the more far-out the better. Hopping from one technique to the next, they snack on the lavish smorgasbord of available approaches, never resting in one place long enough to thoroughly digest any of them. As a result, these spiritual connoisseurs are unable to manifest in their lives the teachings they have tasted.

In spiritual maturity, everything we do becomes part of the path. We are not holy only when we involve ourselves in defined spiritual practice, but also as we demonstrate compassion and kindness at home or at work. Jack Kornfield put it this way, "If you want to know about a Zen master, just ask his wife." What goes on behind the scenes when the doors are closed?

We might also *mistake the path or spiritual practice for the final goal.* We confuse the tool with the result, the map with the territory. Some people might feel that if they meditate, pray, or follow the Twelve Steps perfectly, if they know the Bible or the Alcoholics Anonymous Big Book inside out, they have arrived. Often at the expense of the true experience of the deeper Self, they cling to vehicles that are merely instruments designed to help seekers to find their spiritual identity. As the anthropologist Gregory Bateson said, they end up eating the menu rather than the meal.

Related to this is a certain goal-oriented attitude that many of us bring into our spiritual lives from our materialistic cultural programming. Not only do we want to get to the mountaintop, we want it *now*. In our search for instant gratification, we expect enlightenment overnight, like second-day airmail. Unfortunately, the path of self-discovery does not work that way. Our spiritual journey requires patience, courage, and the willingness to put one foot in front of the other. After a while, we may arrive at the insight that there is nowhere to go and nothing to do. We realize that even though we are attempting to move toward our inner source, it already exists in its fullness and radiance. This is another paradox, one of many: to be diligently involved in working on ourselves, yet to know that it is all right here right now.

Many people also become confused by *the issue of detachment*. If we acknowledge our addictions and attachments and then let them go as fully as we can, we learn how to detach. Surrender implies detachment. In some people's minds, this means we must turn our backs and leave the objects of our attachments behind. If we have devoted ourselves to a materialistic lifestyle, we might feel we must sell the house, leave the powerful job, and give away the bank account. If we have spent years clinging to a spouse as the Higher Power in our lives, we might assume that detachment means divorce. Perhaps, but not necessarily.

Of course, alcoholics or drug addicts must completely let go of their use of alcohol or drugs in order to recover. Their biochemistry, among other factors, requires it. But many other addictions or attachments present the dilemma faced by someone with an eating disorder. A compulsive overeater or a bulimic has an obsessive, addictive association with food. However, they need nourishment in order to stay alive. They cannot give it up completely. In order to recover from their addiction, they must give up their compulsive physical, emotional, mental, and spiritual *attachment* to food. They must change their relationship with it, the way a mother who obsessively clings to her daughter needs to release her emotional grip on her child. This does not necessarily mean ignoring or moving away from the child or the food but inwardly detaching from them.

Unfortunately, in their confusion, some people act out the impulse to completely detach from an unhealthy or dysfunctional situation. A young wife who has lost her own identity through her habitual dependence on her husband suddenly realizes she has become hopelessly attached to him. In the flurry of her revelation, she might easily assume that in order to change her situation, she must end the marriage, even though she loves him. Or a businesswoman may recognize that her nonstop workaholism has led to frequent depression and constant stress. She fears that a healthier life means leaving her creative and consequential job.

Perhaps in some cases, actual physical detachment *is* necessary, but again, it is possible to change the nature of our relationship with the source of many of our attachments or addictions while retaining or evoking their healthy, positive qualities. The original situation, the job or the marriage, remains intact. Now that we are no longer clinging to it, we can relax and feel the love, enthusiasm, and inner strength we obscured with our grasping.

We can also *confuse addiction and attachment*. In *The Diseasing of America*, Stanton Peele writes, "*Everything can be an addiction. This remarkable truth* . . . *has so overwhelmed us as a society that we have gone haywire*. . . . *From this perspective, nearly every American can be said to have an addiction*." Peele points to a very essential problem. I would restate it this way: *everything has the potential to become an attachment*. The tremendous growth of interest in addiction and recovery in America means we are beginning to address the suffering in our lives and the addictions and attachments behind it. Every American *does* have attachments. Every human being, regardless of national, racial, or religious origins, struggles with attachments.

Problems occur when we mistake our attachments for our addictions. It is easy to do. What is the often fine line between an addiction, an attachment, and a source of pleasure? In our confusion, some of us see our lives through the filter of addiction, dysfunction, or disease. This is especially easy for someone who carries a burden of shame. In early recovery, I began to question my every move. My reasoning went something like this: "I am an alcoholic, no doubt about that, and I have some serious codependency issues to address, too. When I am uncomfortable or restless, there are times that I try to satisfy myself or escape my pain with a cookie, a trip to the store, or a dance class. Does this mean that I am a food addict, a shopaholic, and an exercise junkie?" I concluded, "I must be a generic addict. Give me something, and I will become addicted to it." Soon I constructed long mental lists of my myriad addictions. It was not a pretty picture. I felt hopeless.

This identification of myself as a creature of addiction, dysfunctional to the core, fit with my already dismal self-esteem. I had the perfect excuse to beat myself up, something I did well. "I am a terrible person because I like something sweet after dinner. I'm a sweets addict." Yet, as I progressed in my recovery, I began to shift my attitude: "Yes, I am a generic addict, but some of my addictions will kill me faster than others, so I will focus on the most serious ones first."

What was puzzling to me was that not all of my "addictions" had the helpless, out-of-control, progressive, and devastating nature of the alcoholism that had nearly destroyed my life. The substances, relationships, or activities I was labeling as addictions had varying degrees of power over me. In addition, the image of myself as a diseased generic addict did not fit with the healthy inner core that I was discovering. When I began thinking about the relationship between addiction and attachment, many of the missing pieces began to fall into place.

I know that, indeed, I have submitted to serious life-threatening addictions. What made them addictions was that they were progressive in nature, involved compulsive, self-destructive behavior, and rendered me completely out of control. As a normal human being, I also grapple with my attachments, which create varying degrees of discomfort or suffering in my life. In addition, a deep thirst for wholeness propels me. When it stirs, it signals that I am not in touch with the deeper Self. When it becomes obvious and uncomfortable, this undercurrent of yearning lets me know that I need to make an effort to resume conscious contact with my Higher Power. By pathologizing all of this under the umbrella of "disease," I was demeaning it.

A frequently asked question among people who are working on their problems with codependency is, How do I differentiate between an act of compassion and a codependent one? When I help someone because I genuinely want to assist a person in need, am I really giving myself away or trying to control that person's life? Ultimately, each person has the answer to these questions. What do they get out of such an action? What do they go away with: the temporary satisfaction that comes with proving oneself or gaining another's appreciation, or the genuine sense of love and fulfillment that accompanies a compassionate, selfless act?

In presenting this discussion, I do not in any way want to diminish the gravity of the prevalent problem of addiction in the world. I know firsthand how powerful and destructive a true addiction can be. There is no question that severe and dangerous addictions affect millions of people. However, I also have witnessed the unnecessary pain, guilt, and shame heaped upon people, by themselves and others, as they liberally identify every move as potentially addictive. With an understanding of the continuum of addiction and attachment, we can become kinder to ourselves as we continue our quest for freedom from addiction, attachment, and the resultant suffering.

The Pitfalls of the Path

The pitfalls of the spiritual path are the often-hidden difficulties or traps along the way. I like the image conveyed by the original meaning of the word *pitfall:* it is a lightly camouflaged hole in the ground that hunters use to ensnare animals or that the enemy employs to capture members of the opposition. On the spiritual journey, we slip into many pitfalls, and the enemy is usually ourselves. As our egos continue to exert themselves within the spiritual arena, we find ourselves justifying and playing out unfinished personality problems that ensnare us for a while. What are some of the pitfalls so many of us face?

The first pitfall is *using spirituality as part of denial.* Sometimes, we engage in destructive or self-destructive behavior and excuse it by pointing to our religious or spiritual pursuits and interests. Earlier in life, we may have enjoyed true and meaningful encounters with our Higher Power. But as our addictions develop, our self-identification as "a religious person" serves as an impediment to honest recognition of our problem: My spiritual awakening took place years before I became an alcoholic. So as I was dying from my alcoholism, I was telling myself that I was a spiritual person. I went to church regularly, sang the hymns, and recited the prayers. Therefore I could not be a lowly alcoholic.

People who use psychedelic drugs addictively commonly drop into this pitfall. The substances may have initially led them to mystical insights. However, in a desire to repeat their original experiences and to continue their exploration of other realms, they become involved in frequent and obsessive usage that is no different from any other addictive behavior. Eventually, their relationships are threatened, their lives start to fall apart, and their health suffers. In spite of everything, they remain convinced they are participating in consequential cosmic work that is more important than everyday concerns.

Addiction is a condition that hides itself from the addict, and this form of denial, using spirituality or religion, is especially seductive and tricky. We create covers, seemingly sacred masks that identify us as devout seekers. Behind our disguises, we act out our addictions and attachments, all the while convincing ourselves we are heading toward enlightenment. Cloaked in the guise of our supposed holiness, we become certain we are pursuing the most creative possible endeavor, when in reality we are damaging ourselves and others. After coming into recovery or engaging in true spiritual practice, we recognize that our sham has only helped to keep us from true contact with the divine within.

A second pitfall relates to the first one: *using spirituality to avoid everyday reality or basic life issues.* I have heard this described as a "spiritual bypass" or a "spiritual end run." We want to remove ourselves from what we consider to be the mundane level of ordinary existence in favor of the so-called higher, more exotic realms. We meditate, do ceremonies, pray, or become occupied with other sacred activities in order to transcend our emotions. The sixties and seventies labeled such people "bliss ninnies" or "cosmic cabbages." With our feet firmly planted in midair, we escape the pain of everyday reality by retreating into the comfort of our spiritual personas.

Many people who follow the impulse to escape the demands of daily life are thin-skinned and openhearted. They may have endured a history of abuse, and as a result, they simply cannot stand the suffering in the world. Perhaps they learned to dissociate as children and later find themselves attracted to spiritual, religious, or New Age techniques and groups that focus on the light, on the positive and transcendent realities. There they cultivate convenient and consistent ways of resisting or denying difficulties, supported by a larger community of others who are doing the same thing.

Even if such individuals become involved in therapy, they might find it easier to rage at mythological demons or past-life tormentors than to acknowledge and express their well-protected fury toward abusive parents or siblings. They tend to identify the stress or challenges in their lives as coming from astrological influences or archetypal manifestations rather than taking responsibility for their emotional or physical origins. They are more comfortable if they relate to the transpersonal than the personal or interpersonal.

Throughout this book, we have been emphasizing the whole person, who is composed of the small self and the deeper Self. One is no more or less important than the other. Every aspect of the complex and wondrous constellation of who we are is valuable, and exclusive focus on any one part can be constricting. If we concentrate solely on our material, ego-bound identities, access to our spiritual and creative potential becomes limited. On the other hand, transpersonal or spiritual pursuits can function as convenient ways to avoid individual and relationship issues. We find harmony and balance as we are able to recognize, explore, accept, and integrate all facets of ourselves. No matter how many ecstatic transcendental experiences pepper our lives, if we are unwilling to address personal issues, we will never enjoy the true benefits of spiritual maturity.

We may stumble into the pitfall of *spiritual or religious perfectionism*. Many of us come to the spiritual life as perfectionists, and we even try to follow the path flawlessly. Some of us become codependent with God: we are good girls or good boys for God, exemplary churchgoers or perfect devotees. Our unswerving drive toward our sacred ideal only produces undue stress and frustration. The Twelve-Step programs emphasize "spiritual progress rather than spiritual perfection," a daily and continuous practice that is uncomplicated by pressures to do it perfectly.

Indifference may masquerade as serenity or acceptance. When we are indifferent, we are aloof and unconcerned, unable to express interest in or empathy toward others. We keep ourselves emotionally distant from the fluctuations in our lives, our own needs, and the needs of the people around us. By remaining uncommitted, we do not have to accept responsibility for the experience of being in the present, of being open to suffering as well as to joy. We do not have to feel our emotions or our pain. Nothing gets to us. Within a spiritual or religious context, we might convince ourselves that when we feel indifferent, we are demonstrating peace, tranquility, and acceptance. By not becoming involved we appear to be allowing whatever is to be. But this attitude is a trap. Real freedom in the midst of our human drama requires complete involvement, an attitude of surrender, and an honest acceptance of the truth of reality, including our immediate experience.

We may *use spirituality as a way to act out our shame or guilt*. At first glance, shame may simulate humility. Humility is the opposite of pride; a truly humble person is someone who embodies a certain degree of self-acceptance without arrogance. Individuals who already feel deeply flawed can easily assume a seemingly humble role. They might become "martyrs": going without, becoming submissive in the name of religion, or putting others first while sacrificing themselves in the process. They give up possessions or money, allow others to take primary positions, or help those in need, all the while appearing to exude humility. In reality, they feel they do not deserve better. As a result, they often do not adequately care for themselves. Yet, they may secretly feel proud that they are so humble.

If a positive experience comes their way or they receive a compliment from another person, these people cannot let it in. Their shame will not allow it. They feel they do not deserve anything worthwhile. Heavily identified with their drama, with their hardship and suffering, they are afraid of straying too far from it, even into joy or happiness. I have seen many people in the Holotropic Breathwork™ who spend a session waiting for the "real work" to start even though their unconscious is trying to give them a bliss-filled experience. Their mental attitude tells them that in order to accomplish anything, they need to combat painful material, and they feel disappointed with even the most transcendent states.

I have already mentioned people who become hypervigilant about their every activity, labeling them as addictions and berating themselves. This, too, reflects shame. These individuals already feel like a mistake. By becoming obsessed with their attachments and condemning themselves for having them, they reconfirm and add to the profound sense of self-contempt that already exists.

Self-flagellation can also manifest through perfectionism. If we already carry a burden of guilt, we might tell ourselves that, no matter how much we try, we are living our spiritual life incorrectly. "If I do not do the practice or conduct myself perfectly, I am a bad person." We are doing the Twelve Steps wrong; almost everyone else in the program does them right. Our friends use proper language, talk in meetings, maintain the correct relationship with their sponsors, and we do not. They know how to help others, and we feel selfish. Their lives work well, and ours are a mess.

Mental and emotional guilt-tripping can happen anywhere; religious or spiritual contexts are no exception. The people around us in a church, synagogue, or spiritual community pray, sing hymns, and participate in the rituals better than we do. The other meditators in the ashram or the zendo do the practice and have a better relationship with the teacher than we do. They are candidates for sainthood; we are sinners. Again, because of our shame, we miss the fact that because each of us is unique, our spiritual needs and expressions are different. We ignore the reality that every person has his or her own relationship to God (as we each understand God).

The pitfall of *spiritual ambition and competitiveness* appears regularly along the path. Constant comparisons of ourselves with others can originate out of shame and guilt and lead to a sense of competitiveness. The person next to us is having the experience we want: "If he can kneel throughout the whole mass, so can I." "If she can sit motionless on her meditation cushion for an hour, I can do it for two." And we can compete with ourselves: "If I devote more time to my practice, I will become enlightened faster." "If I repeat twice as many 'Hail Marys,' I will become even purer." "If I pray more in the morning, talk to my sponsor more often, and speak more in meetings, then I will be doing *real* recovery work."

Spiritual ambition emanates from our ego-based expectations about the path of self-discovery, mixed with a goal-oriented sense of urgency and our addictive attitude that "more is better." With a vengeance, we set about to have a spiritual awakening, or to become enlightened, or to gain serenity. We become so intent on our objective that we keep ourselves from attaining it; we focus on the future so earnestly that we miss the possibilities of the present. Ironically, when we give up our attempt to control the direction of our journey, the way toward our destination begins to open to us. Our minds and egos have kept us stuck.

One of the things I appreciate about the Twelve-Step programs is that they actively discourage this kind of competitiveness and spiritual ambition. Although spiritual competitiveness is inevitable in these fellowships, as in any path, the emphasis remains on the ability of each person to discover his or her own style of participation in the program. Phrases such as "one day at a time" and "easy does it" remind people to be gentle with themselves and to respect their own timing and needs.

Those who have a problem with *irresponsibility or procrastination* might decide that God will take care of everything, and they can settle back and relax. They may have had the insight that some divine force is running the show, and therefore they are in God's hands. They set out to live their lives accordingly, abdicating personal responsibility and relegating everything to a vague Higher Power. They might suddenly wake up twenty years later and realize that many of their life's dreams have never come true. Suddenly, they recognize that even though they are not in control of the divine order, they need to exercise their capacity to make individual decisions. They need to find a job and a place to call home and start taking some initiative in their lives.

We may run into *codependency in the spiritual world.* A group of leading experts at the First National Symposium on Codependency in 1989 defined codependency as "a pattern of painful dependence upon compulsive behaviors and on approval from others in an attempt to find safety, self-worth, and identity. Recovery is possible." Some manifestations of codependency include caretaking, feeling responsible for other people's needs and well-being, low self-worth, denial, dependency, and obsession with control and attempts to exert it on others. In reviewing these characteristics, we can see that many of the pitfalls of the spiritual path have to do with codependent behaviors. Let us look at a few of them.

One form of spiritual codependency is militant altruism. Militant altruists are individuals who forcefully dive into other people's lives to help, whether they are wanted or not and regardless of others' wishes. This "helping" is different from the compassionate action of selflessly reaching out to someone in distress. Militant altruists respond to another person's needs because of their own needs. They are often controlling and manipulative, becoming involved as a way of proving themselves or gaining love and appreciation.

Related to militant altruism is the practice of serving others in order to avoid or to cope with our own pain. By alleviating the suffering around us, we hope to alleviate our own. If we concentrate on the ills of the world or concoct elaborate plans to save others, we do not have to feel our own distress. We frequently focus on misery elsewhere or on people who appear to be hurting more than we are. This way, we minimize our own anguish and avoid taking it seriously. We might think, "My problems are nothing like my neighbor Mary's; who am I to complain compared with the people in the world who are starving, or the populations who have endured war, or the religious martyrs," and on it goes. Perhaps by some external yardstick, these observations are true. However, each person's experience has validity and weight, and our awareness of the plight of others need not diminish the power of our awareness of our own.

The *need to manipulate* shows up regularly in religious and spiritual circles, from materialistic preachers to assorted gurus. There are people in a position of power who say, essentially, "I am a representative of God, and I can run your life." This form of coercion can also occur in the context of therapy when an unethical therapist assumes the role of the expert who has all the answers. Manipulative teachers and therapists serve as magnets for needy people, playing on their unfulfilled longings, as well as on their guilt, shame, and fear. They often abuse people who place their trust in them, exploiting them financially, sexually, emotionally, and spiritually. In addition, they help to create religious or therapeutic dependence. Any good spiritual teacher will serve only as a guide who always points us toward ourselves, consistently throwing us back on our own resources.

It is the need to manipulate that is surfacing when someone who has found his or her own answers imposes them on someone else. I remember meeting Martha, an alcoholic who was struggling to stay in recovery but had relapsed several times. Brad, her husband, also an alcoholic, had been sober for a couple of years; he worked as a therapist and had become a prominent figure in his recovery groups. When his wife once again fell into her drinking pattern, Brad maintained a superior pose and exhibited little empathy. He would tell her, "It is God's will you're miserable." As though he had been given special information she had yet to discover, he would add, "This is a lesson that you have to learn." Meanwhile, in her addictive hell, Martha felt completely removed from any experience that could be called spiritual. Her already considerable sense of shame mounted as she told herself she could never live up to Brad's expectations. Eventually, she found a therapist who helped her concentrate on herself, her own needs and difficulties, rather than her husband's injunctions. After a while, she gained sobriety for a consistent period.

Like manipulation, the pitfalls of *greed, selfishness, exclusivity, and intolerance* have all been ignoble parts of religious history and spiritual life for centuries. There are all too many accounts of individuals or entire groups of people who exploit a religious context for their own gain. Nations who worship the irrefutable God conquer those who follow another deity, plundering the infidels' lands and wealth. Kings and emperors have killed and tortured people in the name of a certain God because their enemies espouse a different faith. Some notorious modern American televangelists have used their religious charisma to charm their followers out of millions of dollars, which have gone to support their own lavish lifestyles. Fundamentalists of various religions consider themselves to be God's elect, and they condemn those who do not share their beliefs.

Inclinations toward exclusivity and intolerance can surface in our own spiritual lives, even though we do not act them out on such a large stage. At times, we become tempted to judge others who represent something different. As much as we deny or dislike these tendencies in ourselves, sometimes we feel courted by intolerance or prejudice toward others, particularly in the early stages of the spiritual life.

We find an approach that works for us, and our lives change as a result. In our enthusiasm for our new discovery, we tend to hang on to it as *the* way, considering others who do not share it to be inferior. We feel threatened by any system that questions our own, solid, sacred belief system. Our practices, convictions, or creeds may have saved our lives or effected great changes within us. We do not want to hear about anything that might subvert or undermine our faith. The attitudes of greed, selfishness, exclusivity, and intolerance reflect the degree to which we remain attached, as well as our fear of losing what we have. If we fervently hang on to our religious or spiritual path as the only way, we easily regard others as separate or different.

We can also stumble into the pitfall of *spiritual pride*. Spiritual pride might manifest in feelings such as, "Because I have a guru, do meditation, or work the Twelve Steps, because I wear spiritually correct clothes or use holy language, I am special and better than those who don't." Or, "I am important or even exceptional because I have had a spiritual experience." We might feel proud of our sacred accomplishments: proud of how loving and compassionate we are, how much we contribute to others, how pure or serene we have become.

Spiritual pride in the extreme might be, "I am God, and you are not. I have it, and you don't." Or it might take the form of, "I have it, and if you follow me, you will have it too, unlike everyone else." The insight that we are God is a valid and reasonable one. The conclusion that we are unique in that experience indicates an egocentric attitude toward our new awareness. After a while, we might very well come to the point when we realize that, "I am God, but so is everyone else. Everyone is very special and, at the same time, not special at all."

Another pitfall is that of being *spiritually grandiose and messianic*. Spiritual grandiosity is somewhat different from, "I have the way, and you don't." This is, "I have a direct line to God. I have the way, and mine is the only way." A group that espouses a similar belief considers itself to be "the elect." They become transfixed by what the journalist Daniel Goleman calls "a shared delusion of grandeur that there is no Way but this one." And if someone leaves the group, its members often ostracize that individual.

This form of grandiosity takes on a messianic tone when it includes, "And what's more, everyone should know about this way. Finally, we have discovered the answer to the global crisis." If a certain religious or spiritual system has substantially enhanced our life, we naturally feel tempted to enthusiastically recommend it to others. If it has worked for us, it will work for them. Particularly if we have not yet integrated our new revelations into our way of being, we remain elated in the afterglow of their first effect. From that elevated place, we cannot see that each person has her or his own path, and that each journey has its own timing. In reality, we can report only on our own practice and our own relationship with God; we cannot ultimately control the course of anyone else's spiritual development. Perhaps we are content, with humility, to quietly engage in meaningful inner work without discussing it too much.

Many individuals encounter the pitfall of *dogmatizing or literalizing spirituality and its tools*. We might regard a doctrine or scripture as a complete divine authority, worshiping its opinions and missing its message. Saint Paul wrote, "The letter kills, but the spirit gives life." In our enthusiasm, we might take the Bible literally, or the Twelve-Step Big Book, or any other statement of principle, treating its metaphors as facts. This is an easy mistake to make. In the often-ineffable spiritual realm, our minds naturally seek to grasp something concrete and factual. We crave explanations and directions in a context that is so obviously beyond our control. However, we can become so caught up in interpreting, memorizing, and reiterating a point of view that we become lost in it. We are unable to see beyond the doctrine to the deeper Self. Jack Kornfield says, "It is better to become a Buddha than to become a Buddhist." It is more valuable to merge with the Higher Power than to engage in endless discussions about it.

The final pitfall on my list is *spiritual or religious addiction*. Someone who becomes completely, humorlessly obsessed with religion or spirituality is addicted. In his book *When God Becomes a Drug,* Father Leo Booth courageously and insightfully explores this phenomenon. He defines religious addiction as "using God, a church, or a belief system as an escape from reality, in an attempt to find or elevate a sense of self-worth or well-being. It is using God or religion as a fix."

In this context, I believe it is important to distinguish between true addiction and attachment. Some people can become attached to their religious or spiritual system as a normal stage in their development. Their path gives them so much that they become overcommitted or intolerably enthusiastic for a while. Often, newcomers in recovery temporarily cling tightly to their Twelve-Step programs for fear they will slip back into their old ways. If they begin to use religion or spirituality the way an addict uses a drug, however, with all the destructive and self-destructive implications of such use, they have stumbled over the line from attachment into addiction.

True religious addiction takes to the extreme many of the pitfalls we have already discussed: shame and guilt, exclusivity and judgmentalism, obsessive grasping at dogma or precepts, compulsive spiritual practice, isolation from the rest of life, grandiosity, and others. Our search no longer takes the form of a healthy spiritual quest but instead becomes a progressively ruinous dead end. We employ our addictive attitude that "if one is good, two will be better," voraciously gobbling up every practice and teaching within reach. Our religious concerns become the exclusive focus of our lives rather than an inspirational thread that weaves through them. We grimly crave enlightenment or salvation the way an alcoholic craves alcohol. Our thirst for wholeness becomes a distorted, obsessive preoccupation with the *path* toward that divine source of wholeness.

Religious or spiritual addiction can occur both in individuals and in groups. In the last few decades, many time-honored sacred approaches, such as Eastern religions, shamanism, and Western mystical practices, have become available to our contemporary culture. A large number of people have been deeply affected by their quiet involvement in these disciplines, and their lives have changed for the better. Others have met these new paths with the goal-oriented spiritual materialism so prevalent in our addictive society. This approach, along with the egotism of various spiritual leaders, has led to group behavior that looks very much like that of many dysfunctional families, and it has had similar painful consequences.

The press has had a field day with scandals about spiritual or religious groups. Sensationalist journalists liberally label as "cults" groups that may or may not fit that term, often to the discredit of loving, relatively healthy spiritual fellowships. As a result, there has been an increase in public mistrust and resistance to anything that smacks of unfamiliar group activity. This is like focusing on the most blatantly violent families in the country and deducing that all families are abusive. However, in spite of the obvious drawbacks, public exposure of dysfunctional religious or spiritual communities, their leaders, and their activities has been useful. By honestly identifying their symptoms, the reports have helped the public become more aware of pitfalls.

In her article "Encountering the Shadow in Buddhist America," Katy Butler compares the behavior within some spiritual communities with the patterns of "denial, shame, secrecy and invasiveness reminiscent of alcoholic and incestuous families." She mentions her former membership in a Zen center where a teacher violated the ethical principles of the discipline. Expanding upon her own experience, Butler discusses the group tendency to enable its leader to cover up his behavior. This "insulated [him] from the consequences and deprived him of the chance to learn from his mistakes. The process damaged us as well: We habitually denied what was in front of our faces, felt powerless and lost touch with our inner experience."

Similar phenomena exist in other spiritual groups. Recent revelations about sexual abuse of children by Roman Catholic priests has caused alarm throughout America. We must remember that the dysfunction within religious or spiritual contexts is not limited to specific identifiable denominations or religious communities. Whether we enter Buddhist, Christian, Jewish, or other sacred arenas, whether as leaders or as followers, we extend into any organization the lessons we have learned about how to conduct ourselves in our families and communities. We take with us vulnerability, shame and guilt, lack of personal boundaries, dependency, codependency, and a need to control or be controlled. We carry our projections, our need for power, our tendency to idealize, or our unwillingness to doubt. In addition, a spiritual community or therapeutic setting seems to offer a sanctuary from our own pain, our past, and our addictive culture.

Adulation of the spiritual teacher or therapist can occur within a religious or therapeutic context. The devotee or client naturally regards the authority as an expert. The authority radiates an aura of special sacred knowledge, accomplishment, and awareness compared with the fledgling who feels weighted with shame and lack of self-esteem. If, during childhood, their families carefully guarded secrets or treated taboo subject matter as off-limits, the children probably accepted their behavior as normal. Consequently, when as adults these children find themselves in another dysfunctional system, they blindly support or re-create the same dynamics. Individuals who, early in their lives, were sexually molested by older family members or acquaintances frequently repeat the same experience as adults with people in a position of power. If a child learns to idealize an abusive parent in order to survive, as an adult, he or she might easily idealize a therapist or spiritual teacher.

Although the Twelve Steps can be just as subject to misuse as any other path, many of its traditions serve as wise guidelines toward preventing some of the problems that appear in other spiritual communities. They emphasize principles rather than personalities, regarding leaders as servants who do not govern. They steadfastly avoid any involvement in outside enterprises or issues, and do not accept donations from external sources. In addition, they encourage participants to take what they like from the program and leave the rest: nothing is mandatory. They also believe in "attraction rather than promotion," studiously avoiding advertising as well as opening their membership to anyone who has a desire to stop addictive behavior.

In outlining some of the confusions and pitfalls of the spiritual life, I have attempted to report what many people experience and describe as they continue along the path. Some of these challenges are more consequential than others; some are momentary detours, and others are serious obstacles to healthy, mature spirituality. As with so many aspects of our transformational journey, once we are willing to address the confusion and pitfalls honestly, we take the first step toward approaching them differently.

Along the way, we become more discriminating. Discovering, developing, and adhering to our own ethical standards, we learn to set personal boundaries to safeguard our own integrity and well-being. Returning to the guidance that comes from within ourselves, we start to pay attention to our intuition and gain faith in our own experience. We seek out and respond to the wise counsel of trusted friends, as well as those who have navigated the route before us. We begin to treat ourselves gently, realizing that we can relax our need to be perfect without compromising our standards. All the while, we maintain our sense of humor.

II

Acceptance and Forgiveness

Some months ago, a pleasant-looking woman came up to me after a lecture. I had been talking about many of the themes in this book: abuse, addiction, and the spiritual path of recovery. She said sweetly, "Your healing will really begin when you can forgive your abusers and feel love for them. They couldn't help it." She handed me some literature from her religious group and, smiling, continued, "Eventually, you will bless them for all the opportunities for growth they have given to you. You wouldn't be who you are today without them."

I flushed and murmured that her rationale did not fit for me, and as an incest survivor, I found it inappropriate. Only afterward did I realize the extent of my outrage at her suggestion, imagining in retrospect the response I wish I had made. I wondered, Was the woman who spoke to me right? In one sense she was. I would not be who I am today without the influences that molded me, including the difficult ones. Was she malicious? Or was she well-meaning but extremely uncomfortable with my former circumstances? Perhaps she knew something I did not. Or maybe she felt impelled to "fix" my situation, to tidy it up and sugarcoat it. Perhaps she needed to do the same for herself. Her religious belief system, which focused almost exclusively on the light, seemed to have reinforced her opinions.

Hours later, my mind and heart were still replaying similar questions, questions that have been with me ever since I began my own healing process. Within a spiritual path of recovery, what about forgiveness? What is it? Is it imperative? I know that when I feel forgiveness toward myself or someone else, even for the smallest action, I often feel lighter, relieved, and more loving. I have tasted the power of forgiveness, yet I have also seen many people who are bewildered about the issue. I have met individuals who idealize the ease with which it happens, adding pressure and further shame to themselves or others in an effort to force forgiveness. And I have heard people say, "Am I supposed to forgive someone who has robbed me of my childhood and inflicted so many deep wounds? How can anyone suggest that I need to be grateful for a lifetime of fear and shame and confusion and rage?" The answer, for me, has been no. No, I do not *need* to do anything.

In plotting the course for this book, I at first overlooked the possibility of focusing specifically on the topics of acceptance and forgiveness. However, to my surprise, they kept popping up in my life, my recovery, and my discussions with others in relation to much of what we have been addressing here. I believe they deserve their own chapter not only because their roles in the healing process are so frequently discussed but also because there is so much confusion around this issue. What functions do acceptance and forgiveness serve in our lives? Are they necessary for everyone? What are the misconceptions about and the differences between acceptance and forgiveness?

Acceptance

Acceptance is an important theme in many spiritual systems, including the Twelve Steps. To accept literally means "to receive" or "to take." In the context of our discussion, acceptance has to do with admitting something, consenting to receive the truth. Bill Wilson wrote, "Our very first problem is to accept our present circumstances as they are, ourselves as we are, and the people about us as they are. This is to adopt a realistic humility without which no genuine advance can even begin."

Acceptance is related to surrender, and without it, most of us cannot heal. Acceptance requires honesty. When we accept, we surrender our ego-based ideas about how our reality should be. We take the first step: we admit to the truth of our situation. During our recovery, therapy, or spiritual practice, when we let go of denials, expectations, rationalizations, and fears, we begin to acknowledge what is (or was). We affirm what we have done to others and what others have done to us. The past was real, and we cannot change it. As honestly as we can, we admit to our feelings, responses, and behaviors. This is the "realistic humility" that Bill Wilson was writing about.

Acceptance is the first step toward breaking the grip of a memory, emotion, or behavior pattern. It is saying, "Yes, this is real for me, with all that this implies." In the acceptance that comes with surrender, we begin to examine the undisguised truth. We expose the unacceptable, and its tyranny in our unconscious comes to an end. Once this has occurred, we can begin to change the things we are able to change.

We do not have to like what we accept. Without relishing the fact, we can accept that during our addictive careers, we wreaked havoc on ourselves and others. We can accept the anger or sadness within us without becoming enthusiastic about what it does to us. And to accept does not mean to condone. A survivor of childhood abuse can accept the reality of what happened to him or her without agreeing with it or embracing it. We can accept our past destructive and self-destructive addictive tendencies and activities without approving of them.

Nor does acceptance mean giving up, dispassionately enduring a situation that may be harmful. It does not imply that we waive our rights or learn to tolerate something that should not be tolerated. Acceptance is a step toward further strength, not further victimization.

Many of us more easily accept pleasant memories, emotions, and states of mind than difficult ones. Others cling to the pain and misery in their lives rather than admit to periods of happiness. Acceptance applies to the whole range of experience, the positive and the negative, the joy and the grief, the pleasure and the pain. We accept the ride on the roller coaster as it really is, with its ups and downs, its fear and elation. Once we relax into the ride, we can settle into the present moment.

A form of Buddhist meditation teaches people to sit and, without editing, to observe and allow whatever comes into consciousness. As they sit in silence, most people find themselves traveling through states of fear, joy, boredom, happiness, sadness, anger, fatigue, elation, and pain, as well as scenes from their past and present. As this ever-changing review of emotions and memories continues, the task is to make room for all of it, to accept the truth of our own reality without judgment. After some time, many people notice flickers of compassion and humor with regard to their individual dilemmas. Eventually, these feelings extend past the personal toward humanity, with all of our shortcomings, yearnings, suffering, and sacredness.

Acceptance comes about through our life experience and through our inner work, whatever the path we travel. It is an important derivative of recovery, therapy, and spiritual practice. It requires us to be courageous enough to peel away our layers of denial, face hidden memories, and express unexpressed emotions.

Acceptance starts with ourselves. We cannot accept others until we can accept ourselves. In the last couple of decades, a great deal of attention has been paid to the theme of "self-acceptance." How do I stop emulating or comparing myself to the models in the magazines or the jocks on the playing field or the business magnates in the news and accept myself as I am? How do I reconcile myself with the fact that I am short or tall, fat or thin, intuitive or rational, introverted or extroverted? How do I accept my flaws and my gifts? How do I accept who I am? Without necessarily liking them, we can, in the words of the Serenity Prayer, "accept the things we cannot change," such as our height or our past. By honestly recognizing them, we find the courage to change the things we can, such as our tendency to explode at people or our addiction to food. Through increased compassion for ourselves, we can then begin to accept others as *they* are.

Misconceptions About Forgiveness

Sometimes we mistake acceptance for forgiveness. Although acceptance can be the first step toward forgiveness, the two are not interchangeable. In my dictionary *(Webster's Ninth New Collegiate)*, to forgive means "to give up resentment," "to pardon," and "to grant relief of payment." If I forgive, I stop feeling angry and bitter; I excuse, and I expect to receive nothing from the person I am forgiving. This is easier said than done, yet many of us feel impelled to do it. What is forgiveness? What is it not? How does it come about, and when is it appropriate? How it is misunderstood? And what is it good for?

As with a number of experiences related to the spiritual life, forgiveness is difficult to discuss in a linear manner. Like occurrences such as grace, surrender, or mystical states, forgiveness is ineffable. It is impossible to put adequate words around it. But we are attempting to think and write and read about a very important and fruitful process. Perhaps one way of defining it for ourselves is to back into it, to look at what forgiveness is not and review some of the misconceptions about it. By doing so, I do not seek to diminish its potential for increased freedom, joy, and compassion. However, I feel that it is important to clear away some of the conceptual underbrush before we can get to the experience itself.

Let us start with the misconceptions. Many of us live in an atmosphere that embraces forgiveness as something that good and loving people do. Potent sacred examples surround us: during

Jesus' agony on the cross, he intercedes for his executioners, "Father, forgive them, for they know not what they do." In Christian churches and at the end of many Twelve-Step meetings, the Lord's Prayer entreats, "Forgive us our trespasses as we forgive those that trespass against us." Yom Kippur, the Jewish day of atonement, is a day of forgiveness, of releasing the wrongs that others have done to us and the wrongs we have done to others. Some Buddhist and Hindu meditations focus on recognizing our actions and the deeds of others, then extending forgiveness and compassion from ourselves outward until we embrace the whole world.

We may regard forgiveness as a religious and human ideal, thinking, "If I want to be compassionate, I must forgive. If I want to be good, it is my duty to forgive the misdeeds of others." Yet we find we cannot do it. We still feel angry and hurt. Maybe we hate what someone did to us. Within our religious or spiritual surroundings, we might easily assume that if we cannot forgive, we are bad. There is something wrong with us. We are not as holy as the people around us. If forgiveness involves love and compassion, then we must be unfeeling, uncharitable, and heartless.

We easily internalize external pressures to forgive. How many of us have heard sayings such as "Forgive and forget" or "To err is human, to forgive divine"? We may feel prodded by justifications such as "They were doing the best they could," or "They didn't really mean it," or "In spite of it all, he really loved you." In her book *Banished Knowledge,* the psychiatrist Alice Miller lists various injunctions from therapists who pressure clients to forgive their parents. These "pedagogic pronouncements," as she calls them, include statements such as "It's so long ago. Isn't it time to forget?" "Try to see the positive aspects too: Didn't your parents pay for your studies?" "One can't get well as long as one blames other people," "The child is not a victim, but a partner in an interaction," or "Parents are human too; they can't be perfect." Although these comments originally came from therapists, similar assertions may be offered by friends, family members, or religious teachers.

A person who has been abused as a child already possesses a seemingly bottomless pit of shame and guilt. If someone comes along and shames us into forgiving, the experience is familiar. Shaming remarks make sense to us; as children, we heard them much of our lives at home, at school, from our friends. We already feel ashamed of ourselves and laden with guilt. For years, we have found it simpler to blame ourselves than to face the awful truth about the behavior of others. We find it easier to condemn ourselves than to recognize and express our painful emotions.

In reality, however, coercion to forgive is hurtful and insulting. It demonstrates disregard and disrespect for the validity of an individual's unique experience, as well as for her or his feelings. It can also sabotage recovery or therapy. Alice Miller writes, "Since, to me, therapy means a sensory, emotional, and mental discovery of the long repressed truth, *I regard the moral demand for reconciliation with parents as an inevitable blocking and paralyzing of the therapeutic process.*" This statement relates directly to our earlier discussion of acceptance and its necessity in our healing process. A major emphasis in both therapy and recovery is on the discovery and acceptance of long-repressed truth. If a righteous demand for reconciliation blocks or paralyzes this process, it impedes our ability to admit to the reality of our situation.

Pressure to shortcut recovery through premature forgiveness can undermine or obstruct acceptance. It seems like an "easier, softer way," in the words of the Twelve-Step programs. Because acceptance is essential for growth and progress, undermining it can cause our recovery to begin to backslide toward denial. And denial often leads to relapse.

Yet, even with the misconceptions about forgiveness, we feel called by its promise. It must have something to offer if the sacred traditions throughout history have considered it to be worthwhile. Dag Hammarskjöld, former secretary-general of the United Nations and a man known for his humanitarianism, wrote, "Forgiveness is the answer to the child's dream of a miracle by which what is broken is made whole again, what is soiled is again made clean." This sounds enticing. Who has not wished for something shattered to be mended, for something done to be undone, for stains to be wiped away?

What Forgiveness Is Not

As a way of approaching the possible benefits of forgiveness, let us look at what it is not: Forgiveness is not our moral or religious duty. It is not something that others can compel us to do. Nor is it mandatory for everyone or for every situation.

Forgiveness is not a way to deny our experience or mask our own pain, anger, shame, guilt, and sadness. It is not about repressing and forgetting but about revealing and remembering. It is not about avoiding or escaping reality but about accepting it. Covering our emotions and memories with a gesture of forgiveness is like trying to cover an old, discolored wall with a coat of inferior paint. Eventually, the blemishes underneath will seep through.

Forgiveness is not for the benefit of the one who has harmed us. Nor does it come out of pity. It comes about for our own well-being. A common misunderstanding is that we forgive other people because we feel sorry for them or because we want them to feel better. We pardon their wrongdoings to help them or to heal them. If we vindicate them, they will see the error of their ways and change according to our expectations. They will be cured of their abusiveness, and they will be happier as a result. Then everything will be wonderful.

They may even alter their attitudes and feelings toward us; they will like us again. Maybe they will even love and accept us. The tension will be soothed, and "what is broken will be made whole again," as Dag Hammarskjöld said. This is a codependent attitude toward forgiveness: attempting to control others or taking care of others at our own expense. Only they can help or heal or change themselves.

Just as we cannot forgive for the sake of others, so we cannot depend upon others to forgive us. They may or they may not. It is up to us to forgive ourselves.

Forgiveness is not an intentional gesture, a belief, or a cognitive decision. We cannot wake up one day and say, "All right, today I am going to forgive my father or my uncle or myself." We cannot read about the benefits of forgiveness and simply decide to absolve an offense, our own or another person's. However, even though we cannot force forgiveness, for our own sakes, we need to be open to the possibility of forgiveness.

Forgiveness is not a complete, permanent act. It is not something that occurs at one moment in time. It is not a line we step over; on one side, we have not yet forgiven, and on the other, we have thoroughly forgiven, forever. Forgiveness is not an event, it is a process.

How Does Forgiveness Happen?

We forgive, when we are able, for our own benefit and according to our own timing. Around the community of people recovering from addictions, we can hear, "Recovery is a selfish program." At first, this thought may seem contrary to much of what our families, cultures, or religions tell us about loving and helping others. However, many people in recovery understand clearly that they must do their work from the inside out. Those who have brushed up against death, particularly, recognize that if they do not minister to themselves first, often on the most elementary level, they will not even survive. Without some degree of personal healing, they cannot begin to tend to others.

Every individual has a unique relationship to forgiveness. We more readily forgive daily occurrences that have relatively superficial consequences than deep wounds inflicted by ourselves or others. We more easily forgive less severe forms of abuse than extreme forms. Moreover, there are many variations in the way forgiveness happens. Forgiveness, when it occurs, lightens our load. And usually, acceptance comes first. Let me explain.

Forgiveness is the opposite of resentment. Resentment means to "re-feel," to "be emotionally receptive," and "to express annoyance or ill will." It happens when we rehash, recirculate, or hang on to stagnating anger. The Twelve-Step programs tell us that resentment is "a deadly hazard" that keeps us "shut off from the light of the Spirit." Much of recovery centers around identifying and letting go of resentments. This makes sense. Our ill will keeps us from the healing power of the deeper Self, from the possibility of *spiritus contra spiritum*. Resentment is a large part of the dam. By releasing our resentments, not only are we able to live our lives more fully, but we also ultimately assist ourselves toward a reunion with our true Self.

We each carry a burden of varying amounts of pain, fear, shame, guilt, sadness, resentment, and other emotions, as well as the memories and experiences encoded within us. These feelings were appropriate responses to situations that inflicted suffering on our lives, either because of our own actions, the deeds of others, or our life circumstances. A child who was repeatedly told that she was stupid and ugly carries profound shame and anger at not being able to strike back. A young boy whose loving father died when he was little may not have had the opportunity to fully grieve the wrenching loss. Children who are physically or sexually abused bear the weight of fear, shame, rage, and confusion. But, as these children have grown, the emotions have often become toxic, influencing their lives in ways that inflict even more pain.

As we have said, we may become controlled or contaminated by our unexpressed emotions as well as by our unaddressed memories. A loving mother feels regular surges of uncontrollable anger, which floods her family life and business career. A new employee feels continually overwhelmed with anxiety and distress because, with his low self-image, he fears he will not be able to adequately perform his job. A young bride with a history of sexual abuse discovers that during intimate moments with her husband, she is overcome by shame, fear, and disgust.

As we explore ourselves, we begin to acknowledge that we are walking around with an unnecessary load that not only perpetuates past emotions and experiences but also keeps the influence of the former perpetrators firmly embedded in the present. The power of the past restrains us from moving ahead with our lives. If we become uncomfortable enough, we may decide to search for the roots of the pain. When we delve into ourselves through therapy or other forms of self-exploration, we discover undeclared emotions and unrecognized memories. And we realize that in order to be free of their domination, we need to express them. We need to exorcise the old demons, bring them into the light of day, so that we can see them and expel them.

Within a safe environment and with the support and love of others, we shout out our anger, unveil our shame, and relive traumatic memories. We grieve our losses and allow our hearts to feel the impact of our wounds. We experience the guilt and confusion and we face the buried pain. And as we continue to plunge into the stockpile of our unaddressed emotions and experiences, we exhaust them. As we gradually let go of our denials and resistances, they lose their power over us. Our burden is not as heavy.

Immediately behind our fury lies tremendous strength, strength that helps us to heal. Through our ongoing self-exploration, we examine the ways we have been victimized and ways we have victimized others, as well as ourselves. We discover how we have blamed others and how we have blamed ourselves. By facing the truth, working through emotions, and acknowledging the responsibility of those involved, we become increasingly receptive to the truth about ourselves and our circumstances. And our need to blame is replaced with increased understanding.

We cannot love our neighbors until we start to love ourselves. Most of us cannot forgive others until we forgive ourselves, releasing the myriad of emotions that contribute to self-destructive attitudes and behaviors. Forgiving ourselves is not easy. Perhaps we do not feel that we deserve it or that the task is too overwhelming because of our past misdeeds. An important step is to separate a person's behavior, including our own, from his or her true nature, to realize that we can forgive ourselves or someone else without forgiving the deed. As we continue our recovery, therapy, or spiritual practice, step by step, we automatically feel surges of forgiveness toward ourselves. In stages, we absolve ourselves for the anger, the shame, and the hurt, as well as for the personal limitations they brought about. We forgive ourselves for the notion that the abuse imposed on us was our fault. And we pardon ourselves for the suffering we inflicted on others.

Recognizing that we have caused suffering in other people, we learn to make amends to them. We take responsibility for our actions and ask those we have hurt for forgiveness. As much as possible, we do this without expecting a certain outcome, without anticipating that the people we have harmed will immediately grant us amnesty, embrace us, and forget. We make amends for our well-being, to relieve ourselves of the smoldering fear, pain, shame, and guilt over events that may have taken place long ago. We open the way for possible communication with those we may have hurt. And our burden becomes less ponderous.

As we continue, as our load becomes lighter, we feel increasingly relieved not to have to carry the emotions and experiences that used to imprison us. With this sense of relief comes enhanced feelings of personal freedom, hope, and serenity. During our work, we also chip away at the dam between us and the deeper Self. As we confront the barriers and gradually remove them, our inner source of love and inspiration begins to trickle into our lives. We tap the stream of compassion within. Our cognitive and emotional understanding of who we are deepens into an empathic understanding that is beyond logic.

Through this empathic understanding, we may begin to comprehend in our hearts and deep within our souls why things happened as they did. Periodically, we might feel compassion for the circumstances that brought people whom we may have loved to abuse us, or that caused us to victimize ourselves and others. This does not mean we necessarily condone or forgive the behavior. In those moments, we are somehow able to separate an individual's actions from the individual's true identity and feel compassion toward him or her.

Forgiveness is God's work. It may appear as an outgrowth of the hard work of healing, but it also occurs through grace. My son, Than, gave me a definition of luck: luck occurs when preparation meets opportunity. We might say a similar thing about forgiveness: forgiveness occurs when preparation meets grace. Forgiveness arises spontaneously from the deeper Self, sometimes when we least expect it. As our hearts increasingly open, we may begin to feel waves of forgiveness toward others. Like ripples in a pond, true forgiveness begins with ourselves and naturally radiates outward. Because it comes from a place beyond the ego, it cannot be accomplished with the resources of logic and intention specific to the small self. We cannot force it with a goal-oriented attitude. Coercing ourselves to forgive is like trying too hard to surrender. Each person has his or her own timing, which is guided by a deep inner wisdom.

What about those for whom the wounds inflicted by others are so profound that forgiveness seems impossible? In those circumstances, we need to accept that we cannot forgive and that that is all right. We only wound ourselves more if we drive ourselves or allow others to pressure us toward accomplishing something that does not emerge naturally. Even though we may not be able to forgive another person, our healing depends on our discovery of a place of compassion and forgiveness for ourselves.

Should we actually confront the people who have harmed us? Again, this is an individual choice that necessarily reflects compassion toward ourselves and a respect for our own timing and needs. For our own benefit, the decision to confront a perpetrator must come from a place of strength after we have done a substantial amount of our own healing. Some individuals discover

tremendous personal power and freedom through honestly confronting those who have hurt or abused them, expressing their
unadulterated anger, pain, grief, guilt, and shame. Whatever else
happens, they return the burden of imposed emotions and actions
to their original source. They may even contribute to the possibility of increased communication with the perpetrators, during
which the abusers take responsibility for their behavior.

Whether or not the abusers are willing or able to become accountable for their actions, miraculous healing can result when
emotional and psychological barriers are broken down. At the very
least, the removal of our own blockages encourages the emergence
of love and forgiveness toward ourselves.

When there has been extremely damaging abuse, such as physical or sexual violation, many people feel obligated to confront
their perpetrators or report them to the authorities, particularly if
they continue to molest others. They must be stopped in order to
keep them from doing to someone else what they have done to us.

Direct confrontation is not the best choice if it encourages further abuse from the perpetrator toward us or encourages us to per-
petuate our own abusiveness, to the detriment of our own
well-being. Perhaps we are kinder to ourselves by working in therapy and our spiritual practice, where we can freely vent our hurt
and fury without introducing them into an already painful situation. At times there seems to be a fine line between being honest
in order to bring secrets to light and dissolve old patterns and acting in an anger-motivated, abusive manner that serves only to pro-
long our anguish. If we act out our resentment to avoid taking
responsibility for it, we risk the possibility of staying stuck in it.

There are many ways to work internally on old emotions and
experiences, through writing letters that are never mailed, imagining and confronting the abusers in an empty chair, acting out the
original event through psychodrama or reliving it within therapy
sessions, Gestalt practice, Holotropic Breathwork™, or other
forms of expressive self-exploration. The important factor is to release the feelings, confront the memories, and experience these

truths in an effort to free ourselves from them. This way, if we never speak to the perpetrators but we open up the possibility of forgiving them, we can even forgive someone who has died.

I heard someone ask, "Will I be able to forgive before I die? Can I end my life with a clean slate?" Perhaps and perhaps not. Most of us have no idea when we will die. It may happen tomorrow, perhaps years from now. What we do know is that we can commit ourselves to putting one foot in front of the other, continue our healing work with the support and love of others, and remain open for those moments of grace.

Forgiveness is related to acceptance, and acceptance requires surrender. Therefore, through a practice of surrender, forgiveness becomes possible. Just as surrender is a gradual, long-term process, so forgiveness takes time. It does not happen overnight. It comes and goes in waves and trickles. If we practice surrender and acceptance as essential components of our spiritual path of recovery, we continue to lighten our load, to crack through the dam. Compassion and forgiveness become more available. Through acceptance and letting go, we discover freedom: freedom from the past, from our resentments and our self-degradation, from our denials and the secrets we kept from ourselves. Gradually we begin to rediscover the sacred dimensions within us and around us, the divine experience of being human.

12

The Divine Experience of Being Human

IN HIS BEAUTIFUL description of the hero's journey, Joseph Campbell follows the hero or heroine who has left home, the familiar reality, and ventured into mysterious, unknown territories. Having met many challenges and learned many lessons, the time has come for him or her to cross the threshold of return. An important and necessary stage of the adventure is the homecoming from that land of initiation to daily life or, as Campbell describes it, the emergence "out of that yonder zone." After an often difficult period of reentry into ordinary existence, the heroine or hero discovers that "the two kingdoms are actually one. The realm of the gods is a forgotten dimension of the world we know."

Whether we are recovering from addictions or addressing our attachments, we all travel through the lands of initiation. We have slogged our way through the depths and soared through the heights. We have surrendered during arduous battles, overcome significant obstacles, and tasted the sweetness of victory. During our adventure, as we have glimpsed the treasure of our deeper Self, we might have begun to recognize that the realm of the gods exists right here, right now. As prisoners of our false identity, we simply did not recognize it.

Returning to our familiar surroundings, we feel permeated with the wisdom of our journey. Looking around, we suddenly find ourselves in the midst of the world arena, learning to participate in life in an earthbound manner, often for the first time. As our feet touch the ground, our new perspective challenges us to live our lives with more awareness. One day at a time, one moment at a time, our spiritual path of recovery gently nudges us into the present moment. Here, without the protection of our tattered, worn-out escapes and defenses, we tenderly unfurl into a complex environment filled with joy and suffering, miracles and pain.

The world is not an easy place to be. Is "the divine experience of being human" a contradiction in terms? After all, the reality is that we are living in a society of individuals who lack wholeness, "where men who are fractions imagine themselves to be complete," as Joseph Campbell wrote. We exist in an unprecedented period of global crisis, in a culture that is in denial about many issues, including spirituality, and that continues to exploit, exclude, and control others.

On the other hand, there are millions of individuals undergoing dramatic transformations through life experience, with the assistance of many tools for self-exploration, and with the loving support of other people. By becoming courageous enough to begin facing the enemy within, they have tapped into inner harmony, love, and serenity. They eventually translate these qualities into the way in which they live their lives, treat others, and care for the environment.

Fresh from the land of initiation, we return to communities where family structures are breaking apart or are being exposed for their dysfunctional nature. We may encounter difficulties communicating with some family members or friends about our new discoveries. Perhaps we feel we cannot continue the relationships as they were. In our recovery, we recognize the harmful bonds that held us to people who supported our attachments or addictions, participated in them with us, and continue to engage in behavior we can no longer share. Some of these people feel threatened by our new interests and pursuits. And we realize that we must either move away from these relationships or restructure them.

However, we might also forge deeper bonds and receive unsolicited support from individual family members. Some of them may find inspiration in our struggles and victories. There may be others who have preceded us, offering us their heartfelt encouragement, guidance, and experiential wisdom. If we do not find validation from our family of origin, we develop a "family of choice," people who are loving, empathic, and free from hidden agenda. We gain new acquaintances who are truly friends, people who associate with us because they genuinely like or love us and share a similar outlook on life.

On a personal level, living in the world means to become embodied. Many of us have spent years floating in a cloud of dissociation or addictive behavior that removed us from our physical identities. In addition, we might have been uncomfortable in our bodies, felt ashamed of them, even hated them for their height, weight, limitations, or lack of perfection. Now, after so many years of splitting off from our physicality, we incarnate. We commit ourselves to our lives, with their constant waves of fluctuation. Increasingly, we learn to look squarely in the face a world that is full of opposites: suffering as well as joy, pain and pleasure, ups and downs. Even now, we periodically recognize familiar feelings of restlessness brewing inside. Living in the here and now is not always easy.

By keeping our feet on the ground, however, we reclaim our humanness. As we honestly confront our wounds, our behaviors, and the reality of our past, we slowly awaken to the truth of our lives. At the same time, we come out of denial about our spirituality. By continuing our self-exploration, we break through the dam that has kept us separate from our deeper Self, and we begin to identify with our true nature. Kabir said, "If you have not seen your own Self, if you have not pierced the knots of your heart and washed away the filth of your mind, then what does it really matter if you are a human being?" In the process of pulling aside the veils between us and our deeper Selves, we cleanse and heal ourselves.

The power that went toward our addictions or attachments now emanates from within, providing us with a new strength. We learn to love rather than possess, to recognize and respect the sanctity of others rather than disregard or neglect them. We grow to appreciate the wonder of our bodies as sacred instruments that deserve to be finely tuned and nurtured. Expanding in kindness, openheartedness, vitality, and serenity, we begin to satisfy our intense inner craving for wholeness.

At the same time, we more readily perceive the miracle of existence, its vitality and interconnectedness. Our horizons widen, and our perception continues to be cleansed. In his poem of gratitude, "i thank you God," the American poet e. e. cummings writes, "now the ears of my ears awake and now the eyes of my eyes are opened." This is often the point on the spiritual path where those of us who have spent years trying to escape the pain of our lives stop. We take a look around, and we begin to realize the beauty of the world and of our participation in it. The divine manifests all around us. We may have the insight that Jesus' teachings were right, that the kingdom of God is on earth. Or we might realize the truth of shamanic cultures that perceive every part of creation as alive and sacred.

We start to understand that the extraordinary permeates the ordinary, that the material world is suffused with spirit. Our life adventures become exciting and rewarding, and each aspect takes on meaning. We begin to understand that only here can we have certain experiences. Recognizing the importance of staying rooted to the earth, we genuinely participate in the divine experience of being human. We "walk the mystical path with practical feet," as Angeles Arrien calls it. This is the journey home.

Everyday Spirituality

Earlier in the book, we discussed the pitfall of assuming that spirituality is separate from ordinary life, that it has to do with an unreachable, external God who transcends the world. During our recovery, many of us recognize the immanent divine, the Higher Power within and around us. We have a new lease on life, as well as a new strength to live it. Each day, each moment, affords us a fresh start. "i who have died am alive again today and this is the sun's birthday," revels e. e. cummings. But what about the practical mechanics of operating in a way that reflects the lessons we have learned, as well as those we continue to learn?

The most inspirational and authentic spiritual teachers usually appear to be very ordinary. They live outwardly simple lives, instructing their students and writing, cooking, gardening, feeding the animals, taking walks, working with others, or sitting in the same place day after day. Through their example, they teach about love, humility, strength, serenity, and wisdom. Spiritual literature is full of accounts of seemingly simple Zen masters, elders, rabbis, saints, or yogis who, through their actions, quietly and humorously lead seekers to their own truth.

One story describes a dedicated student of Judaism who sets out to meet a great rabbi. Along the way, he meets an old acquaintance on the road and tells him where he is going. "What are you going to learn from your master?" asks the friend. "I am not going to learn the Talmud [the holy scriptures]," the student replies, "I am going to see the way he ties his shoes."

There are many tales like this one. Each action and attitude, no matter what its magnitude, is significant. Mahatma Gandhi once said, "My life is my message." The way in which we live our lives declares our message to the world. The care and attention with which we tend to our daily activities, relate to our children, prepare our meals, interact with the clerks at the grocery store, or drive through traffic demonstrates our inner state. The external often reflects the internal. We betray our level of agitation, fear, or disconnection by the way we treat ourselves, our environment, and those within it. We demonstrate the reservoir of love, respect, and compassion within us as we reach out to others. When I went to alcoholism treatment, my counselor told us that he can always gauge the state of his well-being by noticing the degree of disorder in his automobile. If the seats are littered with papers and old gum wrappers, if the trunk of the car is a mess, he knows that he needs to pay attention to his peace of mind.

Our spiritual path of rediscovery includes profound, life-changing insights and experiences. However, no internal adventures, no matter how grand and glorious, have any value unless we are able to integrate them into our present lives. The Sufi story warns, "Worship Allah, but tie your camel to the post." Do your spiritual practice, but take care of everyday necessities and obligations.

Living in our new world also requires that we become truly alive. During our addictions or because of our attachments, many of us were spaced-out, numb, or asleep. We navigated through our lives on automatic pilot. By committing ourselves to an honest life of surrender and acceptance, we begin to awaken from our deep slumber. We recognize that, although we thought we were enjoying ourselves, in reality we existed within a limited spectrum of experience. And now, we are no longer content to live in a cotton-padded gray zone. Nor do we allow our emotional barometer to drag us to excessive heights and depths. As we claim our center of gravity, as the "eyes of our eyes are opened," we become increasingly enthusiastic about participating more fully in our human adventure.

One woman put it this way, "I spent most of my forty-five years wearing blinders that limited my vision. Now, God has given me a second chance, and my life, with all its faults, is a miracle. I have decided to go for it, to live as fully as I can each day. I've spent enough time in the dark." By this time, we know that a frantic outward search does not lead to fulfillment or satisfaction. Ever more firmly anchored in the ground of our being, we engage in our outer lives from the inside out.

Awakening to Wholeness

Eastern religious and spiritual traditions describe *enlightenment* or *illumination* as the ultimate goal of spiritual development. To be enlightened is to become *fully awake, aware,* or *conscious.* Illumination takes place through removal of layers and layers of blindfolds and becoming open to the clarity of spiritual sight, insight, or vision. Enlightened beings lucidly perceive the world as it is without the distortion of illusions, ignorance, anger, or attachments. They are entirely open to and fully aware of the truth of reality. Completely conscious, they exist free of attachments, hatred, and resentment. Although they have thoughts, emotions, and a physical body, they do not cling to any of them—no attachments, not one shred of resentment, no denials. Imagine that.

Most of us will probably not achieve the final goal of enlightenment. However, by addressing our addictions and working on our attachments, we become freer and our day-to-day routine becomes more illuminated. As we peel away our denials, confront our addictions, and surrender our attachments, we become more honest about our lives. Embracing the truth of suffering as well as joy, we wake up. As we realize and accept the spectrum of the human condition, the door of compassion opens. Recognizing the pain of the world, the disease, warfare, death, and misery, our hearts stir. We are all in the lifeboat together. There but for the grace of God go I.

Chögyam Trungpa said, "I am afraid love is not really the experience of beauty and romantic joy alone. Love is associated with ugliness and pain and aggression, as well as with the beauty of the world. . . . Love or compassion, the open path, is associated with 'what is.'" By accepting what is, we tap the love inherent within us, a deep sense of belonging and relationship with ourselves, others, and our surroundings.

We also feel freer. Our new freedom does not mean we perch on the mountaintop, removed and separate as we savor other realms. On the contrary, we stand in the midst of the rich, dynamic, ever-changing life drama with increasing flexibility, serenity, compassion, humor, and humility. We walk through the storms and see the rainbows with more ease, drawing on the light in our lives as well as the qualities of our spiritual maturity. By regarding our addictions and attachments honestly, we become "happy, joyous, and free," in the words of the Twelve-Step programs.

As we become freer and more accepting, we awaken to our own wholeness. The word *whole* means healthy, free from wound or injury, healed. Wholeness is also defined as the unity or totality of complex components. This is what we have been thirsting for—and it is possible to find it in our everyday world. As we experience the spiritual awakening that the twelfth Step promises, we unite with the divine, we retrieve that core of wholeness within. A life of wholeness is a life of health and balance. In the process of healing from our wounds, we begin to harmonize our physical, emotional, mental, and spiritual parts. During our eleventh-Step work or our spiritual practice and through our actions in the world, we more easily integrate the small self and the deeper Self. The immanent divine meets the transcendent divine, and we become aware of the miracle of our lives.

D. H. Lawrence filled his poems, particularly his later ones, with images of death, rebirth, and spirituality. His *"Pax,"* or "Peace," is one of my favorites. I think of it as I watch my cats serenely curled up or stretched out around the house. The first lines convey the atmosphere of serenity and unity we cultivate as we return home:

All that matters is to be one with the living God
to be a creature in the house of the God of Life.

Like a cat asleep on a chair
at peace, in peace
and at one with the master of the house, with the mistress,
at home, at home in the house of the living,
sleeping on the hearth, and yawning before the fire.

We rest in our divine home, yawning before the fire. We are one with the God who envelops and guides us through the simple tasks of day-to-day living.

And What About the Pitfalls?

During our daily routine, we enjoy periods when we feel content and connected. We also encounter rough spots, pitfalls, and bumps along the way. Drinking or drugging dreams remind us that our addictive tendencies still exist somewhere below the surface. What do we do with the all-too-familiar restlessness that sometimes circulates through us or the periods when our minds work overtime? If we take two steps forward on our journey, what about the times when we take a step back? What do we do to avoid or move past these pitfalls? Here are some suggestions that have been given to me by friends, guides, and colleagues along the way.

We need to *stay in conscious contact with our Higher Power* through regular spiritual practice that includes the elements of surrender, acceptance, and love. Make time each day to pray, meditate, spend time outdoors, go to Twelve-Step meetings, engage in creative activities, or do whatever helps us to contact the deeper Self. Be sure that our path has heart, that we practice the compassion and kindness we are discovering within ourselves. Surrender each day. Turn it over, as the Twelve Steps say. Allow the deeper Self or Higher Power to operate through our actions. Some spiritual teachers say that spiritual practice is not about getting anywhere or accumulating anything but about letting go. Experience each moment as fully as possible, and move on. Accept that "this too shall pass," that times of happiness as well as painful periods are transitory. Ride the waves of change.

Treat restlessness as a signal that we need to do some eleventh-Step work, to consciously contact our Higher Power. Our thirst for wholeness becomes activated when we feel disconnected or out of touch with the deeper Self. As part of our practice, learn to recognize our yearnings when they occur. When we feel that deep hunger, our spirit needs to be fed. It signals us to step back from the business of our lives and reconnect. Replace the misdirected, potentially addictive attempts to quench our thirst with healthy and nourishing endeavors. Even if we cannot directly feel our Higher Power, we can always remind ourselves of its presence.

Develop healthy relationships with other people. One level of our lifelong thirst is a yearning to relate to other people, to love and be loved. Many of us have felt as though we exist separate from the rest of humanity. We have considered ourselves to be different, alienated. Our loneliness and our craving to belong have led to unhealthy, sometimes addictive relationships. Now, we are working to change. When we notice our desire to be included, we reach out. We overcome our fear of rejection and enter into honest, caring interaction with those we can trust. This does not happen overnight. Trust in other people grows as we develop trust in ourselves. Relationships become easier as we continue to do our own healing.

Listen to what others have to say. Around Twelve-Step programs they say, "Get the cotton out of your ears and put it in your mouth." Refrain from focusing solely on ourselves and become attentive to the people around us. Listen to their needs, their stories, the lessons they have to teach us. Resist the urge to give advice and pronounce judgment; instead, offer empathy and kindness.

Work with a spiritual guide, teacher, or sponsor, someone who has done a lot of his or her own healing and understands that we each contain our own answers. Earlier, we discussed some guidelines for finding a therapist. These, too, can assist us in looking for a guide or sponsor: a feeling of personal resonance with the individual and evidence of a broad understanding that includes spirituality, the knowledge that we are our own healers, and respect for boundaries, their own as well as ours. The role of these coadventurers may change at various stages of our development as our needs change.

Augment our spiritual practice with therapy or other forms of self-exploration. This will help us to remove the dam between us and our deeper Self more consistently. We cannot have a full experience of spirituality in our lives without addressing our personal issues. (We addressed this topic more fully in chapter 8.)

Learn to distinguish isolation from solitude. Many of us have lived isolated lives, even though family, friends, schoolmates, and community members surrounded us. We have felt less than other people, different, as though we were on the outside looking in. Those who were abused and betrayed often responded by sequestering ourselves from the rest of the world and creating layers of protection. But when we isolate ourselves, we are left alone with our mental chatter. If we feel shame, anger, or fear, our minds often deceive us. We convince ourselves of our inadequacies, justify harmful actions, or judge and criticize others. We tell ourselves stories that may or may not be true.

Emerging out of our isolation is an important part of our recovery. As we heal our wounds and discover our strengths, we increasingly develop trust in ourselves and others. We risk interaction with other individuals, and our relationships become more comfortable. When our lives become painful, we are tempted to retreat once again into isolation. If we do, we resubmerge ourselves in mistrust, bitterness, and the illusions in our minds.

Solitude is different from isolation. Whereas isolation activates the mind, solitude opens the heart. It is the quality of being alone with ourselves, separate from the rest of the world, and enjoying our own company. Solitude is a voluntary action; isolation is a reaction. Solitude is necessary during our spiritual practice and during other times of regeneration, introspection, and reconnection. It is a healthy retreat. We pray, meditate, walk in the woods, and dream at night in solitude.

Continue to work with our minds as well as our intuition. Learn to watch the mental gymnastics as they occur and recognize them for what they are. Trust our inner voice and distinguish it from "the committee," the mental chatter that only serves to confuse us. Listen to our intuition rather than our thoughts or logic; we all have it, whether we know it or not. Pay attention to the messages of our hearts rather than our heads. True intuition is the deeper wisdom speaking, not the ego.

Engage in regular grounding activities that help us to develop a sense of connection with the earth and work to bring our spiritual insights into daily life. Gardening, actually getting our fingers in the soil, keeps us rooted in the here and now and encourages our reverence for nature. Physical activities such as running, dancing, or manual labor keep us in our bodies and our feet on the ground, as do simple tasks such as cooking or doing odd jobs around the house.

Notice when we are out of balance and correct it. Give equal attention to our physical, emotional, mental, and spiritual needs. Some of us are more rational than emotional, more physical than spiritual, more spiritually oriented than intellectually developed, and vice versa. One aspect of us may be vying for attention today, and another tomorrow. Learn to honor all parts of our nature as important, and tend daily to the ones that appear to be weak. If we need to rest, nap for a couple of hours or take some time off. If we feel troubled or become aware of a specific problem in our lives, find someone who can help us discover the roots of our discomfort. If we feel bored, take action: read something stimulating, study a language, or become involved in a creative project.

Recognize when we need help and be humble enough to ask for and accept it. For years, we may have depended upon ourselves. When others demonstrated that they were untrustworthy, at least we knew we could trust ourselves. If all else failed, we could manage alone. Originally, this may have been an essential survival strategy. However, like so many creative solutions, the fear and mistrust behind it eventually began to hamper our development. We have trouble asking for assistance even when we know others can help. Add to this a certain mask of pride that may be a cover for our shame and low self-image. We are not going to let anyone near us, because we have the answers. What can they add?

Unfortunately, this attitude robs us of the understanding, wisdom, and guidance others have to offer. It encourages isolation. An important factor in changing this attitude is creating a "family of choice," a community of kind and caring individuals who are traveling the same path we are. These are people we can call on the telephone when we are having a bad day, when we need a friendly ear or a loving word. These are friends and family members who allow us to be who we are, respond to us honestly, and love us. When we reach out for help and receive the response we need, we let someone into our world. We open the gates into our isolation with humility and trust.

Accept that we are human and that to be human is to be attached. We are so hard on ourselves. We can become disciplined and responsible without being self-critical. We need to be gentle with ourselves and do the best we can, one moment at a time. We find contentment as we make progress rather than force ourselves toward perfection, as the Twelve Steps say. Develop compassion for our own dilemma and our own path. Forgive ourselves when we need to be forgiven.

Practice service regularly. This is a cornerstone of many spiritual traditions, including the Twelve Steps. Help others without becoming attached to the outcome. Give back some of what we have been given. Do the twelfth-Step work that is so important in Twelve-Step programs. Know that when we do something for another person, we are also doing it for ourselves and for God. Convey through compassionate action the lessons we are learning along the way. We do not have to save the world or do anything grand. Perhaps service is as simple as selflessly paying attention to the needs of those in our family or community or at work.

Develop our sense of humor and learn to play. Lighten up. Do not take everything so seriously. Become able to laugh at ourselves, at our drama, at the dance we are all doing together. Angeles Arrien says where there is no sense of humor, there are attachments. We can take our paths seriously without becoming attached to them.

Discover our role, and play it the best we can. Discern what our bliss is, find our niche. Determine what inspires us and generates our creativity. This has nothing to do with imitating someone else. Although others might serve as role models or exhibit qualities we would like to emulate, they cannot ultimately tell us where we fit. That knowledge comes from looking within and learning where we feel most vital, as well as from finding the courage and self-confidence to act. The human drama requires a wide variety of characters to make it dynamic and meaningful. It is clear to me that I cannot become Martin Luther King, Jr., or Mother Teresa. But I can take inspiration from them and look within to find my own unique purpose.

Continue to awaken to the here and now. This is an extension of all our spiritual practice and therapeutic work. Pay attention. Notice the times when we are lazily lounging in the gray zone or escaping into the ozone. Take risks, be courageous enough to keep moving through whatever our lives bring to us. Recognize our gifts and use them. Stay present for every act of the play.

Keep it simple, a wonderful slogan used by the Twelve-Step programs. *Simple* and *easy* are not always synonymous. Do not be lured into the exaggerations and complexities of the world or our minds. Slow down. Notice the times when we keep ourselves too busy, overengaged, and complicated. Stay in touch with the messages of our hearts and bodies, harmonizing the intricacies of our lives with simple activities. A friend who works as a transpersonal counselor says that after intense interactions with an individual or a group, she often comes home and scrubs the floors whether they need it or not. This practical, down-to-earth exercise brings her into balance, returning her to a sense of harmony and simplicity.

Practice these principles in all our affairs is another phrase from the Twelve Steps. Let everything we do reflect our developing qualities of spiritual maturity. Whether we are chopping vegetables, caring for our children, or addressing the United Nations, let our way of being mirror our spiritual truth. Whether we operate on an individual, family, national, or planetary level, the principles are the same. In an interview for *Time* magazine, the former president of Czechoslovakia, Vaclav Havel, spoke to the need for conscious participation in the world: "I do not think that any more technical tricks or systemic measures could be created capable of preventing [global threats to mankind]. Certain changes of the human mentality are necessary in order to deepen the feeling of global responsibility. The renewal of global responsibility is not thinkable without a certain respect for a higher principle above my own personal existence."

We live in a time when there is, perhaps, an archetypal race taking place. On one side is the personal and collective freedom, unity, love, and understanding that is breaking out all over the world. On the other is the violence, hatred, divisiveness, oppression, and abuse of ourselves, each other, and the environment. The outcome may very well depend on each one of us, on the ways in which we participate in our lives and the consciousness with which we do it.

This list is by no means complete. Although many traditions repeat these guidelines in some form, each one has its distinct principles, precepts, and language. We each find our own direction and tailor our unique spiritual style to our own needs. With the help of some new tools, we continue on our homeward path, taking increasingly confident steps with the support of a community of like-minded companions.

Through our practice of surrender and acceptance, each day we enjoy a reprieve from our addictions. We continue through more adventures with the guidance of new psychological and spiritual maps, wisdom gained from experience, and the help of others. We live our lives a step as a time, making progress but not expecting perfection. In the process of removing the blocks that keep us from knowing our inner possibilities, we satisfy our intense thirst for wholeness and fill our existential emptiness.

We feel waves of serenity, acceptance, and joy as we relax into the flow of our lives. We retrieve the key to heaven, and as we unlock the door, we rediscover the home we did not know we had. We realize that the futile, agonizing, and destructive outward search for meaning has been the wrong strategy. All along, without knowing it, we carried within us all the questions and all the answers. Kabir writes,

> *Are you looking for me? I am in the next seat.*
> *My shoulder is against yours.*
> . . . .
> *When you really look for me, you will see me instantly—*
> *you will find me in the tiniest house of time.*
> *Kabir says: Student, tell me, what is God?*
> *He is the breath inside the breath.*

Our entire journey through life toward home is a heroic journey. In returning to the True Self, we realize that the object of our search has been right here all along. At the end of our adventures, we may very well arrive where we began. As T. S. Eliot writes in the "Four Quartets,"

> *We shall not cease from exploration*
> *And the end of all our exploring*
> *Will be to arrive where we started*
> *And know the place for the first time.*

References

"Alcohol Practices, Policies, and Potentials of American Colleges and Universities." Washington, DC: Office of Substance Abuse Prevention; Alcohol, Drug Abuse and Mental Health Administration; U.S. Department of Health and Human Services, 1991.

Alcoholics Anonymous. New York: Alcoholics Anonymous World Services, 1976.

Arrien, Angeles. *The Fourfold Way.* San Francisco: HarperSanFrancisco, 1993.

Augustine. *The Confessions of St. Augustine.* Translated and note by John K. Ryan. New York: Image Books, a division of Doubleday, 1960.

Aurobindo, Sri. *The Life Divine.* India Library Society, The Colonial Press, 1965.

Bhagavad Gita. Translated by Swami Nikhilananda (New York, 1944), as quoted in *The Hero with a Thousand Faces* by Joseph Campbell. Princeton, NJ: Princeton Univ. Press, 1949.

Bass, Ellen, and Davis, Laura. *The Courage to Heal.* New York: Harper & Row, 1988.

Bateson, Gregory. *Mind and Nature: A Necessary Unity.* New York: E. P. Dutton, 1979.

———. *Steps Toward an Ecology of Mind.* New York: Ballantine, 1972.

Beattie, Melody. *Codependent No More.* Center City, MN: Hazelden Foundation, 1987.

Bolen, Jean Shinoda. *The Tao of Psychology: Synchronicity and the Self.* San Francisco: Harper & Row, 1979.

The Book of Common Prayer, According to the Use of the Church of England. Oxford: Oxford Univ. Press, 1965.

Booth, Father Leo. *When God Becomes a Drug: Breaking the Chains of Religious Addiction and Abuse.* Los Angeles: J. P. Tarcher, 1991.

Bradshaw, John. *Bradshaw On: The Family.* Deerfield Beach, FL: Health Communications, 1988.

———. *Healing the Shame That Binds You.* Deerfield Beach, FL: Health Communications, 1988.

———. *Homecoming: Reclaiming and Championing Your Inner Child.* New York: Bantam Books, 1990.

Butler, Katy. "Encountering the Shadow in Buddhist America." *Common Boundary* 8:3 (May/June 1990).

Campbell, Joseph. *The Hero with a Thousand Faces.* Princeton, NJ: Princeton Univ. Press, 1949.

———. *The Mythic Image.* Princeton, NJ: Princeton Univ. Press, 1974.

Carnes, Patrick. *Out of the Shadows: Understanding Sexual Addiction.* Minneapolis: Comp-Care, 1983.

Carroll, Debra. "Angeles Arrien, Native Basque and Anthropologist." *Shaman's Drum* (Summer 1986).

Eliade, Mircea. *The Encyclopedia of Religion.* New York: Macmillan, 1987.

Feldman, Christina, and Kornfield, Jack. *Stories of the Spirit, Stories of the Heart: Parables of the Spiritual Path from Around the World.* San Francisco: HarperSanFrancisco, 1991.

Friedlander, Ira, ed., *Wisdom Stories for the Planet Earth.* New York: Harper & Row, 1973.

Goldstein, Joseph, and Kornfield, Jack. *Seeking the Heart of Wisdom: The Path of Insight Meditation.* Boston: Shambhala, 1987.

Goleman, Daniel. "Early Warning Signs for the Detection of Spiritual Blight." *Yoga Journal,* no. 63 (July/August 1985).

Graf-Durckheim, Karlfried. *The Way of Transformation.* London: Unwin Paperbacks, 1980.

Grof, Christina. "Rites of Passage: A Necessary Step Toward Wholeness." Paper presented at New York Legislature symposium Rites of Passage: A Comprehensive Approach to Adolescent Development. Albany, NY, February 1992.

Grof, Christina, and Grof, Stanislav. *The Stormy Search for the Self.* Los Angeles: J. P. Tarcher, 1990.

Grof, Stanislav. *The Adventure of Self-Discovery.* Albany, NY: State University of New York Press, 1988.

———. *The Holotropic Mind.* San Francisco: HarperSanFrancisco, 1992.

Grof, Stanislav, and Grof, Christina. *Beyond Death.* London: Thames & Hudson, 1980.

———. *Spiritual Emergency: When Personal Transformation Becomes a Crisis.* Los Angeles: J. P. Tarcher, 1989.

Guru Rinpoche. According to Karma Lingpa, *The Tibetan Book of the Dead,* translation and commentary by Francesca Fremantle and Chögyam Trungpa. Boulder, CO: Shambhala Publications, 1975.

Hammarskjöld, Dag. "1956" in *Markings.* Translated by Leif Sjoberg and W. H. Auden. New York: Knopf, 1969.

Harman, Willis, and Rheingold, Howard. *Higher Creativity.* An Institute of Noetic Sciences Book. Los Angeles: J. P. Tarcher, 1984.

Huxley, Aldous. *Moksha.* Los Angeles: J. P. Tarcher, 1982.

James, William. *The Varieties of Religious Experience.* New York: Collier, 1961.

Jung, C. G. Letter to Bill Wilson. In *"Pass It On": The Story of Bill Wilson and How the A.A. Message Reached the World,* pp. 382–85. New York: Alcoholics Anonymous World Services, 1984.

———. *Memories, Dreams, and Reflections.* New York: Random House, 1989.

Kabir. *The Kabir Book: Forty-four of the Ecstatic Poems of Kabir,* versions by Robert Bly. Boston: Beacon Press, 1977.

Kapleau, Philip, ed. *The Wheel of Death.* New York: Harper & Row, 1971.

Kasl, Charlotte Davis. *Women, Sex, and Addiction.* New York: Ticknor & Fields, 1989.

Keen, Sam. *Faces of the Enemy: Reflections of the Hostile Imagination.* San Francisco: Harper & Row, 1986.

Keyes, Ken, Jr. *Handbook to Higher Consciousness.* Coos Bay, OR: Love Line Books, 1975.

Kornfield, Jack. *A Path with Heart: A Guide Through the Perils and Promises of the Spiritual Life.* New York: Bantam, 1993.

Kornfield, Jack, and Breiter, Paul, eds. *A Still Forest Pool.* Wheaton, IL: The Theosophical Publishing House, 1985.

Kübler-Ross, Elisabeth. *On Death and Dying.* New York: Macmillan, 1969.

Kurtz, Ernie. *Not God: A History of Alcoholics Anonymous.* Center City, MN: Hazelden Publications, 1969.

Lawrence, D. H. *The Complete Poems of D. H. Lawrence,* edited by Vivian de Sola Pinto and Warren Roberts. New York: Penguin Books, 1964.

Leonard, Linda Schierse. *Witness to the Fire: Creativity and the Veil of Addiction.* Boston and Shaftesbury: Shambhala, 1989.

Levine, Stephen. *A Gradual Awakening.* New York: Doubleday, 1979.

"Lick Toads at Your Own Risk." Hofsess, Diane. *Marin Independent Journal,* November 2, 1989.

Maslow, Abraham, *Religions, Values, and Peak Experiences.* Cleveland: State University of Ohio, 1964.

———. *Toward a Psychology of Being.* Princeton, NJ: Van Nostrand, 1962.

May, Gerald G. *Addiction and Grace.* San Francisco: Harper & Row, 1988.

Merton, Father Thomas. *New Seeds of Contemplation.* A New Directions Paperbook. New York: Penguin Books, 1961.

Middleton-Moz, Jane. *Children of Trauma: Rediscovering the Discarded Self.* Deerfield Beach, FL: Health Communications, 1989.

———. *Shame and Guilt: Masters of Disguise.* Deerfield Beach, FL: Health Communications, 1990.

———. *Will to Survive: Affirming the Positive Power of the Human Spirit.* Deerfield Beach, FL: Health Communications, 1992.

Miller, Alice. *Banished Knowledge.* New York: Anchor Books, 1991.

———. *The Drama of the Gifted Child.* New York: Basic Books, 1982.

———. *The Untouched Key: Tracing Childhood Trauma in Creativity and Destructiveness,* translated by Hildegarde Hannum and Hunter Hannum. New York: Doubleday, 1990.

Mirabai. *The Devotional Poems of Mirabai,* translated by A. J. Alston. Delhi, India: Motilal Banarsidass Publishers, 1980.

Moody, Raymond. *Life After Life.* Atlanta, GA: Mockingbird Books, 1975.

Muktananda, Swami. *Kundalini: The Secret of Life.* South Fallsburg, NY: SYDA Foundation, 1979.

———. *The Mystery of the Mind.* South Fallsburg, NY: SYDA Foundation, 1981.

———. *The Perfect Relationship.* South Fallsburg, NY: SYDA Foundation, 1980.

———. *Satsang with Baba.* Vol. 1. Ganeshpuri, India: Shree Gurudev Ashram, 1974.

"Pass It On": The Story of Bill Wilson and How the A.A. Message Reached the World. New York: Alcoholics Anonymous World Services, 1984.

Pearce, Joseph Chilton. *Magical Child.* New York: Bantam Books, 1980.

Peele, Stanton. *The Diseasing of America: How the Addiction Industry Captured Our Souls.* Lexington, MA: Lexington Books, 1989.

Peterson, Betsy. *Dancing with Daddy.* New York: Bantam Books, 1991.

Ram Dass, and Gorman, P. *How Can I Help? Stories and Reflections on Service.* New York: A. A. Knopf, 1985.

Ring, Kenneth. *The Omega Project: Human Evolution in an Ecological Age.* New York: William Morrow, 1992.

Ring, Kenneth, and Rosing, Christopher J. "The Omega Project: An Empirical Study of the NDE-Prone Personality." *Journal of Near-Death Studies* 8:4 (Summer 1990).

Sanders, Joanne, ed. "Why Spiritual Groups Go Awry." *Common Boundary* 8:3 (May/June 1990).

Sargant, W. *Battle for the Mind.* New York: Random House, 1957.

Satir, Virginia. *Conjoint Family Therapy: Your Many Faces.* Palo Alto, CA: Science and Behavior Books, 1967.

Schaef, Anne Wilson. *Co-Dependence: Misunderstood, Mistreated.* San Francisco: Harper & Row, 1986.

———. *Escape from Intimacy.* San Francisco: Harper & Row, 1989.

———. *When Society Becomes an Addict.* San Francisco: Harper & Row, 1987.

Schweickart, Russell L. "Space-Age and Planetary Awareness." In *Human Survival and Consciousness Evolution,* edited by Stanislav Grof. Albany, NY: State University of New York Press, 1988.

Seymour, Richard B., and Smith, David E. *Drugfree: A Unique, Positive Approach to Staying Off Alcohol and Other Drugs.* New York: Sarah Lazin Books, 1987.

Singer, June. *Boundaries of the Soul: The Practice of Jung's Psychology.* Garden City, NY: Anchor Books, 1973.

Sparks, Tav. *The Wide Open Door: The Twelve Steps, Spiritual Tradition, and the New Psychology.* Center City, MN: Hazelden, forthcoming.

Steindl-Rast, Brother David. *Gratefulness, the Heart of Prayer: An Approach to Life in Fullness.* New York/Ramsey: Paulist Press, 1984.

Trungpa, Chögyam. *Cutting Through Spiritual Materialism.* Berkeley, CA: Shambhala Publications, 1973.

Twelve Steps and Twelve Traditions. New York: Alcoholics Anonymous World Services, 1953.

V., Rachel. *A Woman Like You: Life Stories of Women Recovering from Alcoholism and Addiction.* San Francisco: Harper & Row, 1985.

———. *Family Secrets: Life Stories of Adult Children of Alcoholics.* San Francisco: Harper & Row, 1987.

Vaughan, Frances. *The Inward Arc: Healing and Wholeness in Psychotherapy and Spirituality.* Boston: Shambhala, 1985.

Walsh, Roger, and Vaughan, Frances. *Beyond Ego: Transpersonal Dimensions in Psychology.* Los Angeles: J. P. Tarcher, 1980.

Watts, Alan. *God.* Millbrae, CA: Celestial Arts, 1974.

Wegscheider-Cruse, Sharon. *Choicemaking.* Pompano Beach, FL: Health Communications, 1985.

Weil, Andrew. *The Natural Mind.* Boston: Houghton Mifflin, 1972.

Whitfield, Charles L. *Alcoholism and Spirituality: A Transpersonal Approach.* East Rutherford, NJ: Perrin and Treggett, 1985.

———. *Codependence: Healing the Human Condition.* Deerfield Beach, FL: Health Communications, 1991.

———. *A Gift to Myself.* Deerfield Beach, FL: Health Communications, 1990.

———. *Healing the Child Within.* Pompano Beach, FL: Health Communications, 1987.

Wilber, Kenneth. *No Boundary.* Boulder, CO: Shambhala Publications, 1979.

———. *The Spectrum of Consciousness.* Wheaton, IL: The Theosophical Publication House, 1977.

W[ilson], Bill. *As Bill Sees It.* New York: Alcoholics Anonymous World Services, 1967.

Woititz, Janet G. *Adult Children of Alcoholics.* Pompano Beach, FL: Health Communications, 1983.

———. *Struggle for Intimacy.* Deerfield Beach, FL: Health Communications, 1985.

Woodman, Marion. *Addiction to Perfection.* Toronto: Inner City Books, 1982.

———. *The Owl Was a Baker's Daughter.* Toronto: Inner City Books, 1980.